THE SOCIOLOGY
OF THE PROFESSIONS

Keith M. Macdonald

SAGE Publications
London • Thousand Oaks • New Delhi

SAGE Publications Ltd
6 Bonhill Street
London EC2A 4PU

SAGE Publications Inc
2455 Teller Road
Thousand Oaks, California 91320

SAGE Publications India Pvt Ltd
32, M-Block Market
Greater Kailash - I
New Delhi 110 048

British Library Cataloguing in Publication data

A catalogue record for this book is available from the
British Library.

ISBN 0 8039 8633-5
ISBN 0 8039 86534-3 (pbk)

Library of Congress catalog record available

Typeset by Photoprint, Torquay, S. Devon
Printed in Greater Britain by Redwood Books, Trowbridge,
Wiltshire

THE SOCIOLOGY
OF THE PROFESSIONS

Contents

To Eric Norman Macdonald:
true professional and great amateur

To Eric Norman Macdonald:
true professional and great amateur

We trust our health to the physician; our fortune and sometimes our life and reputation to the lawyer and attorney. Such confidence could not safely be reposed in people of a very mean or low condition. Their reward must be such, therefore, as may give them that rank in society which so important a trust requires. The long time and great expense which must be laid out in their education, when combined with this circumstance, necessarily enhance still further the price of their labour.

(Adam Smith, *Wealth of Nations*, BK 1 Ch. 10)

Preface

The decline and near disappearance of papers on the professions would make it appear that this category of occupations is no longer meaningful to sociologists. (Hall, 1983).

The announcement of death of the sociology of the professions now appears every bit as exaggerated as the report of his own death seemed to Mark Twain, when he read of it in the newspapers; but at the time, the supposed demise of that branch of sociology had the warrant of a content analysis of American sociological journals (as well as the French journal *Sociologie du Travail*), which was then compared with similar studies that had been carried out some years earlier (Smigel, 1954; Smigel et al., 1963). The viewpoint therefore carried considerable weight, and although the criticism was raised that Hall's method had limited him to an inappropriate sample and that there was plenty of material being published elsewhere, if he only looked for it (Macdonald and Ritzer, 1988), it certainly seemed as though some sort of change had come over the sociology of occupations.

What now seems likely is that the decline of interest in the professions in the principal journals of sociology in America was a consequence of the major shift in theoretical orientation, particularly in American sociology, from the structural functionalist orthodoxy of the 1960s, to a much more pluralistic scene, in which action-based theory in a variety of forms played an important part. The change was of consequence for the sociology of the professions, because this topic had played an important role in the functionalist depiction of modern society: while work and occupations in general were ethically neutral, the professions were seen as being ethically positive and (as will be seen in the Chapter 1) embodiments of the 'central values' of the society. The father figure of functionalism, Emile Durkheim, had written on professional ethics (1957), while the doyen of mid-century structural-functionalism, Talcott Parsons, had also made important contributions to the topic. At the same time the preoccupation with legal-rational bureaucracy (an action-based idea that had been hi-jacked by the structuralist opposition!), provoked a concern that the values of professionalism were in danger of being seriously restricted by the 'Iron Cage' of bureaucracy.

With the demise of functionalism, the professions left the centre of the sociological stage – or so it would appear from Hall's study quoted above. It would probably be more accurate to see the sociological enterprise as becoming multi-centred, rather than dominated by one paradigm, with the result that professionalism became no longer a topic ancillary to a central theoretical theme, but part of a number of areas of interest, that combined theoretical and empirical material. Amongst these are social stratification, the state, the social division of labour, and patriarchy as well as the continuation (with rather different emphases from those of the 1960s) of the interest in professional ethics and the relationship between professionalism and bureaucracy. Most important, however, was the removal of the professions from their privileged position in the sociological order of things: with this shift in emphasis from structure to action the sociological question changed from 'What part do the professions play in the established order of society?' to 'How do such occupations manage to persuade society to grant them a privileged position?'

An account of this sea-change is the starting point for the present work (Chapter 1), and in particular the emergence of a conceptual framework which has as its central feature the notion of a 'professional project'. This approach is concerned with the ways in which the possessors of specialist knowledge set about building up a monopoly of their knowledge and, on this basis, establish a monopoly of the services that derive from it. This draws on a mainly Weberian tradition, especially the concepts of 'exclusion' and 'social closure' as mechanisms whereby the social standing of a group is achieved and maintained. The work of Larson (1977) in developing this approach and applying it to the achievement of monopoly of services based on the exclusive use of a particular field of 'scientific' knowledge, is particularly important. The relevance of these ideas for the study of social stratification is then pursued in Chapter 2.

Chapter 3 widens the scope of the study by comparing the historical development of professions in four Western cultures – Britain, the United States of America, France and Germany. The objective is to draw attention to the variety of ways in which professions have developed and to the crucial place of the state and political culture in any explanation of this variation. At the same time this material is intended to meet the criticism raised by some sociologists, that the lack of development of professionalism on Anglo-American lines, in for example Germany and Scandinavia, casts serious doubt on the utility, and even the validity of the 'professional project' as a concept for societal and intercultural analysis.

No monopoly can be obtained and guaranteed in a modern society (nor probably in any other) without the active cooperation of the state – or at the least, a very benign neglect. Chapter 4 therefore builds on the foregoing cross-cultural comparison and examines the relation between the state and professional occupations and in particular the nature of the 'regulative bargain' that exists between them. This term refers to the almost inevitable consequence that a bid for monopoly will, if successful, elicit from the state the imposition of a number of restrictions and requirements. The particular examples considered are those of medicine, accountancy and architecture in Britain.

A special case of exclusion is the way in which male professionals have excluded women – a theme that is taken up in Chapter 5. The concept of the professional project is not only valuable in exploring the exercise of patriarchal power, but it is equally useful in understanding the attempts of professional groups with female membership to advance their cause in an inherently hostile environment.

If the state is the omnipresent external feature of the professional project, the *sine qua non* of its internal structure is knowledge. The origins of any profession lie in the existence of an area of knowledge which those who possess it are able to isolate from social knowledge generally, and establish a special claim to. As important as retaining control of it, is its development and presentation to society as the special province of the members, who alone can be trusted to use it in an ethical manner. The way that this constitutes part of the professional project is the subject matter of Chapter 6, together with a consideration of the way that the social influence of a profession varies according to the nature of its knowledge base.

Finally, Chapter 7 draws these themes together to present a synthetic model of the professional project and illustrates its practical applicability to empirical cases.

The theme of this book is therefore a consideration of the '**professional project**' as a means of understanding and explaining professions and professionalization. It is a concept that comes from the 'Chicago School' of American sociology, and more particularly its Symbolic Interactionist tradition; and from the action orientation to be found in the work of Max Weber. Both schools of thought emphasize 'action', with *how* things get done in society and a concern with the social construction of reality. Glaser and Strauss (1965) convey this idea by saying that this kind of sociologist wants answers to the question 'What is going on here?', while Larson (1977: xii), paraphrasing Everett C. Hughes, asks 'What do professions actually do to negotiate and maintain their special position?'; and Abbott (1988: 310) declares that 'Case studies of professions are both the raw material of theory and the audience that [gives] thumbs up or down.' It is this kind of sociological work that will be attempted in what follows.

Before proceeding further, I must acknowledge a debt to my colleagues at the University of Surrey, who for years have listened patiently to my seminars on professions and who have responded helpfully. Thanks are especially due to Martin O'Brien and Nigel Fielding, who read and commented on earlier versions of Chapters 3 and 4 respectively. Crucial to my decision to pursue this topic was George Ritzer (University of Maryland) who, (some years ago now!) provided both general encourage-ment and the particular stimulus of asking me to collaborate with him on *The Sociology of the Professions – Dead or Alive?* But neither he nor my other colleagues are responsible for the shortcomings in what follows.

1

Sociological analysis of the professions

The subject of this book is what the English-speaking world calls 'professions', and which for the sake of sociological clarity we should refer to as 'occupations based on advanced, or complex, or esoteric, or arcane knowledge'; or better still (although this has the disadvantage of excluding the priesthood) to follow Murphy (1988: 245) and to speak of 'formally rational abstract utilitarian knowledge'. 'Professional' and similar terms have a wide range of uses in everyday speech, many of which are value-laden, while in some European languages the Anglo-American usage has no direct equivalent (Geison, 1984: 3, 10). So when the word 'professions' is used in this book, it is as a kind of shorthand, not as a closely defined technical term.[1]

Another way of looking at the subject matter of the present study is to say that it deals with those occupations to which the concept 'professional project' can be usefully applied. This is a term employed by Larson (1977), which forms the linchpin of her study of professionalization, and which has been used as the basis for much important work on the professions. This is not to say that it has been taken without comment or criticism as the foundation of a sociological orthodoxy, but it is the case that many sociologists and social historians working in this area since its publication acknowledge a debt to it, or offer constructive criticism or modification. Some work on the professions may be said to talk past it, and indeed some comments have been strongly critical; but all these assessments, positive and negative, will be reviewed and put in context later in this chapter.

The review of the theoretical work on the professions which follows falls into three sections, of which the discussion of Larson's work is the central one: it is preceded by an outline of earlier theories, to show how Larson (1977) represented a significant departure from some of these theories and an important development of others. The final section reviews and evaluates research and analysis published since Larson's, and considers the extent to which her model requires modification or extension in order to provide the basis for a workable theory of the professions. Of particular relevance to this exercise is the writing of Weber and neo-Weberians and their use and development of the notion of social closure. In this, as in the rest of the book, the theme will be to argue for the advantages of theories of action as opposed to those of structure; and for multiplicity of the bases of action, rather than for the predominance of material interests.

Functionalist sociology and the professions

The sociological study of the professions has, in the past decade or so, been strongly influenced by the model of professionalization formulated by Larson (1977), in *The Rise of Professionalism*. This took as its starting point the work of Freidson (1970a, 1970b) and was wholeheartedly endorsed by him (on the cover of the paperback edition) as being 'the most important book on professions to be published in years'. It represents a development of and a divergence from the 'power' approach to the sociology of the professions that was in vogue at that time and represented a complete break from the functionalism that dominated mid-twentieth-century social theory and which traced its origins back to Durkheim (1958).

Until the late 1960s the sociology of the professions was an area in which functionalist theory flourished, due in large measure to the emphasis which Durkheim (1957) put on professional ethics. His view that the division of labour and occupational groups represented the moral basis for modern society led him to focus on professions as entities which embodied all the eufunctional social forces which he valued and which would provide the model for *corps-intermediaires*, that is, those institutions which are to be found at a level between the individual and the state. These he believed would save modern society from the breakdown in moral authority, which in his view threatened it. The development of this view by a variety of sociologists in the middle years of this century has been admirably summarized by Johnson (1972). They range from Tawney ([1921] 1982) to Halmos (1970) and in some cases reach a level of uncriticality that is hard to credit. Carr-Saunders and Wilson (1933: 497), for instance, saw professions as being one of the most stable elements in society which

> inherit, preserve and pass on a tradition ... they engender modes of life, habits of thought and standards of judgement which render them centres of resistance to crude forces which threaten steady and peaceful evolution ... The family, the church and the universities, certain associations of intellectuals, and above all the great professions, stand like rocks against which the waves raised by these forces beat in vain.

Johnson goes on to quote another author writing thirty years later:

> Our professional institutions are ... an important stabilizing factor in our whole society and through their international associations they provide an important channel of communication with the intellectual leaders of other countries, thereby helping to maintain world order. (Lynn, 1963: 653)

Other writers brought a more reasoned approach to the professions, but most emphasized their socially functional traits such as altruism (Marshall, 1963: 158–9) or 'collectivity-orientation' (Parsons, 1954). This school of thought also included most of those writers who took the 'traits' approach to the professions and believed the sociological task on this topic to consist of listing the characteristics of an ideal-typical profession against which actual examples of occupational groups could then be assessed as more or less professional. Goode (1957) is a prime example of this approach, while Etzioni (1969) takes the step of classifying occupations into 'professions', 'semi-profesions' and (presumably) 'non-professions'. In a more positivistic vein still, Hickson and Thomas (1969) produced a Guttman scale of professionalism.

However, by the early 1970s, functionalist orthodoxy and to some extent the positivism that had been its counterpart since the days of Durkheim, were being increasingly criticized and rejected. Up to that date, the mainstream of the sociology of the professions was concerned with the 'traits' of professionalism, their definition and their use in classifying occupations or placing them on a continuum of which only one end was specified. This concern was not only tied in with functionalism but, as I shall argue below, was not really a proper sociological enterprise.

The functionalist view of the professions never completely dominated this area of sociology, partly because some functionalists were aware of what they called its bias, partly because the study of professions rubbed shoulders with other aspects of sociology, where a less euphoric view of their role in society obtained, and most importantly because, especially in the USA, a variety of sociology with a quite different approach was also interested in the professions.

Robert Merton was more aware than most of his contemporaries that the functionalist approach was not beyond criticism. In fact, he set out (Merton, 1957) a detailed defence against its critics, but as Gouldner (1970: 334) points out, his defence is against a charge of bias, not against fundamental criticisms, and even the defence against this bias is flawed.

None the less, Merton's position hinges on the need to distinguish between eufunction and dysfunction and this formed the basis for his own and others' (for example, Blau, 1955) studies which showed the less than functional aspects of bureaucracy. These studies included work on professionals, and he is quite scathing about some groups, coining the well-known phrase about 'trained incapacity' (Merton, 1947: 79–81) and writing of those who 'come to be indoctrinated with an ethical sense of limited responsibility' (1947: 80).

The same kind of critique was levelled at professions by other non-functionalist sociologists, such as Mills (1956) who, like Merton and the functionalists, were interested in organizations, bureaucracy and bureaucrats. Mills's view was that bureaucracy and managerialism were becoming such dominant forces in modern society that professions were increasingly being sucked into administrative machines, where knowledge is standardized and routinized into the administrative apparatus and professionals become mere managers (1956: 112). Professionals are certainly not eulogized in work of this kind, but in addition to taking a critical approach, it gives a new importance to the question of 'knowledge' in relation to professional occupations. This matter was adumbrated but not explored by

Weber (1978: 220–2), when he introduces technical qualifications as a characteristic and a basis for promotion of bureaucrats. What later writers – starting with Mills (1956) and continuing with, for example, Oppenheimer (1973) – observed was that professions like other organizational entities in modern society are under pressure to systematize their knowledge and thereby make it potentially accessible to lay members of society, or at least to less skilled occupations.

Interactionist alternatives

Although functionalism dominated mid-century sociology and social anthropology and still casts its long shadow over textbooks, the school of symbolic interactionism in America always maintained an alternative view and tacitly contradicted the theme of ASA President, Kingsley Davis (1959: 757–73) that 'we are all functionalists now'. This was particularly true for the sociology of occupations, in which Everett Hughes (1958, 1971) was pre-eminent and which gave rise to such significant works in the sociology of the professions as Becker et al.'s *Boys in White* (1961) and Freidson's *The Profession of Medicine* (1970b). These studies were the outcome of a tradition which took as its subject matter the actions and interactions of individuals and groups, how they constituted their social worlds as participants and how they constructed their careers. The professional principles of altruism, service and high ethical standards were therefore seen as aspects of the day-to-day world within which members lived, worked and strove and which therefore appeared as less than perfect human social constructs rather than as abstract standards which characterized a formal collectivity. Trainee physicians were portrayed as developing cynicism rather than altruism (Becker et al., 1961), doctors appeared as wielders of power, not servants of the social good (Freidson, 1970a) and most of the professional 'traits' were shown to have an ideological tinge (Daniels, 1973) or even to be characterized as 'mythology' (McKinlay, 1973b: 62).

Professional power

It was this tradition which gave rise to one version of the 'power' approach that a decade later came to dominate sociological writing on the professions (Hall, 1983: 11). In the hands of Freidson (1970a), for example, this gave a strong impetus to a new kind of study of the professions, although it was the same author who recognized that there was a real danger, that in the work of some writers, the multi-trait approach had merely been replaced by 'a single … explanatory trait or characteristic' (Freidson, 1983: 33).

In fact, the so-called power approach included quite a range of emphases from different authors and came close to being a mere label to refer to all those who had abandoned the earlier orthodoxy. Freidson himself makes very little use of the word 'power', preferring the term 'organized autonomy' (1970b: 71), reflecting its 'licence and mandate' to control its work (Hughes, 1958: 78–80), granted by society (or in effect the state), by virtue of winning the support of a political, economic or social elite (Freidson, 1970b: 188). Freidson actually comes close to overusing 'autonomy', in the same way as some others overuse 'power', when he refers to medicine's 'autonomy *to* influence or exercise power over others' (1970b[1988: 383]). This is more accurately described as 'dominance', as indeed his book with this title would suggest. The main themes in this strand of his work are how the medical profession has attained its autonomy, especially in the US and British contexts, and the way in which this is extended into 'dominance' over kindred occupations; and further, the exercise of autonomy to prevent outside interference and supervision, while at the same time failing to exert formal control over members, relying merely on the informal private ostracism of non-compliant members.

One can see how such an analysis of a profession came to be labelled 'the power approach', even though the author rarely used the term himself, and how it was extended to others working on the same general theme. What is more surprising is that it became applied to nearly all post-functionalists, and that this has led some later writers, such as Abbott (1988) and of course Hall (1983), to regard Berlant (1975) and Larson (1977) as cast in the same mould. From the point of view to be developed in the present work and in the eyes of others (such as Witz, 1992), Berlant, Larson, Parry and Parry (1976) (et cetera) were developing a neo-Weberian line of analysis, which certainly concerned itself with power, but chiefly in so far as power cannot be separated from the conflicts that constitute the main focus of such studies, in the sense that the outcome of conflict will often result in one of the protagonists achieving a superior and therefore more powerful position.

But while this new orthodoxy deriving from interactionism and the work of Freidson became an important model for the sociology of the professions in the USA, in Britain a rather different power approach came to be accepted, deriving from Johnson's (1972) analysis. This approach focused on the relations between producer and consumer of professional services and the extent to which the producer could or could not control the relationship and thereby benefit from it. While Marx is not referred to in this context, the centrality of the 'producers' and their relationships, together with the tenor of other work by this author, (e.g. Johnson, 1977, 1980) leads one to see it as deriving more from a Marxian tradition.

However, although the Johnson approach became accepted on one side of the Atlantic, it was rarely acted upon. Heraud (1973) refers to the Johnson schema, but references by other writers are often to other points made by Johnson rather than his typology (Fielding and Portwood, 1980; McKinlay, 1973a). Works originating in the United States often ignore Johnson completely and while that may be the consequence of a kind of

academic Monroe Doctrine,[2] absence from the pages of Spencer and
Podmore (1986), for example, suggests his typology is more intellectually
interesting than it is empirically relevant. This may well be because, as
Freidson (1983: 33) implies, it is a variant on the trait approach; but
the problem of its value as a research model may well lie in the fact that
the relationship of producer/consumer of professional services is itself a
product of the availability of a number of power resources on either side,
and of historical/cultural circumstances, for all of which the producer/
consumer relationship is only a sort of shorthand. The interactionist
version of the power paradigm attained considerably more popularity
among American researchers; even so Freidson (1983: 33) was cautious
about it, while Hall (1988: 273) thought that it appeared to be 'no longer
meaningful to sociologists' and believed that other authorities, such as
Rueschemeyer (1987: 461–2), thought likewise.

Professions as social actors

The 'power approach', whether derived from interactionist or Marxian
traditions, was undoubtedly more fruitful than the work of functionalists
and the related delineation of professional 'traits'. However, within
interactionism another line of thought was coming to the fore, one which
developed more slowly, more insightfully and, most important, more
radically. This was the view that basically *sociologists were asking the
wrong question.*

Like the Magrathean computer, Deep Thought, sociologists had, in
many respects, got the answer, although it was rather more complex than
'forty-two', and probably less elegant (Adams, 1979). The question eluded
them and it was only by degrees that the sociological community, or that
part of it interested in occupations, realized the significance of what
Everett C. Hughes (1963) had written:

> in my own studies I passed from the false question 'Is this occupation a
> profession' to the more fundamental one 'what are the circumstances in which
> people in an occupation attempt to turn it into a profession and themselves into
> professional people?'

Some sociologists realized that Hughes was saying something radical
about the sociology of the professions, but it seems that they did not really
understand *what*. Jackson (1970) quotes this passage from Hughes and so
does McKinlay (1973a: 66) but both fail to grasp the fact that Hughes is
talking in terms of *action*, not structure. Both appear to think that to shift
from 'structure' terminology to that of 'process' is to have adopted a new
paradigm whereas they are basically the same. Observe the terminology
used by McKinlay:

> several dominant occupations (especially medicine and law) *have come to
> occupy* uniquely powerful positions in Western societies from which they
> monopolistically initiate, direct and regulate widespread social change. Several
> of the *mechanisms which have facilitated* these developments have been

identified and discussed. Principal among them are *the emergence of a mythology concerning professionalism . . .* (1973a: 77, emphases added)

Although words such as 'initiate' and 'direct' refer to action, the phrases emphasized imply the existence of a structure or a system within which *things happen*. In the passage quoted from Hughes *people act.*

In spite of this misperception, McKinlay does make the important point that from the sociological point of view 'there is no logical basis for distinguishing between so-called professions and other occupations' (McKinlay, 1973a: 65). McKinlay goes on to argue that the definitions of 'traits' are basically 'myths' imposed on 'a gullible public', which is perhaps no more than to put flesh on the bones of George Bernard Shaw's bald assertion in *The Doctor's Dilemma* (1906) that 'all professions are conspiracies against the laity'. But he omits to emphasize the counterpart to the point he makes, something which can be found in Becker (1970: 91) and rather later in Freidson (1983: 27); namely that 'profession' is a lay or folk term and that assessing whether an occupation is or is not a profession, is a 'semi-profession', or is more or less professional than other occupations, is what the '*folk*' do, and it is not the real task of sociology to try to do it for them scientifically. Sociology should do something different from what the lay members of society do.

> If 'profession' may be defined as a folk concept then the research strategy appropriate to it is phenomenological in character. One does not attempt to determine what a profession is in an absolute sense so much as how people in a society determine who is a professional and who is not, how they 'make' or 'accomplish' professions by their activities. (Freidson, 1983: 27)

Lay members of society assess the 'traits' of occupations sometimes in a rough and ready way, sometimes with great precision. Customers, patients and clients are continuously aware of the performance in all manner of aspects of members of occupations: they monitor, assess and evaluate and thereby produce the climate of opinion which provides the background for 'professional' standing and at certain junctures may become quite crucial. In much more precise and consequential ways employers, agents of the state, other professional bodies assess the claims of occupational groups and make specific decisions which affect their 'professional' standing. So society, in one guise or another, is continuously engaged in defining and evaluating 'professional traits' or for that matter 'professional power'. What then should sociologists do? What can they do that is distinct from what the folk do already?

The answer is to be found in the interactionist tradition. It is implicit in the oft-quoted remark of Hughes (1963) cited above, in the remarks of Becker and Freidson and is explicit in the research objectives of Larson:

> ideal-typical constructions do not tell us what a profession is, only what it pretends to be . . . Everett C. Hughes and his followers are the principal critics of the 'trait' approach and ask instead *what professions actually do in everyday*

life to negotiate and maintain their special position ... My intention here is to examine *how* the occupations we call professions organized themselves to attain market power. (1977: xii, xiv, emphases added)

As Larson states in this passage, the roots of her line of enquiry lie in the Chicago school of sociology and its successors, such as Hughes, Becker, Freidson and others. This style of sociology, for all its merits, attracted criticism for its failure to pay sufficient attention to the larger social structure and in particular to the exercise of power in society, although this latter point cannot be levelled at Freidson. None the less, reference to theoretical work at the societal level is decidedly lacking from, say, his *Profession of Medicine* (1970b) which contains no reference at all to the work of Max Weber. This is something that was remedied in the work of Larson, who by incorporating the insights of Marx, Weber and other European social theorists into her innovative development of the interactionist position, started the sociological analysis of the professions off on a new and rewarding theme.

The professional project

Larson's conceptualization builds on the work of Freidson (1970b), starting with his clarification of the nature of professional prestige and the processes by which it is asserted. In this connection he argues that the distinctive autonomy of a profession depends upon the power of the state and that its privileged position is secured by the influence of the elite that sponsors it. Secondly he emphasizes that the cognitive and normative features of professions, which are conventionally used as elements in the definition of professions, are in the first place not stable and fixed characteristics, and are furthermore used as the basis of arguments to establish the boundaries of their domains and the membership who belong within them. The third important element in Freidson's analysis is that professions have to strive to gain autonomy and, having once done so they can begin to establish a position of social prestige independent of their original sponsoring elite and with its own distinctive niche in the system of social stratification. Lastly and most importantly Freidson examines the potentiality for producing an ideology possessed by a successful profession. The successful deployment of its cognitive and normative aspects not only allows the occupation to establish its social status, it also provides the potential for defining social reality in the area in which members of the profession function, and the opportunity to use their technical expertise as the basis for a claim to a universal validity for their public pronouncements. While they may in some circumstances extend this well beyond their particular domain, they typically use it to define the standards by which their competence will be judged and the extent to which the laity enter their domain.

Larson then goes on to show that most previous sociology of the professions (other than the interactionist school), for example that of

Talcott Parsons, has taken the technical, social, cultural and ideological achievement of the successful professional groups as if it were a natural-historical fact about modern society. In contrast to Friedson's emphasis on the need for aspirant professional groups to secure the support of strategic social or political elites, Larson notes as typical of the 'institutional approach' the view of Karl Mannheim, in which professionals would be seen as placed in the stratum of educated and socially unattached intellectuals, 'increasingly detached from a given class'.

Larson contrasts this assessment with that of the Marxian tradition and in particular refers to the work of Gramsci. From this viewpoint any appearance of 'detachment' of professionals from the class system of the structure of power is largely an illusion that results from the 'tradition-alism' of professional groups which they acquired from their association with elites of an earlier period in the course of their rise to prominence. But, says Larson, 'this traditional presentation is contradicted by the professions' involvement in the everyday life of modern societies and also by the proximity to power of many professional elites'. Furthermore, the need to defend their privileges counteracts any tendency towards tradi-tionalism.

The historical theme of this aspect of Larson's conceptualization is continued in her examination of the significance of 'the great transforma-tion' (Polyani, 1957) for the emergence of professional groups, and here she emphasizes two aspects of modernity that are crucial in this connection, namely scientific knowledge and the existence of free markets. At this point she introduces Max Weber's ideas on social stratification and the importance of qualifications and expertise as well as property as 'opportunities for income' in a market society; and she quotes Parkin (1971) to emphasize the need not only to possess such opportunities, but to strive to maximize them.

Stated at its simplest, the formulation of her research problem follows the path of Freidson (1970a, 1970b), while her conceptualization of the 'professional project' draws directly on Weber's view of stratification and brings together his ideas of the economic order and the social order, and the notion that specialist knowledge constitutes an 'opportunity for income'. Larson summarizes her approach as follows:

> Professionalization is thus an attempt to translate one order of scarce resources – special knowledge and skills – into another – social and economic rewards. To maintain scarcity implies a tendency to monopoly: monopoly of expertise in the market, monopoly of status in a system of stratification. The focus on the constitution of professional markets leads to comparing different professions in terms of the 'marketability' of their specific cognitive resources. It determines the exclusion of professions like the military and the clergy, which do not transact their services on the market. The focus on collective social mobility accentuates the relations that professions form with different systems of social stratification; in particular, it accentuates the role that educational systems play in different structures of social inequality.

> These are two different readings of the same phenomenon: profession-alization and its outcome. The focus of each reading is analytically distinct. In practice, however, the two dimensions – market control and social mobility – are inseparable; they converge in the institutional areas of the market and the educational system, spelling out similar results but also generating tensions and contradictions which we find, unresolved or only partially reconciled, in the contemporary model of profession. (Larson 1977: xvii)

Throughout Larson's work there is an emphasis on the fact that social mobility and market control are not mere facts of social life; that is, they are not straightforward reflections of skill, expertise or ethical standards. They are the outcome of 'the professional project', a term which 'emphasizes the coherence and consistence' of a particular course of action, even though 'the goals and strategies pursued by a given group are not entirely clear or deliberate for all the members' (1977: 6). She also quotes Parkin (1971: 212) to the effect that 'positions which rank high in expertise generally attempt to maintain or enhance their scarcity, and thus their reward power by various institutional means ... it is no simple matter for an occupation to restrict its supply in this way'.

This theme is also apparent in the summary statement of her theoretical model:

> The process of organization for a market of services, which I have analyzed in the first part of this study, has theoretical precedence: for indeed, in order to use occupational roles for the conquest of social status, it was necessary first to build a solid base in the social division of labor. Without a relatively secure market the new pattern of mobility inaugurated by the nineteenth-century professions would have been meaningless. Actually, all the devices mobilized for the construction of a professional market and the organization of the corresponding area of the social division of labor also served the professions' drive towards respectability and social standing. I have attempted to show ... that this relation was reciprocal: the success of the professional mobility project depended on the existence of a stable market; but also, in the process of securing a market, the professions variously incorporated ideological supports connected with the 'anti-market' structures of stratification. These pre-industrial structures provided both models of gentility toward which nineteenth-century professional men aspired and images which legitimized status inequality. Because these models evoked legitimizing notions of disinterestedness and noblesse oblige, they helped to guarantee on the market the professions' ethicality. In so far as the professions relied on these guarantees, they reinforced the ideological persistence of 'old' stratification structures. (Larson, 1977: 66)

The market control aspect of the 'project' requires that there should be a body of relatively abstract knowledge, susceptible of practical application, and a market, or market potential, given the social, economic and ideological climate of the time. If the possessors of this knowledge can form themselves into a group, which can then begin to standardize and control the dissemination of the knowledge base and dominate the market in knowledge-based services, they will then be in a position to enter into a 'regulative bargain' (Cooper et al., 1988: 8) with the state. This will allow them to standardize and restrict access to their knowledge, to control their market and supervise the 'production of producers' (Larson 1977: 71).

These dimensions of market control are interlocked with the dimensions of social prestige to such an extent that Larson describes them as 'two ... distinct analytical constructs which can be "read" out of the same empirical material' (1977: 66). The sources of prestige which are tapped or incorporated as means of social mobility in the professional project can be schematically differentiated along the following three main dimensions.

1   Independent of or dependent on an achieved market position.
2   Modern/traditional.
3   Autonomous/heteronomous, i.e. defined by the group/defined by (other parts of) society.

Larson sets these dimensions out as a matrix (Table 1.1).

One can envisage ways in which this scheme could be criticized. It takes as given the social, economic and ideological climate referred to above, which might be thought to give it a level of generality that would diminish its applicability to specific topics of empirical research. More importantly those who, in writing about professions, emphasize the role of the state (for example, Johnson, 1980, 1982), or the importance of the ownership of the means of production (Murphy, 1984) might find it seriously deficient, while those scholars whose concern is with the nature – inherent or contrived – of professional knowledge bases – (Boreham, 1983; Halliday, 1985;

Table 1.1   *Means or sources of professional prestige*

	Autonomous Means	Heteronomous Means
1. Independent of the professional market		
'Traditional means'	Aristocratic or liberal education. (Institutionally located in corporate bodies like the Inns of Court, Royal Colleges, academic bodies, or in 'ancient' universities)	Aristocratic or gentlemanly characteristics (noblesse oblíge). (Structurally located in 'aristocratic' or 'old' elites)
'Modern' means	Systematic training and testing. (Institutionally located in professional schools and 'modern' universities)	Registration, licensing. (Institutionally located in the state)
II Dependent upon an established professional market	Cognitive exclusiveness. (Institutionally located in professional associations, 'modern' universities)	Higher incomes and prestige than most other occupations. Connections with 'extra-professional' power. (Institutionally located in the state corporations, and universities)

Source: Larson, 1977: 68.

Jamous and Peloille, 1970) – might well feel that the content of this dimension – as opposed to the form – had been omitted.

On the other hand no one to my knowledge has in fact made any adverse comment, while in my own work I have found it a useful starting point (Macdonald, 1984, 1985a, 1989) and in one instance (Macdonald, 1989) cell 2 of the matrix has been the topic for investigation.

Larson's conceptualization can therefore be seen to arise out of the main schools of interactionist theory and to give rise to categories that provide the means of formulating research problems in the sociology of the professions.

One further feature of Larson's scheme should be emphasized; namely the importance she gives to the link between individual aspirations and collective action, in this case the drive for collective mobility (1977: 66–74). She also notes the importance of relations between rank and file members and the elite of the profession. Her own research work has little to say about individuals because she is working from the kind of documentary material which deals with collectivities and their elites. However, these points would be significant for any future study which used data from individual members, because theoretical guidelines for relating individuals to collectivities are stated.

To conclude this review of Larson's theoretical centre-piece one should note that there is a wealth of empirical analysis in her book, which makes use of the concept of the 'professional project' as well as dealing with other important themes in the sociology of the professions. She examines the success of medicine, the relative failure of engineering, the ideological functions of professionalism as well as the different ways in which professions have responded to challenges at various periods in modern society. Nor should one overlook the way in which the theoretical base appears to shift during the course of the book, so that the emphasis becomes much more Marxian in the later chapters. While full of interest for the sociologist of the professions, this part of Larson's material diverges from the theme to be pursued in the present work, and so has not been covered in the foregoing presentation of her ideas.

The professional project as a research focus

Hopefully, the value of Larson's conceptualization can be seen from the work in the sociology of the professions presented here, but given the level of generality at which it is expressed, additional, more detailed categories are needed in order to bring it to bear on specific problems. My work on professional aspirations and the importance of respectability (Macdonald, 1984, 1989) and on professional/state relations (Macdonald, 1985a, and Chapter 4 below) exemplify this point.

Larson's interactionist approach encourages the researcher to regard social processes as the product of individual and collective actions, and 'respectability' (cell 2 of the matrix in Table 1.1) as something which is actively pursued. This is in contrast to most stratification theory and research which (a) considers the atomized individual or possibly the family as the unit of analysis and says nothing of larger categories, such as occupational groups; and (b) is totally static. Such theories seem to imply that a social 'big bang' known as 'industrialism' or 'capitalism' brought into existence 'the three great classes' (*Capital*) – or two (*The Communist Manifesto*) (Marx in McLellan, 1977: 222, 506), or the Registrar General's five categories. Any change in the class structure is explained in terms of individuals moving from one category to another as a consequence of changes in 'mode of production' or economic structure. Exceptions to this atomistic approach to class structure are rare, but one may be found in Stinchcombe, who writes: 'Many of the important stratification phenomena in modern society have to do with the ranking of organizations' (1965: 172).

The researcher starting from interactionist assumptions finds that members of society, often working in pressure groups and occupational associations, are actively striving to change the system of stratification to their own advantage. A clear example of such a process (in a traditional society) is the activity undertaken by Indian castes or *jatis* known as 'sanskritization' (Abercrombie et al., 1988: 29), while historical studies of stratification in the nineteenth century show not that middle classes 'emerge' but they actively strive to achieve new status in the face of rearguard actions by the aristocracy and gentry (Foster, 1974; Rubenstein, 1977). The study of achievement of professional monopoly and status therefore supplements Larson's categories with stratification theory, albeit in modified form. The actual form taken by certain aspects of status-striving benefits from the ideas of Veblen (1970).

Similarly the empirical study of professional/state relations from the interactionist perspective makes the societal level analysis of (for example) Johnson (1980, 1982) seem implausibly mechanistic. In the perspective advocated here, professional/state interactions are seen as the outcome of actions and reactions on the part of the officers of a professional body, their counterparts in other professional bodies and in various Civil Service departments. Crucial to that outcome are the legislative strategies of both profession and state, as well as the skill displayed by the protagonists on either side on particular occasions. The study of material of cell 4 of Larson's matrix needs to draw on such concepts as professional dominance (Freidson, 1970a), professional imperialism (Larkin, 1983) and the 'regulative bargain' (Cooper et al., 1988).

The need to elaborate the basic categories of Larson's model would appear even more pressing if one wished to formulate a research design to study a contemporary profession's pursuit and maintenance of monopoly and status. The design must be one that not only covers the profession's official actions and pronouncements, but the ways in which 'professional' behaviour is enacted and displayed to various appropriate publics by the professional body itself and by the constituent firms and individuals. So, for example, the study of a profession's concern with ethics may start with an official code and the punishment of offenders but it must also follow through the ways in which firms and individuals (in a variety of work contexts) act ethically and make those actions visible.

To conclude, the work presented here, while drawing inspiration from a variety of theorists, aims to follow the lines laid down by Freidson and Larson. In my view these concepts have proved robust enough to carry through research on a number of facets of the sociology of the professions with the main emphasis on accountancy. The main rival is Abbott's (1988) conceptualization of a 'system of professions' and it is to this and to two other possible contenders – Burrage (1988, 1990) and Halliday (1987) – that we must now turn.

The system of the professions

Most writers in this field have indeed made use of Larson's approach, if only in a general way; a few, however, have ignored it and some, while referring to it, have been dismissive even though their own work seems to have affinities with hers. An example of the latter is the work of Abbott, particularly in *The System of the Professions* (1988). The significance of Abbott's work lies in his review of sociological work on the professions and his attempt to put forward a scheme for the study of the professions which shifts the emphasis from those adopted by previous writers and aims to remedy the deficiencies which he finds in them generally. He then presents three case studies of expert occupations – information, law and personal problems – and after a short concluding chapter leaves it to the reader to give 'thumbs up or down' (1988: 31). This admirable enterprise is, however, not assisted by what seems to be the author's intellectual journey from his Chicago School origins (p. vx) to an uneasy resting place in a kind of neo-functionalism – as the title of his book suggests. Nevertheless, he appears to balance the relative significance of actor and system when he writes that: 'the writer must disentangle the threads of determinants, structures and intentions, then reweave them into an analysis, and then recount that analysis in some readable form – arduous tasks indeed' (p. 319), which leaves the explanatory priority of structure and action unsettled.

Abbott's starting point is pure Chicago School sociology, namely 'what work do professionals do?' His own research style seems to be in line with Glaser and Strauss's objective; to hang around a workplace (preferably a hospital) and to find out what is going on (Glaser and Strauss, 1965: vii, 288). This clearly informs his view that to study professionalization was misleading, for it looked at form rather than content: it ignored who was doing what to whom and how (p. 1). The importance of professional work and the professional claim to exclusive rights over certain kinds of work leads Abbott to assert that 'a fundamental fact of professional life [is] interprofessional competition ... It is the history of jurisdictional disputes that is the real, the determining history of professions' (p. 2).

Although there is no need to read this emphasis on history as 'determining', as historicist, Abbott seems to favour the structural factors, for he goes on to say that 'the movement from an individualistic to a systematic view of professions organizes this book' (p. 2), and that it theorizes the systematic relations of the professions and analyses the external forces bearing on the system. The need for this theoretical shift arises, Abbott argues, because all existing sociological work is more or less directed towards the theme of professionalization, and this comprises a certain sequence of development which he sees both as misleading and as inhibiting methodologically sound generalizations about sequences of events.

To provide the basis for this critique and to justify the theoretical shift he proposes, Abbott categorizes existing sociological work on professionalization in two ways. First he shows that sociological conceptions of professionalization vary in their formal properties and then he proceeds to demonstrate their substantive differences. His examples of 'formal' variation, with typical authors, are as follows:

1 A series of steps – Wilensky (1964).
2 A sequence of functions – Caplow (1954).
3 Each case is unique – Millerson (1964).
4 Stages to a steady state – Larson (1977).

Substantively, views on professionalization are grouped by Abbott into:

1 Functionalist – Carr-Saunders and Wilson (1933); Marshall (1963); Parsons (1954).
2 Structuralist – Caplow (1954); Millerson(1964); Wilensky (1964).
3 Monopoly – Berlant (1975); Johnson (1972); Larson (1977).
4 Cultural – Arney (1982); Bledstein (1976); Haskell (1984).

There is no doubt of the value of this re-classification as it draws attention to features of these theories and to their similiarities and differences, which had been glossed over previously. Similarly, one must applaud the theoretical alternative to professionalization that he offers, 'that accounts for idiosyncratic developments in individual professions without invoking a social trend' (p. 33). This theory begins with a focus on work. It is the content of work and the control of work and the differentiation of work, which give rise to internal occupational divisions and to conflict with other occupations, conflict over *jurisdiction*.

> The central phenomenon of professional life is thus the link between a profession and its work, a link I shall call jurisdiction To analyse professional development is to analyse how this link is created in work, how it is anchored in formal and informal social structure and how the interplay of jurisdictional links

between the professions determines the history of the individual professions themselves. (p. 20)

Abbott then proceeds to examine professional work and the professions' claims to their jurisdictions and to put forward his view of a 'system of professions'. He goes on to examine the internal differentiation of professions and their social and cultural context. This is followed by the three case studies referred to above and some general concluding remarks.

In spite of the value of Abbott's insights there are a number of problems with his analysis which may be thought to diminish its value as a basis for research and to confirm a preference for Larson as a starting point.

First of all, his concern to dismiss 'professionalization' from centre stage seems to me to be out of proportion. Agreed it is important to remove the notion of an ineluctable process at work in society, but the extreme form of this idea is not to be found in any recent work. In a weak form – as an observation that most professions have grown in size and influence – it seems to be quite true. When constructed into a straw man as a series of propositions based primarily on Wilensky (1964) it is soon demolished – too easily indeed to provide the support for his case that Abbott seems to feel it achieves.

Secondly, the classification of formal variation in theories of professionalization into sets of properties seems less than convincing, while the classification of Larson (1977) as 'stages to a steady state' does not do justice to a piece of well-researched and soundly reasoned sociological history. Larson's emphasis on the 'professional project' carries with it the explicit expectation of an endless effort on the part of an occupation to defend, maintain and improve its position.

My third point concerns the classification of substantive issues. It clearly differs from that outlined earlier in this chapter and particularly in the division of functionalism from structuralism (the two normally being grouped together), with the absence of the 'power' model except in so far as it is subsumed under 'monopoly' and with the notion of a 'cultural' model which, it could be argued, crops up in various contexts where sociologists have concerned themselves with legitimacy. Once again, I feel justice has not been done to Larson (1977) in particular by these procrustean categories.

Lastly and most importantly, I take issue with the basic premise of Abbott's thesis, that professions constitute a system, for a number of reasons. First, that the concept of system seems to me to imply either intentionality lying behind it (as in 'a legislative system') or a considerable degree of interrelatedness and interaction between the component parts, (as in 'an eco-system' or the digestive system). Professions, by contrast, are competing in a market place where they may or may not impinge on each other and where they also compete, conflict and collaborate, in a quite non-systematic way with non-professionals, with their clients and with the state. Secondly, theoretically the notion of 'system' is associated with structure and function, which Abbott has apparently dismissed as inappropriate early on in his discussion. Thirdly, the notion of a system of professions, even when linked to emphases on jurisdiction and professional work, is cut off from that aspect of sociological explanation that is at the heart of Weber's work, namely the meanings and motives of the actors.

It is this last point which is of greatest significance in the decision not to include Abbott's conceptualization as basic for the work envisaged here. The lack of compatibility with Larson's scheme is exemplified by the way Abbott (1988: 15) refers to the nub of Larson's work by saying 'Professions were corporate groups with "mobility projects" aimed at control of work.' This not only does no justice to the complexity of Larson's ideas, but also sums them up in a way which entirely omits Larson's concerns with both how and why certain occupations acted the way they did, and thus bypasses the whole question of the motives and meanings of members and their embodiment in a 'professional project' (not a 'mobility project').

In deciding not to utilize Abbott's conceptualization (while acknowledging the stimulus provided by his work) I find myself in broad agreement with a number of reviewers of this work. Turner (1989: 473) is perhaps most favourable, criticizing him only for not addressing certain topics. DiMaggio (1989: 535) is more incisive and complains that Abbott 'brackets the question of how professions achieve collective rationality' and points out that to an important extent his own accounts do not differ from those he criticizes. Johnson (1989: 413) is more emphatic still: 'Abbott's achievement is finally weakened by the obsession with competition as the overriding dynamic, and with the formal systems model ...'.

For the present purpose, therefore, Abbott (1988) provides a very useful source of data and insights, but his theoretical destination in (a weak version of) systems theory is conceptually too disparate from the theoretical sources on which I draw to be of assistance: furthermore, his data seem to be as readily analysable from my perspective as from his own – as DiMaggio (1989) implies.

Revolutions and social actors

The theme of 'jurisdiction' that is central to Abbott's study is not incompatible with Larson's concept of the 'professional project' for all that Abbott regards the latter as merely part of the misguided 'monopolization' school. This inclination to ignore or to 'talk past' the Larson approach can also be found in another writer who has made a major contribution to the study of the development of professional occupations, both empirically and theoretically, namely Burrage (1988; Burrage et al., 1990). In the first of these papers, Burrage examines the goals pursued by the legal professions in three societies while in the second, the authors put forward an actor-based framework for the study of the professions; both themes seem to be compatible with the notion of a 'professional project' but Larson is not mentioned in either and in fact the first-mentioned only quotes two sociological works in all.

None the less, the professional project seems to be at the heart of Burrage's suggestion that we analyse professional behaviour, not by inferences or assumptions about lawyers' underlying interests or motives, but by observation of what they collectively have done or tried to do, that is, by their *goals*.

> In my judgement, four goals have been constant and preeminent in the history of the legal profession, or at least of those I am concerned with here. First, lawyers have sought to control admission to, and training for, legal practice. Second, they have tried to demarcate and protect jurisdiction within which they alone are entitled to practice. Third, they have tried to impose their own rules of etiquette, ethics or practice on one another. Finally, they have tried to defend, and if possible enhance their status. (Burrage, 1988: 228)

These objectives seem entirely consistent with Larson's analysis except that there is no mention of monopoly and that economic aims are specifically excluded; which raises the question of why lawyers should strive so purposefully for these objectives? While the idea of monopoly does not exclude the achievement of power for its own sake, it is hard to avoid the conclusion that the legal profession, like any other group, were, and still are, interested in these goals so that they might secure a monopoly and achieve autonomy in order, in part at least, to improve their economic position. However, this apparent avoidance of Larson's topic does not affect the value of Burrage's study of the comparative success or failure of the legal professions in England, France and the USA in their pursuit of these goals, nor his analysis which shows the explanatory value of political culture as manifested in the effects of the revolutions experienced by these three societies.

The efforts of these legal professions to achieve their goals, their successes and failures and the circumstances surrounding them, not only provide valuable evidence for Burrage's thesis, but they also illustrate the need to be aware of the way that cultural differences affect professions. The details of Burrage's data will be reviewed in the chapter on cross-cultural comparisons of professions, but his conclusions may be considered here. He finds that, on the one hand, there was striking similarity in the goals pursued by the three professions prior to the revolutions in their respective societies and in the attacks that were mounted against them, which can be summarized as aspiring to a new legal order – 'law without lawyers'. On the other hand, those attacks differed in form; for in France the widespread desire for reform was translated by the revolutionary assemblies into a decision to abolish existing legal institutions altogether, while in the USA legislatures were only persuaded to take action after a considerable lapse of time. In England, Parliament was almost entirely unresponsive. The consequences for professional legal organizations also varied: in France, in the short term at least, they were destroyed while in America they were undermined and eventually removed over a period of decades, and in England they survived intact and were even reinforced.

Burrage claims, with justice, that his comparative study helps us to understand and explain the contemporary differences between these three professions, but in considering hypotheses put forward by some other writers he is obliged to concede that other historical explanations, going even further back in time, have some validity.

This line of enquiry might suggest that Larson's model requires some elaboration to be an effective research tool and it is in some sense provided by Burrage et al. (1990), in 'An actor-based framework for the study of the professions.' Apart from a passing reference to Abbott who is thereafter ignored, Burrage and his co-authors make no use of the authors referred to above and their 'actor-based framework' owes little if anything to Weber. The actors here are four in number; the practising members, the state, the users and the universities. A study of the interactions of these four parties over time would, write Burrage et al., enable us 'to advance general propositions about professionalization and be on our way to a general theory of the professions'. There are, however, a number of points about their 'framework' which might lead to some tempering of such optimism.

1   It is unusual in view of all the research that portrays the professions as the protagonists in this particular social drama that they are not given any kind of priority over the other actors, other than being put first in the list. However, such a de-emphasis might be thought to be justified by the relatively weak position in which some European professions have found themselves, in certain epochs.
2   Also unsatisfactory is the eliding of any distinction between the 'practising members' and the professional body. Sometimes there is no difference to be found but many empirical studies take the professional body as the object for study, and it is often the case that this is controlled by the elite members of the profession, who can find themselves in bitter conflict with the general membership, who may in fact defeat them on particular issues. The classic case is, perhaps, the British architectural profession which has been divided for most of its history, sometimes amicably, but at others bitterly, and publicly split.
3   Again it is curious, in view of the weight of empirical work, to accord no special position to the state, especially in the light of Burrage's own work on this topic; and to deliberately exclude other professions, which are seen by Abbott as occupying centre-stage.

However, it would be a mistake to make too much of these points which are largely matters of emphasis rather than serious criticism. The value of Burrage's two papers lies in drawing attention to the other protagonists in the arena in which the professions are pursuing their goals. This is particularly true of Burrage (1988), which draws our attention in a lucid and erudite manner to the importance of the political culture of the society in which a profession exists. As Johnson (1982) says, 'Professions are a product of state formation.' Hence nothing can be more crucial for a professional occupation than political culture.

Beyond monopoly

One of the alternatives to his hypothesis that Burrage reviews is that of Abel-Smith and Stevens (1967: 459–68), which includes an emphasis on the unique position, as compared with other professions, that the legal profession occupies, in relation to the state, a point which Burrage himself makes in analysing the legal profession in nineteenth-century France (1988: 238). All professions, in their pursuit of monopoly and privilege, have to enter into a special relation with the state, but lawyers in all parts of the division of legal labour have a specific relationship to an arm of the state – the judicature – and in some cases are unambiguously integrated into the state apparatus. This unique situation has led another sociologist of the professions, Halliday (1987), to argue that this gives lawyers an interest in the law itself which leads them to act in ways which have nothing to do with the pursuit of monopoly and may in fact be entirely public-spirited.

Halliday's (1987) work is a continuation of the themes of the professions in relation to social class and to knowledge to be found in Halliday (1983, 1985), but now directed to an examination of the topical social (as well as sociological) question of the governability of a modern society (the USA) and the role of the legal profession in this context as exemplified by the Chicago Bar Association. It seems that he also continues to cast his work in a Weberian or neo-Weberian mould (1983: 340, 1987: 24), which is why he regards Larson's focus on monopoly as too narrow, and, in company with Berlant (1975) and Parry and Parry (1976), as subscribing to a view in which 'professions are preoccupied with pecuniary interests, committed to the protection of their economic domains, enamoured of the pursuit of upward collective mobility and of the consolidation of their class position and of those whom they disproportionately represent'. By contrast, Halliday describes his own work (1987: 3) as

> a study of how such associations build the resources and construct the authority on which their macrosocial role rests; it is an analysis of the potential scope of professional action, especially *vis-à-vis* the state; and it is an examination of the conditions under which bar associations, or any other comprehensive pro-fessional bodies, may act collectively. Ultimately, it is an exploration of the conditions under and for which arcane knowledge can be mobilized for political action in contemporary democracies. (1987: xix)

Halliday acknowledges the value of the Weberian theme in Berlant (1975) and of the neo-Marxism of Larson (1984), albeit with some reservations, especially about the latter. But he feels that there are strains of thought in these theoretical traditions which may be 'loosely woven into a new conjunction'. Of these the most potent is that of Weber, not merely his work on interest groups and their exclusionary and monopolistic strategies but more importantly his theory of rationalization in modern society. Part of this work is concerned quite specifically with the rationalization of law and his comparative study of England and Germany in this regard provides Halliday with an ideal basis for his analysis of the US legal profession's development and its relation to government. While on the one hand this connects with his major theme of the importance of the legal profession to the problem of 'governability' and legitimacy, on the other it allows him to follow the Chicago School tradition of staying close to primary data – participant observation, interviewing combined with historical and documentary research. This 'methodological catholicity', he believes, avoids the shortcomings of Larson and others who mainly rely on secondary literature and of whom 'none is sufficiently proximate to the organizations from which it derives or substantiates its theories' (1987: xiv). By contrast, Halliday's access to the archives of the Chicago Bar Association gives him the full story, allows him to assess the proportion of the organization's effort that went into monopolization as compared with other activities, and to perceive 'the lack of congruence between what the professional association does and what it reports it does' (1987: xiv). Halliday's impressive work in operationalizing Weber's concepts of rationalization and in analysing the mass of local and national data that was available to him, leads to the conclusion 'at the very least that the organized bar has committed its resources quite emphatically to the value of a limited rationalization' – limited because the logical conclusion of such a process would lead to a purely administrative system which would not conform to the principles of liberal democracy. This is not to deny that over the past century collegial legal associations have been pursuing a professional project, but rather that the success of their activities has allowed them in recent decades 'to move beyond a preoccupation with monopoly, occupational closure, and the defence of work domains to courses of action more concerned with the functioning of the state itself'. In contrast to Johnson (1982: 208) who sees all 'modern professions [as] a product of state formation', Halliday regards the legal profession as having a distinctive relation with the state because it stands astride the public–private boundary. Once the US legal profession had achieved its professional and market control, it was able to exemplify its 'collective interests in an efficient and effective legal system, in the legitimacy of law as an institution, and in the intrinsic merits of procedural justice and legalism' (1987: 369). '[I]t is unlikely that professions will serve the state without any consideration of cost to themselves. But it is equally implausible to believe that the only driving motivation of professions is an unbridled bid for collective gain' (1987: 370).

One of Halliday's starting points is that the rejection of the overly benign stance of functionalist sociology in favour of the 'professional project' approach has led to a totally cynical sociological view of the professions which does not reflect the true state of affairs. His own case that professions have moved beyond monopoly is put with great cogency and clarity, and is soundly based in empirical data, but the reader sometimes begins to feel that Halliday, like the functionalists before him, has begun to take the professions at their own valuation; or alternatively, that his conclusions are too broad to be sustained by data from one society only. But no sooner does such a suspicion arise than the author enters a timely *caveat* or a cross-cultural comparison. Even if such an opinion were indeed justified, Halliday's analysis is well enough founded, methodologically and theoretically, to provide the basis for further work.

Marxian theory and the professions

The work reviewed above is based on concepts which derive more or less directly from the writings of Max Weber or from the Chicago School of sociology, even though Burrage mentions neither, and Larson is often taken to be Marxian because of the tenor of her later writings. Other themes certainly exist in the sociology of the professions, although there is the view that there is a kind of orthodoxy in the sociology of the professions known as the 'power approach'; '[i]n the minds of experts in the field, the power approach to the professions is itself in power' (Hall, 1983: 12). In Hall's mind, this school of thought springs primarily from the work of Freidson, with his interest in professional dominance and professional powers (as the titles of two of his books suggest), together with his concern with the internal regulation of professional bodies as an exercise of power. But power is actually just one of a number of topics which have been pursued in the sociology of the professions (Macdonald and Ritzer, 1988) and indeed a number of theoretical approaches have been used in the study of professional power (or lack of it) as they have in other areas. The most prominent are those deriving from Marx and from Foucault, and it is to these that we now turn.

The Marxian sociology of the professions is mainly concerned with two problems; professions in relation to the state and the proletarianization of professional occupations. As Marxian sociology is primarily structuralist in nature, the explanation of what happens to the professions in these contexts is seen as the outcome of the workings of a society based on capitalist relations of production. The clearest example of the former is to be found in Johnson (1980), who examines the relative merits of Marxian and Weberian analyses of the development of the professions and comes down in favour of the former. In his discussion of professions Johnson is at pains to emphasize the plurality of processes at work in a modern society and the lack of coherence of the objectives of dominant groups and the state. But in later work he seems inclined to give weight to the 'articulation which involved the interrelated processes of state formation and professionalization' and the 'processes of professionalization [which] are integral to state formation' (1982: 188). Explanations of this kind which identify 'processes' are seen by Marxians as superior to those of a Weberian kind, because the latter are said to frame their explanations in terms of concepts, such as the market and other forms of social competition, which are themselves left unexplained. The importance of the state in relation to the professions is also the concern of Fielding and Portwood (1980), though not from such an overtly Marxian viewpoint as Johnson, while analyses of the professions in Europe, such as Geison (1984) and Cocks and Jarauch (1990), also see the state as a dominating actor in the story of professional development, but in a rather atheoretical manner.

The other principal theme in Marxian analyses of the professions is the application of the 'labour process' debate to professions, with bureaucratization and the market power of a knowledge base as sub-themes. The question of whether professions were becoming 'proletarianized' has been debated by sociologists for some time (Oppenheimer, 1973), but since the publication of *Labour and Monopoly Capital* (Braverman, 1974) the issue has acquired more prominence, perhaps reaching something of a peak with the publication of *Professionals as Workers* (Derber, 1982), but none the less continuing to receive attention from sociologists such as Haug (1988), McKinlay and Arches (1985) and Murphy (1990) – although the last-mentioned argues against the proletarianization hypothesis. Allied to this is the question as to whether the professions are being radically transformed as a result of general social change, namely a trend towards increasing bureaucracy which draws a growing number of professionals into non-professional organizations (Murphy, 1990: 82–90). The problem of proletarianization is linked to the more basic question of the nature of social stratification in modern society and the conflicting views of Marx and Weber on knowledge and credentials as a basis for class position (Boreham, 1983; Murphy, 1988, 1990).

Marxian theory clearly raises important issues in the sociology of the professions and the problems outlined here will be dealt with in later chapters; but the Marxian approach differs from the other approaches discussed so far, in that Marxian and neo-Marxian sociology is a sociology of structure and system. In a modern society there are, in this view, 'processes' at work which are the consequences of the capitalist mode of production on which the society is based and for which Marx had worked out an economic theory which he believed explained the laws of motion of that society. Furthermore, his materialist theory of human society argues that the basis of stratification (and every other aspect of society) is to be found in the means of production and the relations of production that are based on them. It follows that state formation, polarization of social classes, monopolization of the means of production (and other topics explored by Marxians) are all *processes* in which the professions are bound up. While no sociologist will deny that societies develop in ways that no one specifically intends nor that there are unintended consequences to collective action that nobody wants, many are disinclined to take these features of social life as being the whole, and to attribute the entire social fabric to the working of ineluctable processes.

In the work of some sociologists, who wish to look for larger scale explanations (Johnson, 1980, 1982; Larson, 1977), a tension can be discerned between the study of the purposive action of groups and organizations and the use, for purposes of explanation, of the terminology of social 'processes', which Johnson in particular refers to repeatedly. Others prefer to focus on the actions of individuals and collectivities and to see trends which emerge in society as the consequences, intended or otherwise, of such action and not as the working out of the logic of exploitative relations of production.

Professions or disciplines?

In her more recent work Larson (1990) has continued to search for a theoretical base which will provide a wider explanatory scope than the Weberian concepts with which she started (1977). Moving on from the Marxian ideas which she explored in the 1980s, she has turned instead to the work of the French ex-Marxist Michel Foucault. His ideas have appeal for the sociologist of the professions because his central concern is with the relationship between knowledge and power; but he tackles it not in the limited way to be found in the Anglo-American power approach to the professions of, say, Freidson (1970a) or Johnson (1972), but on a societal scale. Foucault's view is that the emergence of modern society was accompanied by an epistemic shift from a 'classic' to a 'modern' form of knowledge, which is organized into 'disciplines'. Now this term has two meanings, and as Goldstein (1984: 178) observes, 'The term "discipline" has, in both French and English, the perfect ambiguous resonance for this conflation of a social power-wielding activity and knowledge.' While 'discipline' has a wider scope of meaning than 'profession', both Goldstein and Larson find it useful to apply concepts implied in the former to the study of the latter.

For Larson it seems that the attraction of Foucault's conceptualization lies in the way it coincides with the topics dealt with in the later part of *The Rise of Professionalism*, namely structured inequality and ideology, with the advantage that it provides an even more coherent, comprehensive picture than that of Marxism, without being entangled with problematic Marxian economic theory, but resting rather on detailed historical study of the very subject matter that concerns Larson. At the time of writing Larson has not published any empirical work using Foucault's concepts although she adds some reflections on medical knowledge and contemporary problems (1990: 35). Goldstein, on the other hand, follows her exposition of Foucault's ideas with a study (admittedly very brief) in which she applies them to three episodes in the emergence of French psychiatry. She concludes:

> this venture has had, I believe, a not insubstantial yield. It has offered historians a way of conceptualizing the relationship between forms of applied knowledge and their external environment, between the constitution of professional expertise and the organization of professions as social entities.

However she continues that she does not want to overstate her case, and points out that as her examples are from precisely the same French context that Foucault studied, it was not the most stringent test that could be applied, which would have to come from farther afield. German material would probably provide confirmatory evidence, while in 'the much less bureaucratized Anglo-American milieu the "fit" of the Foucauldian model is inherently more problematic'.

Foucault's work has been described as 'brilliant' (Goldstein, 1984: 170) and 'penetrating' (Ramsey, 1988: 8), but some authors have found him opaque (Goldstein, 1984: 171). Goldstein goes on to remark that his model is 'perhaps too brilliant to be entirely credible' while Ramsey (1988: 9) writes that there is something of Foucault in his work; 'anyone who works on French medicine in the late eighteenth and early nineteenth centuries must try to come to terms with him and winds up, almost inevitably, appropriating some of his insights', but thereafter Foucault only appears in his work as a source of empirical reference, not as a theorist.

The originality of Foucault makes it difficult to place his work clearly in any sociological tradition but there are certain respects in which his approach may be seen as having limitations. One of these can be seen above in the quotation from Goldstein, who has reservations about the applicability of the Foucault model to other societies. It is significant that in an article on the history of psychiatry in France Goldstein (1984) makes only one reference to his work, empirical not theoretical, as in the case of Ramsey mentioned above. The same is true of all the contributions to *French Professions and the State* (Geison, 1984) and, if one excludes the contributions of Larson, there are practically none in all the papers collected in Geison (1984), Haskell (1984), Cocks and Jarauch (1990), Burrage and Torstendahl (1990) and Torstendahl and Burrage (1990), which include studies of the professions in the USA, Britain, Germany and Sweden. Sociologists and historians of the professions (outside France), therefore, seem to have little enthusiasm for applying Foucault's concepts to non-French contexts. This may be because much of his work is concerned with the body and doctors' relation to it via what he calls 'the gaze' (*le regard medical*), so that it is actually of more interest to sociologists of medicine and of health and illness – for instance Armstrong (1983) or Nettleton (1992).

The second problem is the structuralist cast of Foucault's theory, which gives the impression that while he is no longer Marxist the model of society with which he operates comes from that stable and certainly not an action-based one. 'Devoid of significant flesh-and-blood actors', and 'the theme of anonymity and impersonality' are comments of Goldstein (1984: 172–4) on the activity that Foucault refers to as archaeology and which 'seeks to reveal relations between discursive formations and non-discursive domains (institutions, political events, economic practices and processes)' (Foucault, 1977a: 162). The level of abstraction at which Foucault operates may be gauged from the terms in which he sets out the purpose of *Discipline and Punish,* namely to provide 'a genealogy of the present scientific-legal complex from which the power to punish derives its bases, justifications, and rules' in order to understand how 'a specific mode of subjection was able to give birth to man as an object of knowledge for a discourse with a scientific status' (Foucault, 1977b: 23–4). Or to take another example from the same work, where Foucault defines one of the instruments of disciplinary power, 'normalizing judgement':

> the workshop, the school, the army were subject to a whole micro-penalty of time (lateness, absences, interruptions of tasks), of activity (inattention, negligence, lack of zeal) of behaviour (impoliteness, disobedience) of speech (idle chatter, insolence), of the body ('incorrect' attitudes, irregular gestures, lack of cleanliness), of sexuality (impurity, indecency). (1977b: 178)

This structuralist language, in which abstract nouns predominate, is echoed by Larson who writes in similarly impersonal terms, such as 'institutional domains which issue and apply authoritative practices' (1990: 37) and goes on to sketch an outline of a profession in terms of a set of concentric circles from the core of which 'true discourses' are issued. Even so, the professional domain is subordinate to the larger structure of power: 'The modern state and the capitalist corporation mobilize the expert information needed to govern society or to control production and markets' (1990: 48). Her paper concludes with what appears to be a dismissal of symbolic interactionism because it studies merely actions and interactions, failing to reveal the 'lies' of professionals or 'to understand the real significance of the experts' collective appropriation of knowledge'.

What renders Foucault even more problematic as a source of theoretical insight is what appears to be an unacknowledged idealism (in the philosophical sense) lurking in his thought – something not entirely unexpected in an ex-Marxist. This is apparent in one sense in his use of metaphors such as 'archive', 'genealogy' or 'gaze' to indicate the nature of his subject matter. But much more serious for a sociological enterprise which attempts to use his conceptualization as a starting point is the way in which 'discipline' for example appears to be a metaphysical entity, an element of the *zeitgeist,* manifesting itself in particular social phenomena; something which can be detected in the passage quoted above.

It is probably for reasons such as this that some sociologists and social historians, such as Ramsey (1988), acknowledge his work, but do not actually build on it, while others such as Larson (1990) espouse his cause but seem not to have made empirical headway, or like Hopwood (1987) embark on 'archaeology' and 'genealogy' but in fact engage in a much more phenomenological enterprise.

Social closure and the 'neo-Weberians'

This review of sociological work on the professions has had as its fulcrum the work of Larson, because of the value of her development of the concept of the 'professional project'. The early sections of this chapter outlined the background and antecedents to this innovation, and after presenting her own ideas, the later sections dealt with certain writers who followed a broadly similar tradition (Abbott and Halliday) and with two quite distinct perspectives – those of Marx and Foucault. What must be added now is an indication of how the Weberian reading of Larson's work presented here is part of a theme in sociology, which draws its inspiration fairly directly from Weber's ideas, and which has made notable contributions to the study of stratification and occupations, especially professions.

The ideas of Max Weber that are relevant here are, first, that society is to be seen as individuals pursuing their interests, and that this activity generates more or less collectively conscious groups, who are the bearers of ideas that legitimate the pursuit of their interests. Such ideas may become as important as the material interests that stimulated them in the first place. Indeed, Weber accords an important place to 'ideas' as metaphorical 'switchmen' that direct the interests and activities of members of society down particular tracks at certain points in time, but having done so, are left behind in the historical past, as the real-life switchmen are left behind in space (Weber, 1978: 280). Secondly, social groups engage in social closure in the course of furthering their interests and they both attempt to exclude others from their group and to usurp the privileges of other groups. Thirdly, Weber distinguishes three dimensions of reward on which groups are differentiated, and for which they strive; economic, social and power.

Larson's development of the concept of the professional project coincided with other work that was based on these Weberian ideas; work which can be roughly grouped into that which dealt with historical development of professions and that which primarily focused on social stratification, but which recognized the importance of groups and particularly the existence of collective social mobility. This side of social mobility is often neglected and there are indeed at least two reasons why this should be so. In the first place there is the strong emphasis in Western culture on individualism, which tends to manifest itself in sociological theory as in other areas of life and scholarship. Society tends to be seen as made up of individuals, who then happen to work in groups, form families and join associations. This may be particularly true of the USA and of France, whose political cultures emphasize populism and 'the General Will', respectively. Certainly one cannot imagine any more individualist social theory than 'rational choice', which in the hands of Elster (1989), for example, seems to regard 'collective' action as being merely the decisions of more than one person to act in the same way. Secondly, there is the practice, not universal, but none the less widespread, of conducting research into social stratification and social mobility entirely in terms of responses to questionnaires filled in by individuals about themselves. Such a procedure is legitimated by statistical theory, which requires a random sample of units drawn from a sampling frame that represents the 'population' as accurately as possible; and that is almost inevitably a list of individuals such as the Electoral Roll.

In contrast to this, Weber's analysis draws attention to the way in which *groups* with interests in common, or even people who share a religious belief, or have racial or other characteristics in common, can act in such a way as to circumscribe their membership so that they may either pursue their collective interest, or, as is often the case, respond defensively to the attempts of others to secure an advantage at their expense. In fact it becomes clear from this approach that social stratification, for all that it has, even in the Weberian perspective, a basis in the structure of capitalist market society, is none the less something that in important ways is the outcome of the actions of the members of society, especially their collective actions. However a group may originate, if it has an interest to pursue, it will probably endeavour to become 'a legally privileged group', it will aim for a closed monopoly and 'its purpose is always the closure of social and economic opportunities to *outsiders*' (Weber, 1978: 342).

This concept has its reflection in Freidson's (1970b: 159–60) character- ization of the medical profession as having gained 'organized autonomy', which is bolstered by

> barriers to communication and co-operation within a functional division of labour . . . structures of evasion . . . and the reduction of the client to an object . . . This imperialistic ideology . . . hardens when an occupation develops the autonomy of a profession and a place of dominance in a division of labour.

But Freidson's roots were in Chicago School sociology, and he was not concerned with the more general issues raised by Weber, and so did not link his penetrating critique to a conception of social stratification. But this soon appeared in the work of Berlant (1975) and Parry and Parry (1976) who made the connection between a critical historical analysis and the Weberian picture of the collective action of professional groups and, more importantly, collective social mobility. Parry and Parry actually went further than this in their attempt to round out their analysis with Giddens's (1973) conceptualization of class structuration, but despite their best endeavours, this does not really come off, not least because Giddens concludes that 'although there are certainly controversial problems of sociological analysis posed by the existence of the professions, profession-alization does not offer any major problems for class theory' (1973: 186). Berlant (1975), by contrast, directs his efforts to drawing the sociology of the professions out of the long shadow cast by the functionalism of Talcott Parsons, and bases his work on his clear and vigorous development of Weberian ideas. His book was apparently published too late for his ideas to play any part in Larson's (1977) framework, but for most subsequent writers they have considerable significance.

Theories of stratification will be discussed in the next chapter, but it should be noted that the work of Parkin (1971, 1979) and Murphy (1984, 1988) effectively redressed the individualistic emphasis of so much writing on stratification, especially that of a Marxian complexion. In addition, they provided valuable and welcome conceptual tools for sociologists of the professions to apply in their empirical studies, and thereby to refine and extend the concepts of Weber. This can be seen in the work of Larkin (1983), Waddington (1984) and Macdonald (1984, 1985a, 1989), but the most notable advances both conceptually and in the empirical application of concepts came first from their extension by Crompton (1987) to the question of gender and their further elaboration and development by Witz (1992).

Detailed consideration of this work will follow in later chapters; the point to emphasize here is that as developed by these writers, social closure is one of the most important means by which the professional project is pursued, and constitutes the conceptual counterpart to Larson's model. The occupation and its organization attempts to close access to the occupation, to its knowledge, to its education, training and credentials and to its markets in services and jobs; only 'eligibles' will be admitted. In so doing it may well exclude those of a particular race, gender or religion and thus play a part in the structured inequality of society. Exclusion is aimed not only at the attainment and maintenance of monopoly, but also at the usurpation of the existing jurisdiction of others and at the upward social mobility of the whole group.

A working theory of the professions

In the foregoing review of sociological work on the professions a critical tone has often been in evidence, but it should not therefore be assumed that such work may be dismissed as valueless. On the contrary, one of the joys of sociology is the richness of theoretical perspectives, which is stimulating in its own right as well as reminding us that it is rare that there is only one valid view of a social action or a social phenomenon.

The approach in this book will be open-minded but not totally eclectic. The emphasis will be on action rather than structure as a means of understanding the social world: in a word, it will be Weberian. The nodal point of analysis and discussion will be 'the professional project' (Larson, 1977) which embodies the Weberian notion of conflict and competition very neatly. As noted above, Larson's critics often see her as Marxian in orientation but this does not apply to the early part of *The Rise of Professionalism* where the nineteenth-century professions in Britain and the USA are depicted in a typically Weberian style as social actors. Furthermore, this depiction draws on a number of other features of Weber's thought.

1   Professions are interest groups and are therefore typical of the components that Weber sees as making up society. As such, they are engaged in competition with each other and with other groups in society, up to and including the state, thus forming part of the conflict that Weber sees as the inherent nature of society.

2   Such groups may pursue economic interests, but may well have other motives for their collective actions as well. This is true of professions in a particularly interesting fashion, for the drive for economic advantages is linked to the pursuit of social status in a quite distinctive manner. In terms of Weber's model of social stratification, professions operate in both the economic order and in the social order.

3   Professions have a distinctive place in the class system, because their 'opportunities for income' derive from their knowledge and qualifications, and as Weber sees it, this gives them a significance on a par with those whose class position derives from either their capital or their labour power.

4   This class position is to some extent determined by the structural features of industrial society, but the actions of members of society, especially the collective action of groups, are always of significance and can usefully be conceptualized as a strategy of social closure.

It is these last two features that may be seen as lying at the heart of the 'professional project' in the sense that they demonstrate the professions' need to strive both economically and socially. The services that professionals provide are characteristically different from the goods that are sold by a manufacturer, a merchant or a retailer in that they are intangible and the purchaser has to take them on trust; to take an extreme case, the faithful have no means of verifying that the priest has ensured their salvation. Furthermore, it is in the nature of some of these services that they are going to be unsuccessful: it is a foregone conclusion that half the advocates are going to lose their cases and that eventually the doctor will lose every patient. In such circumstances how can the laity be persuaded to trust the professionals with their money, their property, their lives or even their immortal souls? The professional's possession of knowledge and expertise can be warranted by diplomas, certificates and degrees, but only up to a point. Thereafter, trust becomes extremely important and trust will be accorded to those whose outward appearance and manner fits in with the socially accepted standards of repute and respectability. Professionals' motivation and action in this matter have been documented by many writers on the professions (e.g. Berlant, 1975; Macdonald, 1984, 1989; Parry and Parry, 1976), but graphic accounts of professionals' social status and the way their clients and patients assessed them can be found in nineteenth-century novels, especially in the work of Trollope (for example, *Dr Thorne*). In short, gentlemen wished to have their money, their property, their bodies and their souls dealt with by gentlemen, and ordinary people followed their example if they could afford to. Professional bodies therefore strove to display their respectability and to achieve upward social mobility.

But this is only one side of the coin: the collective pursuit of economic advantage is, in a sense, more important, but cannot in the nature of things be separated from the drive for respectability. In the economic order, to use Weber's term, the professional project is pursued in two main areas: the legal closure and monopolization of the market and the occupation; and the exclusive acquisition of the knowledge and education on which the profession is based. While this is the 'practical' as opposed to the evaluative side of the project, it also has its value as a source of prestige. Possession of education is itself prestigeful and its value can be enhanced still further if the certification can be obtained from a highly regarded institution – Ivy League, Oxbridge or *grande écôle*.

The professional project can be represented diagrammatically as in Figure 1.1.

Larson's conceptualization clearly has value for social historians (Geison, 1984; Goldstein, 1984; Ramsey, 1988) who use it as a general starting point rather than as a research model, while Macdonald (1984, 1985a, 1989) and Witz (1992) have followed it in a more detailed fashion. On the other hand, some writers have found it less than satisfactory, and in order to keep a balanced view of the conceptualization that will be the central theme in the chapters that follow, it is important to review their objections (which are sometimes implied rather than explicit). It must be remembered that we are only dealing here with the Weberian part of Larson's work, not that part where she shifts to Marxian concepts nor indeed her later Foucauldian formulations. These later changes of direction by Larson mean that she might be regarded as her own most serious critic, because these two theoretical positions are fundamentally at odds with the neo-Weberian stance adopted here. But for that very reason – that is, the theoretical distance between them and the approach to be taken in the following chapters – there is little to be gained from an attempt to accommodate to their point of view; the differences that exist are disagreements, not critiques.

So what are the lines of enquiry that offer a critique, rather than a rejection of the profesional project? Probably the most explicit comes from Halliday (1983, 1987). The first of these tackles Larson's treatment of professions on a number of points, but the latter, *Beyond Monopoly*, as its title suggests, is concerned with a perceived deficiency in the 'professional project'. Halliday argues that Larson, like most other writers on the professions, has not used primary sources in her work and therefore has not had the opportunity to observe how little time a professional body actually spends on the pursuit of monopoly. His own work has given him access to the archives of the Chicago Bar Association and from his study of these he concludes that not only did the quest for monopoly take up a relatively small proportion of the Association's time, but also that much of its effort could be seen as public spirited in that it was directed towards the improvement of the law and of the legal system.

These points are well made, but it is also true that Halliday himself shows that at certain stages in its history the Association acted vigorously in the interest of its monopoly. Abbott (1988) likewise shows that lawyers in New York and in England have had to exert themselves considerably to obtain and preserve their monopolies. Furthermore one must consider how far efforts to improve the law and the legal system are entirely disinterested, for success in this regard will have a practical pay-off for the

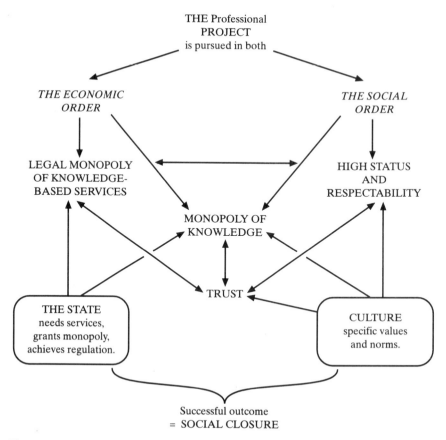

Figure 1.1 *A working theory of the professions: a conceptual outline*

lawyers as well as giving them a share in one aspect of the functioning of the state.

All in all, one may conclude that Larson may have overstated her case somewhat, but that this does not represent a serious flaw because the 'professional project' is an 'ideal type' (Weber, 1978) and therefore the extent of the drive for monopoly in any particular case is a matter for empirical investigation. If it were absent altogether, that would be another matter, and one which will be considered in a later chapter. This question is connected to another which emerges clearly from Halliday's work and that is that the legal profession is normally in a different relationship to the state from that of other professions. This is something which will be examined in later chapters, but for the time being it should just be noted that this special relationship with the state must be borne in mind when evaluating the supposed altruism of the actions of the legal profession to improve the law.

The depth of Halliday's analysis of one metropolitan legal association is matched by the breadth of Abbott's scholarship in *The System of the Professions* (1988) – which should not be taken to mean that he skims across the surface of his subject matter; far from it. Abbott does not offer an explicit critique of Larson in the way that Halliday does, but he does in a sense talk past her by treating the study of the professions from the point of view of a weak version of systems theory. But the system in question is one of competition, in which occupations vie with one another to obtain control of a 'jurisdiction' and to defend and if possible to extend its boundaries. It is therefore quite simple to see Abbott's data as examples of Larson's thesis and the fact that there is not unlimited professional work and that professions compete vigorously for it, does nothing to undermine the validity of the 'professional project'. In fact there seems to be no significant difference between a 'jurisdiction' and a 'monopoly'. What needs to be added to Larson's formulation is the recognition that a profession does not merely mark out its domain in a bargain with the state; it has to fight other occupations for it, not only at the time, but before and after as well.

A third source of possible modification to Larson's model is to be found in the work of Burrage (1988) and Burrage, Jarausch and Siegrist (1990). While neither of these papers refers explicitly to Larson, there is nothing that makes them incompatible with the latter; in fact both may be fruitfully used to modify the concept of a 'professional project'. Burrage (1988) has been discussed above: nothing in it conflicts with the Larson model but it becomes patently clear that there is in the latter a distinct underemphasis on inter-societal differences, on the role of the state and on the whole question of political culture. The differences that Burrage discusses between Britain, the USA, France and Germany are profound and, at the least, cast a shadow on the validity of much Anglo-American writing on the professions. So the theoretical sociological concept of the professional project has to handle empirical problems that range from the

systematic demolition, in the USA in the first half of the nineteenth
century, of any conception of elitism whether of birth, education or
expertise, and hence the removal of the most important rungs in the
ladder of social prestige, to the almost complete domination of professional occupations and education by the Prussian state of the same
period and the consequent near-impossibility of a professional group being
able to strike a bargain with the state (a situation that was even more
clearly observable in the former USSR in the present century).

But once again one must remember that the 'professional project' is an
'ideal type', and the phrase in Weber's original definition to the effect that
the ideal type contains elements that are 'more or less present and
occasionally absent'. So aberrations of the kind just outlined do not
invalidate the concept; they merely make it clear that a heuristic concept
is doing its job and the model requires some elaboration to continue to
function as a research tool.

Conclusion

To understand how those knowledge-based occupations that aspire to be
accepted in society as professions set about achieving their goal, the
concept of a **'professional project'** promises to be more fruitful than most
and has a clear affinity with a Weberian action approach. As formulated
by Larson it has considerable analytical power, but needs some modification and amplification to handle the breadth of data to be covered in this
book. So the following points must be appended to the original structure;
thus buttressed, it will serve as the theoretical framework for the material
presented in succeeding chapters.

1 In order to achieve a monopoly, or at least licensure, an occupation
   must have a special relation with the state. Many writers have made
   this point but the phrase that conveys it best is perhaps **'the regulative
   bargain'** (Cooper et al., 1988: 8). But the style of 'the regulative
   bargain' will be strongly conditioned by the **political culture** (Burrage,
   1988; Joppke, 1992), or the **political power network** (Mann, 1986, 1993)
   and this must be seen as an ever-present feature of the world in which
   the profession has its being.
2 Although a profession may be granted or may secure for itself a
   monopoly, it still must strive in the arena or compete in the market
   place against others who can provide similar or substitute or complementary services. It must, therefore, at the least defend and
   probably enlarge the scope of its activities; or to adopt Abbott's apt
   term, its **jurisdiction**.
3 Halliday's (1987) point that professions are not entirely self-seeking
   must be kept in mind. While there is no need to revert to the
   functionalist view, which takes professions entirely at their own
   evaluation, these occupations are providing the services that they claim

to provide in relation to the life, health, property and other matters of crucial importance to their clientele. It is, after all, essential that they do so, because they cannot keep afloat on ideology alone. Some of their actions may be mere self-enhancement, economic or social, but by far the greater part of the actions of members of professions are providing a service for their patients or clients. The actions of professional bodies are more likely to be self-seeking, but even here the profession must be able to persuade the public and the legislators that there is a reasonable quantum of altruism and public spirit in their motivation, and these audiences are not totally gullible.

4   The overall strategy of a professional group is best understood in terms of **social closure**. Especially as developed by Witz, this Weberian concept offers a basis for understanding the progress (or otherwise) of the professional project, the conflicts and interaction that develop between and within occupations, and a means of grasping the nature of their discriminatory actions, and the way they contribute to the structured disadvantages of gender, race, ethnicity and so on.

In the chapters that follow, the concept of the 'professional project', expanded and modified as outlined above, will be the guiding principle in the selection, presentation and analysis of material on the professions. Theoretical presentation will not obtrude nor, it is hoped, obscure the flow of argument; but these will be what Gouldner (1970) terms 'the domain assumptions'.

Notes

1   In taking a pragmatic line on the use of the word 'professional', I am following Abbott (1988), but one must be aware of the rather different slant to be found in Kimball (1992). In a sense, both writers are following the dictum of Wittgenstein: 'Don't ask for the meaning, ask for the use.' Abbott's mode of following this prescription is to say, 'There are so many uses, many of them tendentious, that one has to take as part of one's inquiry the problem of how and why these uses come to exist, and leave the matter of "meaning" to one side.' Kimball, by contrast, while accepting 'use' as the starting point, examines the way in which the 'meaning' of the term has changed over the past four centuries, as a way of exploring historical cultural change. This is certainly a worthwhile endeavour and of considerable interest to the sociologist of the professions, but the dismissal of most sociological work as 'presentist' (i.e. ignoring historical development) seems to undervalue the sociologists' point of view (of which Kimball is well aware). However, discourse analysts might think that he is bent on reinventing the wheel with his study of 'rhetoric'; on the other hand he gives a strongly reasoned argument for preferring his concept of 'archetectonic' to 'ideology' and 'cultural hegemony'.

2   Declared by President Monroe in 1823: it stated *inter alia* that the American continent was no territory for future European colonization.

2
Professions and social stratification

The sociology of the professions makes an important contribution to the study of stratification – more important than is often realized (Macdonald and Ritzer, 1988). One reason for this is that the professions started to appear in their present form contemporaneously with modern capitalist industrial society; in fact, since modern society is knowledge based, professions, as knowledge-based occupations, are an integral part of the modern social formation. The study of professions, especially of the history of their professional projects, therefore sheds light on the way that part of the modern class system developed.

Secondly, the professional project has the market as one of its main themes and this draws attention to an aspect of modern society omitted from the usual terminology, as employed in the previous paragraph; modern, industrial, capitalist society is a *market* society. The debate between Marxian and Weberian sociologists, on the nature of social class, hinges to an important extent on the former's insistence that Marx was correct to give social production a unique position in sociological explanation, and that capitalism has an inherent tendency to monopoly, which enables the owners of the means of production to dominate all markets and therefore society. Weber's definition of capitalism, on the other hand, emphasizes a number of features – rationality, the capitalist spirit *and* formally free markets in capital, labour, goods, services and raw materials; and it does not suggest that the owners of the means of production achieve monopolistic positions in any of these.

The emphasis on market, in addition to shifting the prime focus from relations of production, has two other important consequences; it facilitates the introduction of the gender dimension to social stratification, and it dispenses with the Marxian lumber (or 'blindfold', as Murphy, 1990: 87, terms it) of surplus value in service occupations and 'non-productive labour'. These are given considerable attention by Larson (1977), but it is the market that is of more importance in understanding modern society.

Theorizing social class

The professional project has as its objectives the securing, enhancement and maintenance of the social and economic standing of its members, and thus the achievement of a relative advantage in the structure of inequality. It therefore plays a part in the social stratification of society, and the purpose of this chapter is to consider what that role is, how significant it is, and what light can be shed on social stratification, when approached from this point of view.

Social class is the usual term for stratification in modern society, and is contrasted with the systems of caste and estate that characterized agrarian society. But class is different from most areas of sociological study in its intangibility: the sociologist studying work, crime, organizations, the family or religion has the object of investigation immediately to hand – cops and robbers, cathedrals and ritual, conformers and rate-busters. As Roberts et al. (1977) put it:

> The question 'what is a social class' is really incapable of definitive answer ... It is worth pointing out the fundamental concern of the classical writers, including Marx, in expounding the definition of social class, was to explore the inter-relationships between the economic, political and other factors involved in systems of stratification. These are the real issues ... Arguing about definitions is an unnecessary distraction. (1977: 17–18)

In the words of Abercrombie et al. (1988: 36–7), 'this means that identifying just a few major classes is a matter of interpretation rather than being self-evident and objectively determined'. Penn (1985: 12–13) like-wise notes that for many sociologists 'class is theoretically derived and appropriate consciousness is sought among its supposed members, and discrepancies are explained away by mediating or obscuring factors. This analysis puts the cart before the horse ...'; he therefore recommends that social class is a matter for investigation, rather than *a priori* assumptions. Finally, Savage et al. go even further when they state that 'the very status of class analysis is uncertain' (1992: 219).

There is a certain irony about this lack of objectivity of social class, because it is only as society emerged into modernity that people began to use the term in its current sense, and it is only with *The Manifesto of the Communist Party* in 1848 that a conceptualization is formally set out – albeit in decidedly polemical terms. Agrarian society is regarded by historical sociologists as unequivocally a class society, in which the ruling class of warriors and literati ruthlessly exploited the peasant producers, and that all three categories (and sometimes more) were clearly – even legally and possibly ritually – defined, and it is only as these certainties disappear that it apparently becomes necessary to theorize social class. Marx, of course, was sure that the old certainties were in the process of re-establishing themselves in a new form, but reality became, if anything, more fluid and the growth of stratification theory correspondingly lush.

The view from Marx

In many respects the work of Marx continues to set the agenda for discussion of and research into social class, and in particular the question of the validity of his conceptualization of the structure of inequality provides one of the main foci of sociological work on this topic. Other important topics are, first, the use of social class as an independent variable in the study of other social phenomena, and secondly, the degree of social mobility in a society which has as a background the political question of whether there is the degree of 'openness' that is often claimed for modern democracy. But even in these last two topics, the debate over the best way to characterize and measure this less than wholly empirical feature of society inevitably comes to the surface for the reason that it is not verifiable, in the way that other social characteristics are – gender, ethnicity or religious affiliation for example.

This debate hinges on the value of Marx's theory, and that is particularly contentious because it claims, in effect, not to be more accurate, or more insightful (etc.), but that it is *right* (and others are wrong), because it is founded upon a correct (scientific) perception of human nature, and therefore of the deep structure of human society. In this view, the fact that human beings have to *produce* the means of their livelihood is the essential feature of human existence and hence the determining feature of human society.

> In the social production which men carry on they enter into definite relations that are indispensable and independent of their will; these relations of production correspond to a definite stage of development of their material powers of production. The totality of these relations of production constitutes the economic structure of society – the real foundation on which legal and political superstructures arise and to which definite forms of social consciousness correspond. The mode of production of material life determines the general character of the social, political and spiritual processes of life. (Bottomore and Rubel, 1963: 67)[1]

Now in a sense Marx *is* right: human beings *do* have to produce in a way that no other species does. Owing to their basic nature, humans do have to cooperate, and they do indeed have to enter into 'relations of production': this is a salient feature of all societies. Furthermore, with the advent of industrialism, the nature of production relations took a significant turn, because it was no longer possible for ordinary producers to own or control the means of production; the concentration of capital required was beyond their reach. The propertyless industrial worker was the norm in contrast to the feudal peasant of the preceding era, who may have been in a servile status, but in the ordinary way could not be turned off his land or out of his cottage, and who owned his own tools and sometimes a share in a plough team. Marx indeed recognized that, however bleak the lot of the feudal peasant, that of the industrial worker was more alienating: the feudal lord had at least a number of non-financial relationships with his serfs – 'relations of respect, subordination and duty. His relation to them is therefore directly political, and even has an *agreeable* side' (Bottomore and Rubel, 1963: 134: emphasis in the original).

But in spite of recognizing the drastic change that industrial capitalism was bringing about, Marx turned to the past for his projection of future society. 'The history of all hitherto existing society is the history of the class struggles' he wrote in the *Manifesto of the Communist Party*, (McLellan, 1980: 188), and what he predicted was that confusions of his contemporary world would be resolved into an increasing polarization of classes and the simple confrontation that had, according to him, characterized earlier social formations. His later writings did not rely on this simple extrapolation from the past, but on his theory of the development of monopoly capitalism, and therefore by-passed the implausibility that this distinctive new form of society would adhere to the regularities of the past. But the dominance that Marx predicted would accrue to capital was based on the premise that material factors and the resultant relations of production were, in accordance with his view of human nature, paramount. In fact Marx had misread the nature of agrarian society. Because the ruling class had either controlled the system of economic production, or had successfully exploited the producers, he attributed their dominance to economic power. In fact it was their control of political, military and ideological power networks that gave them control over the economic sphere, and the great change in the shift to modernity was that for the first time since the neolithic revolution the ruling class allowed the holders of economic power freedom of action, and economic power came into its own.

So although Marx may have been misled by the contemporary salience of economic power into giving it a more universal importance than it had in fact enjoyed, there is no doubt of its significance in the mid-nineteenth century nor in the period since then. Nor can one dispute the importance of the 'relations of production' in determining the structure of inequality in modern society. The division between management and workers is manifested not merely in a difference in the levels of financial reward; the nature of the work, the degree of danger (both of accident and disease), the fringe benefits, the nature of controls, the hours worked (especially shift-work), the degree of trust (Fox, 1974), the freedom of action, the time-span of control (Jaques, 1976) – and many other things – locate these two groups in totally different social positions. These differences are the practical consequences of the relations of production and are rooted in the authority/subordination that they entail and the exploitation that they allow: from them flow clearly disparate life situations and life-chances, and round them distinctive class cultures develop.

There is no doubt that this division is the salient fact of the structure of inequality in Western societies at the height of their first and second industrial revolutions, and its practical details can be found in the graphic prose of novelists such as Dickens (*Hard Times*), Zola (*Germinal*), Upton Sinclair (*The Jungle*). But that is not the whole story, as is apparent from (for example) Lockwood's ([1958] 1992) depiction of the 'Blackcoated Worker'. The toiling industrial masses were never more that 35 per cent of the working population, and while theirs was the archetype of the position of the propertyless worker, that of the clerk was just one of the categories that resulted from other features of modern society that must rank in importance with capitalism *per se*, namely the new mode of cognition, the market and bureaucratic authority and organization, which as the embodiment of formal rationality, Murphy (1988) sees as the most important of all. Tied up in all of these is the active spirit of inquiry and expansion that distinguishes modern from agrarian society – and which Marx recognized (ironically enough) when he wrote that 'the bourgeoisie cannot exist without constantly revolutionizing the instruments of production and thereby the relations of production, and with them the whole relations of society' (Marx, 1958: 37). Indeed they must, but knowledge, markets, the state, the military and many other aspects of society were (and are) also being revolutionized, and whatever the tendency or potentiality for capital to achieve monopoly in particular markets, other aspects of social life are on the move.

Some of these mitigate the severity or nakedness of exploitation, but what is significant for our present purpose is the fact that many of them provide the rich soil from which the middle class grew, long before modern society became industrial. In mid-seventeenth-century Britain, with agrarian society a century and a half in the past, there was a significant middle class, ranging from the owners/managers of modest craft enterprises to substantial entrepreneurs, from the penurious younger sons of the gentry to the wealthy bankers and ship-owners, from the scriveners at the lower end of the professional scale to the judges and fashionable doctors at the other. This class had a broad base because at the lower end it recruited from yeomen, craftsmen and the younger sons of the gentry, while at the top its successful members brought landed estates, with the later possibility of a knighthood or even a baronetcy (Earle, 1989). These were not displaced or supplanted by the emergence of industrial capitalists in the next century, and in fact the steady growth of the state during the eighteenth century and its rapid growth during the Revolutionary and Napoleonic wars increased the numbers of civil servants, and of the agents and factors through whom they operated and on whom the military depended – all of whom fall into this class. The nineteenth century saw the emergence of a whole new category of managers for the industrial enterprises, and the new occupations of engineering, accountancy, architecture and so on swelled the ranks of the middle class still further. In the twentieth century, far from shrinking, the growth continued as the huge bureaucracies of the state and of private enterprise arose.

But the important features of modern society besides industrial growth, which lie behind this expansion of the middle class, are the knowledge/ cognitive revolution and the existence of the (relatively) free market. This means that not only is there scope and encouragement for invention and innovation, but those who can acquire or develop aspects of esoteric knowledge that can be translated into a marketable service are free to do so (especially if it can be credentialled), provided the state will allow them to. So while Marx had correctly identified the most important feature of industrial society, with an analysis that is still valid a century and a half later, he made it paramount and monocausal in a way that could not, and still cannot, be justified.

The Neo-Marxian perspective

It has already been noted, in Chapter 1, that Larson's (1977) treatment of the class position of the professions owed more to Weber than to Marx, although she herself clearly thought otherwise. At this date the work of Carchedi (1977) and Wright (1979) was not available, and although Larson in some of her later work (1980) takes up some of their ideas, it is in Johnson (1980) that the professions are examined for the first time from this neo-Marxian perspective. Johnson's paper actually draws on an earlier essay of Carchedi's (1975) which deals specifically with the middle class and with the awkward problem for Marxian theory of the persistence and indeed the efflorescence of the middle class. He points out that Weber's model of the class position of the professions (1978: 304) bases their power on knowledge, which, he argues, cannot enable them to compete on equal terms with those whose position is based on the ownership of capital. Furthermore, the Weberian analysis fails to indicate what kind of knowledge or skill would be of sufficient social value to give professional groups a secure place in the class system of modern societies, and is thus merely a variety of technological determinism. Johnson's application of neo-Marxian thinking, on the other hand, has the relations of production and the division of labour as the focus of analysis and thereby deduces what forms of knowledge and expertise are seen as socially important. The power of professionals is therefore merely contingent on the imperatives of the capitalist system. Professions are thus part of a comprehensive view of class structure and play their role in three particular aspects of class relations, namely, appropriation, realization of capital and reproduction of relations of production.

Johnson's view of the class position of professional occupations is therefore much more complex than the original Marxian prediction of the absorption of the middle classes into the proletariat. In this formulation such strata will continue to exist because they are part of the essential processes of capital, and Johnson pays particular attention to the accountancy profession as being the crucial element in the 'realization' of capital. Johnson concludes:

> the authority of 'professionals' within bureaucratic contexts will be determined by the manner in which their work activities articulate with or relate to these dual processes: in carrying out the functions of capital or the collective labourer at the level of appropriation or realization. Thus, any analysis of the relationship between the organization of occupational knowledge as work, and social class formation must consider the complex outcome of these dual processes. (1980: 361)

So it is not knowledge *per se* that gives professionals their relatively high status in society, but the value that such knowledge has for the capitalist system.

A similar view can be found in the work of Boreham (1983) who also takes the neo-Marxianism of Carchedi and Wright as his starting point. These writers contend that the power of professionals, however sophisticated or arcane their knowledge, can never equal that of the owners of capital, and that the success of professionals is only countenanced by 'capital' in so far as it fits the requirements of the system: 'capitalist domination ... is ... exercised not only through control of commodities and the reproduction of commodity relations at the point of production but also the integration of new occupational strata into class alliances' (Boreham, 1983: 714). By this stage in his argument Boreham has reached that pitch of abstraction where empirical data are apparently no longer necessary, in the manner castigated by Sacks (1983: 16–17). Murphy (1988, 1990) argues the case in a manner both more moderate and more lucid; but his work is concerned with social closure and will be dealt with later in this chapter.

But before assessing just how much of Marx's conception can be usefully retained, it is necessary to sketch in the Weberian viewpoint.

Weber on stratification

The important distinction between Marx and Weber is that the former insists on the primacy of material factors. He adopted this stance in opposition to the Hegelian idealist orthodoxy of the intellectual environment of his university days, and no one today would quarrel with the way he 'stood Hegel on his head'.[2] Weber is equally renowned for asserting that he did not 'aim to substitute for a one-sided materialistic an equally one-sided spiritualistic causal interpretation of culture and of history' (1976: 183); and in fact one finds in his work (whether empirical description or causal analysis) a balance between material and other factors.

In dealing with stratification, Weber puts economic factors first, which like Marx, he terms social class; but he goes on to elaborate it in a way quite different from Marx and to add two other semi-independent dimensions. First of all, he does not conceptualize class as dichotomized simply into capital and labour: both camps lack homogeneity and divide up at various times and places according to their common interests or antipathies. Furthermore, he specifically provides for the existence of a middle group – those with qualifications and credentials. This provides a picture of a society that is divided by its material interests, which, at the same time, provide members with their 'opportunities for income'. Secondly, Weber gives an independent significance to those factors that Marx would see as mere epiphenomena of the relations of production or inconsequential hangovers from an earlier era; that is, groupings or categories that exist by virtue of social values and evaluation, or in other words status groups. Religiosity, militarism, learning, leisure and various other qualities can provide a basis for social grouping whose members have common interests and which have the capacity to act collectively; and to whom the other members of society react. Both classes and status groups may engage in the collective pursuit of their interests and thereby enter into the third dimension of stratification, the political order (1978: 926–38).

Now this conceptualization of the structure of inequality remedies a number of the problems that inhere in the Marxian account. While still giving pride of place to material and economic factors, it allows room for others, removing the need to strain for economic explanations for events and situations which can be accounted for more parsimoniously in (for example) religious or military terms. It envisages less than cohesive classes and, most important for the present purpose, it gives an independent existence to the middle class.

It is this independent existence that is a problem for Marxian writers, one which they sometimes deal with by theoretical elaboration and sometimes by denying it. The first course has been adopted by those who write, under one rubric or another, of the new middle class (NMC). Wright (1985), Carchedi (1977), Carter (1985), Crompton and Jones (1984) and many others have attempted to deal with the middle class that intractably refuses to be proletarianized, and cannot in any strict sense be said to be capitalist. Even by extending 'ownership' of capital to include those who manage, control and co-ordinate, the resulting ambiguous or contradictory categories tend to remain theoretical, in spite of the laudable efforts of some – especially Wright – to verify them empirically. In real life they (and particularly the professions) seem as obstinate as the working class (Penn, 1985) in their lack of fit with Marx's conception.

Those who would deny the independence of middle-class locations follow the route of monocausality, exemplified by Johnson (1980), who starts his essay with the words 'Work is a relation of power', but continues in a vein that implies that it is *the* relation of power. In the context of the professions, knowledge is clearly another candidate (and as we have seen in Chapter 1, Foucault and his followers give it the same over-riding causality as Johnson would ascribe to work). But to accord to knowledge the potential for a basis for social power is, according to Johnson, to fall into the heresy of technological determinism (1980: 342), a lapse so fundamental, it seems, that nothing more need be said.

Weber and Marx

The study of professions adds an important dimension to the under-standing of social stratification, namely that of action. Action is certainly supposed to be present in the Weberian approach and that might even be expected to be found in the Marxian approach also, to judge from such phrases as 'Men make their own history . . .' or 'Philosophers have only interpreted the world differently; the point is, however, to change it.' But Marxian theory is, however, likely to be interpreted in structuralist terms, in which the capitalist mode of production is seen as generating inevitable class divisions. The Weberian approach on the other hand conceptualizes class as having a number of components which derive from the market and from status honour, both of which involve the notion of social actors, in the first instance as competitors and in the second as participants in mutual evaluation.

The nature and extent of the divergence between the two viewpoints has been reviewed by Marshall et al., who conclude that:

> differences between Marxian and Weberian theory . . . can be magnified or minimized according to which of the several Marxian and Weberian accounts of class one elects to pursue. . . . In practice, therefore, the differences between Marxian and Weberian frameworks are more obvious from the details of research procedure than from the axioms of class theory itself. . . . the major traditions of class theory are sufficiently ambiguous as to make any appeal to first principles wholly inconclusive in the attempt to apportion relative merit. (1988: 13–26)

But studies of social class are often carried out for the purpose of explaining some other feature of society, with the result that social class becomes an independent variable, which influences (for example) voting behaviour (Rose and McAllister, 1986) or 'disparity and discord' (Marshall et al., 1988: 1). Even though these studies employ categories that originate from an action approach, and can certainly avoid the criticism of 'crude determinism' that has been levelled at Wright (1985) by Marshall et al., they none the less acquire an unavoidably static quality, as a result of a concern to put individuals in the correct category, sociologically, or to trace their social mobility from one category to another. Given their theoretical and research concerns, they do not have the space to attend to the fact that the existence of some social categories at least requires constant work by their occupants, nor that the passage of certain individuals from one category to another is achieved by the collective efforts of members of a group. This omission may be remedied by considering the work on the rise of occupational groups.

It would not be fruitful for our present purposes to refight these old battles; the background on social stratification required for the sociological study of the professions can be found in the reviews provided, for example, by Abercrombie and Urry (1983) and Savage et al. (1992), and the way forward in the present context would be to attempt to build on some of the essential points of the classic theorists, in order to obtain a realistic framework in which to place contemporary professional occupations, and thereby to enlarge our understanding of both 'classes' and 'professions'.

Historical classes

It is important to remember that 'class' as a concept was invoked and developed by Marx as an essential element in a **dynamic** theory of social change – a point that is easily lost to sight in studies that are concerned with the here and now, as represented by cross-sectional survey data. As Savage et al. (1992: 227) comment:

> It is very difficult to integrate a theory of class based on a synchronic examination of class positions into an account of diachronic historical change. As G. Marshall et al. (1988: 84) point out, it tends to lead to a mode of class analysis in which the structure of class positions is taken as given and is not itself subject to enquiry.

So their essential character is that they are features of the pattern of inequality in a society that persist over time, and that while they may be regarded as historical actors with 'causal powers' (Savage et al., 1992: 6), they lack the empirical existence of a ruling house, a church, an army, or a trade union.

Once human society had passed through the neolithic revolution and had developed settled agriculture of grain crops, there was a storable surplus that could be appropriated. Any group powerful enough to do so thereby immediately reinforced its power and became a dominant class, exploiting the remaining producing part of society. Although Marx's assertion (quoted above) that 'The history of all hitherto existing society is the history of class struggles', is a gross overstatement, dominant classes have certainly existed in agrarian society ever since that time.[3] The dialectic relation with subordinate classes, however, was, for the most part, lacking: in most societies for most of the time the characteristics that Marx saw as defining a class can only be applied to the exploiters. The exploited rarely conceived of themselves as anything like a class, identifying and acting as part of a 'segment' (Mann, 1993: 3, 8), and more often than not a segment which would include their local upper class representatives. And so, as noted above, class relations were exploitative, but had a human face.

It is with the advent of capitalism, as Marx correctly noted, that the situation changes. Commodity production, private, exclusive ownership of the means of production and propertyless, 'free' labour are the essential features of a system in which Marx believed dialectical struggle would steadily develop. The 'laws' of capitalist accumulation would lead to the emergence of monopoly on one hand and miserization on the other, making the exploitation inherent in capitalist relations of production painfully apparent, and generating the class consciousness necessary for the revolution that would sweep away the social formation based on exploitation. Mann (1973: 13) succinctly outlines the components of this consciousness, and his later work (1993: 28) goes on to show how other, more immediate memberships tend to moderate the potency of class consiousness, so that it is only on rare occasions that convinced and convincing militants are able 'to move large numbers by persuading them that their class sentiments are a more significant part of themselves than they had previously believed'.

Mann identifies six main class actors in the emergence of modern society: the old regime and the *petite bourgeoisie*, the capitalist class and the working class, the middle class and the peasantry. But as he emphasizes at the outset of his study of the sources of social power (vol. I, 1986: 4), 'Societies are much *messier* that our theories of them', and social classes are no exception. In particular he notes four 'fault lines' that may weaken the solidarity of whole social classes, namely, the economic sector, the economic enterprise, the nation state and, of particular relevance for the middle class, strata and fractions. The early modern bourgeoisie contained many sub-strata and the later 'middle class contained an elongated hierarchy and three distinct fractions (professionals, careerists and *petite bourgeoisie*) ... Such differences lead to distinct organizations (including) the profession.' Mann continues:

> For these four reasons, the relations of production do not merely generate whole classes. They too are a confused battleground on which our identities are fought over. Purely economic actors have been normally smaller, more specific, and more fragmented by internal sectionalism and crosscutting segmentalism than Marx's great classes. None the less, his classes have played important historical roles. Why? Not because the 'law of value' or some other economic law polarized all these economic particularities into great class camps. Instead, *non-economic* organizations have welded solidarities among these economically heterogenous fractions, strata, and segments. (1993: 29)

Here, I believe, is a theoretical approach to stratification, which clearly makes use of insights from the classic formulations of Marx and Weber, but is basically starting afresh, because it is part of a theory of society which has its own objectives and agenda; it is not trying to hammer the old concepts into a different shape for new purposes. It provides an appropriate backdrop to the notion of the professional project because it paints a sociological scene which is populated by actors, whose exercise of power give society its dynamic quality, and allows for a diachronic analysis. It is not monocausal, it comes to grips with the messiness of society and while it conceives of the structure of inequality as based in exploitation, it acknowledges that the 'roundaboutness' of market society obscures the nature of that exploitation and allows it to go unchallenged. At the same time it includes the theorizing of the middle class, and their existence and ability to secure an enviable slice of social and economic rewards, because it is not wedded to the idea of dialectical conflict between two 'great classes'. It therefore does not have to resort to explaining the middle class as a 'problem' with ambiguous or contradictory locations in the scheme of things: it does not have to insist on their subservience to capital, or their imminent proletarianization.

However, Mann's theory aims for explanation at the societal level, and to focus on a particular segment of the middle class, such as the professions, other concepts must be invoked, and to these we now turn.

Contemporary classes

Much work on the middle classes in recent decades has focused on the notion of the 'service class' – an idea that was introduced to the English-speaking world by Dahrendorf (1959), who took the idea from the Austrian Marxist Karl Renner. Savage et al. (1992) examine the value of this concept, which in its original sense implied providing services for the capitalist class and facilitating, or even making possible, the exploitation of the working class. They show that although it has moved in the hands of later writers, such as Goldthorpe (1982), to a more neutral meaning and a conceptualization that allows the class an independent existence, it still lacks the wherewithal to theorize the middle class in a way that accounts for its formation and for 'the forms of exploitation that may give rise to actual social class collectivities' (Savage et al., 1992: 18). Although these authors could not refer to Mann (1993), their own account of the dynamics of service class formation, the historical formation and the contemporary restructuring of the British middle class has an undeniable affinity with his ideas.[4] Both review existing class analysis as it relates to the middle class, and propose a reformulation of those ideas which accounts for the independent reality of that class, and which attributes the same kind of value to particular historical, contextual factors. Mann's is a broad-brush picture of modern Western society as a whole: Savage et al. provide the concepts for theorizing the middle class in a particular society, and for distinguishing its constituent parts; and this provides one facet of the means for analysing the professions in social class terms. The other, to which we shall turn in due course, is 'social closure'.

After reviewing the numerous meanings that have been ascribed to the term 'service class', Savage et al. turn to the work of Eric Olin Wright (1985, 1989). While not attempting to defend him against the many shortcomings that his critics have pointed out, Savage et al. argue that his starting point has considerable value for a valid theorizing of social class. This is that, in order for one class to exploit another it must possess **assets**, which give this advantage, and which constitute an axis around which class formation can take place. Wright proposes three types of such assets; property (or economic assets), organization and skill.

The first of these is no novelty, and follows the basic Marxian proposition that class is based on the ownership of the means of production. This type of asset enables the bourgeoisie to exploit the propertyless workers, and the *petite bourgeoisie* to exploit members of the family. The second, organization, is not normally to be found in Marxian analysis, nor is it even specifically theorized in the work of non-Marxists, although Salaman (1981) gets close. Wright points to the significance of power relations within organizations as a major axis of class formation, and shows that organizations constitute productive resources for their higher ranking members.

> the asset is organization. The activity of using that asset is co-ordinated decision making over a complex division of labour. When the asset is distributed unequally, so that some positions have effective control over much more of the asset than others, the social relation with respect to that asset takes the form of hierarchical authority. (Wright, 1985: 80)

The important change of emphasis, as compared with Weber, for example, is that it is no longer on the instrumental aspect or the technical efficiency, but rather on the way in which they have become embodiments of inequalities of power; as noted earlier in this chapter, these inequalities start with the differential in economic rewards and culminate in a vast divergence of culture and life chances.

Wright's third asset is only a novelty in that it is incorporated into a Marxian account of class, for it clearly has a place in Weber's analysis. However, although Wright introduces the idea that organization and skill are potential bases for class divisions (and therefore a way of conceptualizing a differentiation within the 'service class'), he tends to see skill merely as way in which its possessors can secure 'strategic' positions within organizations, and this, he believes, is not enough to put them in an exploitative relation to holders of 'non-strategic' positions. He concludes that this potential axis of class relations must therefore be abandoned. Thus organization and skills assets seem rather more problematic than the ownership of capital: organizational position is something which gives power, but is highly context-specific and cannot readily be stored; skill, on the other hand is 'owned' by the individual, but does not necessarily put him/her in an exploitative relation to the unskilled.

Savage et al. resolve this conundrum by borrowing the concept of 'cultural capital' from Pierre Bourdieu.

Economic and cultural capital

Bourdieu (1973) has an original approach to the problem of theorizing social class which plausibly combines the structural and relational emphasis of Marx with the evaluative and status-related features of Weber's 'opportunities for income'. For Bourdieu, capital is 'the set of actually usable resources and powers': this can be viewed as economic resources on the one hand – capital in the Marxist sense – while the socially valued attributes and credentialled knowledge that characterize Weber's status order and the middle class respectively, are brought together into a credible alternative basis for exploitation and social power. Economic capital becomes a means of exploitation when it can be used to dominate those who lack it and who have to work under conditions set by the

owners of capital: likewise cultural capital accrues to those who successfully impose their values on other groups and legitimates its culture
through the processes of 'symbolic violence'.

Wright's difficulty in showing that skills could be regarded as an asset, by
which exploitation could be achieved, is now resolved, because skills
themselves are not an axis of exploitation: rather, they are a valued activity
that is legitimated by a cultural 'field'. Cultural capital, while less tangible
than financial, economic capital, is none the less real. It is stored in
peoples' heads and minds, and manifested in their physical behaviour and
appearance; as such it can be passed on to offspring. The concept of
cultural assets was originally used by Bourdieu to account for educational
inequality, and to show that those children who had acquired cultural
assets from their parents were better able to succeed educationally. By the
same token, they are more likely to be successful in acquiring skills which
form the bases of professional and managerial tasks and which can thus be
deployed in the labour market, and can be used to obtain access to
organizational assets. In this sense they have an indirect relation to social
inequality, for they do not directly exploit the propertyless worker, nor do
they directly bestow authority over inferiors. The place of cultural assets is
summed up by Savage et al.:

> We can now begin to piece together the respective causal powers of the assets
> underlying middle class formation. Organization assets allow superordinates to
> control and exploit the labour of subordinates but cannot be stored easily.
> Cultural assets can be stored more readily, through the 'habitus' (Bourdieu's
> term for the set of internalized dispositions that govern people's behaviour), but
> in order to reap economic rewards have to be deployed in other fields in which
> their value has to be established, rather than assumed. In this respect cultural
> assets are almost the mirror image of organization assets. In order for cultural
> assets to become axes of exploitation of labour they need to be applied, often in
> organization contexts. Hence, those with cultural assets often have to acquire
> organization assets in order to transform them into assets that allow them to
> exploit others. On the other hand, those with organization assets often have to
> transform them into cultural assets in order to store them and hence transmit
> them. This dynamic is the central feature of middle-class formation, and the way
> in which this evolves in any particular society will lay the foundations for
> patterns of middle class formation. (1992: 17)

The bases of class formation are therefore threefold.

1 Property assets are the most robust basis for class formation, because
  they are most readily stored and are applicable to almost any kind of
  undertaking.
2 Organization assets may give considerable advantage to incumbents of
  high positions, but these are very context-specific and cannot be easily
  stored or transmitted.
3 Cultural assets can be stored and transmitted, but not as easily as
  property assets; and they need to be deployed in the labour market,
  organizations or other contexts, if they are to produce material, rather
  than status rewards.

The foregoing theorizing of social class has the following notable advantages:

1 Not only does it fit with the multi-stranded view of society, in that a plurality of social powers is reflected in the several axes of class inequality; it also gives a certain primacy to economic assets while at the same time depicting the independent significance of other assets, and the way the two interrelate.
2 Furthermore, the notion of social causal powers is combined with a very real sense of the need for social actors to put their assets to work, in competition with other actors, if their assets are to pay dividends. The silver spoon, if left in the mouth, will not feed its inheritor.
3 Most importantly for the present purpose, this theorizing of the middle class specifically allows for the conceptualization of different segments, one of which is the professionals.

Social closure

Now although Savage et al. (1992) build on their theory of the middle class by showing its historical development, with divisions that reflect the assets available to different segments, and with an examination of the contemporary changes that are occurring, they do not devote much attention to the actual tactics employed by individuals, families or collectivities. Their references to social closure are almost exclusively concerned with gender divisions, even though the source of these references, Witz (1992), is one of a number of recent writers on the professions who see it as the principal method of professional, and therefore class, formation. These students of the professions represent one of three broadly distinguishable areas of sociological work on this concept: in addition, there is the rather more anthropological and social psychological use to be found in some mid-century American urban sociology and whose most lucid exponent is Beshers (1962); and finally there is the rather more theoretically orientated work of Parkin (1979), Collins (1979, 1986) and Murphy (1988, 1990). As the first school of thought has already been introduced in the previous chapter, the main attention here will be directed to the last two, looking first at Beshers.

Social action and stratification

Sociologists who are closer to Weber than to Marx would argue that the realities of social stratification require the analysis of 'social closure' based not only on property in the means of production but on other criteria as well (Collins, 1975, 1979, 1981; Murphy, 1988; Parkin, 1979). The most important of these criteria is 'credentialism' which is seen as being of the essence of 'collective social mobility' of professions (Hughes, 1971) – although Parkin regards it rather differently, as part of bourgeois individualism. Studies of the 'professional project' provide a useful counter-balance to the more usual concerns with individual social mobility, for their concern is precisely with 'collective social mobility'. Historical studies, for example, those of Parry and Parry (1976), Larson (1977) and Macdonald (1984) are important because they give one an opportunity to see *how an occupational group deploys its resources* (that is, its 'assets', in Savages's usage) *in its struggle for collective social mobility.*

Although the concept of social closure has come to be regarded as important since the mid-1970s, there is an earlier and insightful use of the idea by Beshers (1962), who was working in the tradition of urban sociology associated with Lynd and Lynd (1929), Warner and Lunt (1941) and others, who studied 'Yankee City', 'Middletown', 'Elmtown', 'Jonesville' etc. This is a study of urban social structure in the sense of the relations between the multiplicity of economic, ethnic, religious and other groups to be found in a large American city. Beshers argues that such groups employ a variety of strategies to maintain and enhance their status position *vis-à-vis* each other and that they employ precisely those strategies of exclusion and usurpation that have been applied more recently to professions (Larson, 1977), gender (Witz, 1992) and stratification generally (Murphy, 1988). Beshers (1962) emphasizes those aspects of everyday life and behaviour which at first glance seem quite trivial until one realizes that these are precisely the clues that one uses all the time to place other members of one's society, in order to formulate one's mode of action towards them. In the professional context this is borne out by the work of Dingwall (1979), whose study shows how health visitors 'accomplish profession' by the acquisition of a repertoire of behaviours and a knowledge of norms and mores appropriate to their occupation, and that their professional tutors are meticulous in instilling these codes. Health visitors' professional socialization, like any other, is not merely the learning of an occupation's special, esoteric knowledge; it is the assimilation of a comprehensive style of providing a service based on that knowledge, which helps to convey the impression to the recipients and the public at large that the service is special and its practitioners are special people. In a later chapter we shall see how the longer-established and more dominant professional occupations emphasized their 'specialness' by insisting that their members were *gentlemen*, thereby establishing their superior status *and* exclusion based on gender.

Beshers's interest in the social psychology of stratification leads him to express his overall view of stratification in terms of symbols and behaviour, which would be anathema to the Marxian school, as would his emphasis on race and ethnicity as more important than class in American society.

> When we turn to the relationship between the stratification system and the system of values, we are really dealing with the internal mechanisms of the stratification system itself. For the over-all stratification system consists of symbols, not persons, and the symbols reflect the values of the society. Thus, the definition of a stratification system is dependent upon a certain minimum of

common values. The persistence of the stratification system therefore depends
on the communication of these values to subsequent generations. (Beshers,
1962: 54)

Beshers is mainly interested in the perception of the value/stratification
system by families and the way their symbol-orientated action affects their
position within the system, and reproduces that system. He does not
concern himself with organized occupational groups, but there is no
reason why they should not be included in his scheme of things. The fact
that his work is not pitched at a high theoretical level means that he does
not really have an equivalent term to 'assets', focusing rather on the
symbols of prestige and repute and on the means of obtaining, deploying
and retaining them by families. None the less, his topic is essentially the
way that cultural assets are used and the pattern of stratification that
emerges.

The point to be learned from Beshers (1962) is that in addition to the
large-scale moves and conflicts on which studies of social closure in
professional occupations concentrate, there are a hundred and one ways of
self-presentation and behaviour which professions deploy to achieve and
maintain social closure: and that these range from the style of building
they choose for their headquarters (Macdonald, 1989) to not leaning on
the furniture while speaking to clients (Dingwall, 1979).

The theory of social closure

The work of Murphy on social closure and kindred topics is worthy of
special note, because his aim is to bring the essence of Weber's thinking to
bear on the contemporary world, in a manner that does justice to the
scope of his thought. At the same time he takes advantage of the insights
of Parkin (1979) and of Collins (1975, 1979, 1986). Like Mann, whose
model of society starts from 'circuits of praxis' on which are built 'power
networks', Murphy's sociology starts from 'the pursuit of the mastery and
control of nature and other people' (1988: 250). The major shift in the
nature of human society comes with the advent of the application of
rationality as opposed to tradition to the principal means of pursuing this
objective, namely social closure.

The value of Murphy's treament is that it gives a broad theoretical base
to the concepts employed in the analysis of the middle class and the professions, and while he probably would not entirely agree with the general
conclusions to be found in Savage, Witz and the present work, that has
more to do with the assessment of the empirical evidence than with
fundamental divergence of theoretical perspectives.

Social closure has always been the means by which dominant –
originally conquering – groups have achieved and maintained their
position. 'In the past exclusionary codes were explicitly related to the
collectivity within which one was born . . . lineage, caste, racial, ethnic and
gender exclusion etc. Historically these exclusionary forms arose as a

result of the conquest of one collectivity by another' (1988: 219). Murphy then goes on to say that 'exclusion provoked powerful usurpationary movements', but those he cites are all phenomena of the modern period, and its seems that he has inadvertently slipped out of the traditional world that he was discussing. In fact there were very few usurpationary movements in agrarian society, partly because, as Murphy himself notes, that society was wholeheartedly devoted to the maintenance of the status quo; and partly because, as was noted earlier in this chapter, there was little class consciousness or class formation outside the ruling class. But the exclusion rules of modern society are based on rationality, which means that their basis is open to rational challenge – the elite no longer have a monopoly of truth and knowledge; and the modern world is conscious of those class and segmental divisions that provide the social basis for the movements that he mentions, such as civil rights, anti-apartheid, feminism etc. Thus in modern society usurpation is now the counterpart to exclusion in a way not characteristic of traditional society.

Despite such challenges, however, social closure operates successfully in a number of important ways, and in this Murphy's account parallels that of Savage et al. (1992), on the whole. The former puts decidedly more emphasis on the exclusionary nature of property and its importance for the ruling/capitalist class, but this difference is due to the fact that Murphy's subject matter is the whole of society, while Savage et al. are focusing on the middle class. But both point to the way in which capitalism and the state create bureaucracies, which function in an exclusionary manner, which while intended to be in the interest of the capitalists and the political elite, also redounds to the benefit of the managers and professionals that staff these organizations. Likewise there is in both treatments an importance attached to cultural capital and to credentials.

Savage et al. do not in fact give any prominence to Murphy's ideas, and refer to him in only the most general way; so it should be made clear that Murphy's work has a distinct theme that does not appear in Savage et al. at all – namely the bureaucratization and formal rationalization of society. While Murphy considers that Weber's work is less well developed than it might be, this is merely a sin of omission, and Murphy's objective is to develop the Weberian tradition: one way in which he does this is to link up the study of class formation with the process of formal rationalization – for Weber, the 'ghost in the machine' of modern society.

Murphy's central points are, first, that property exclusion cannot be taken as the *fons et origo* of class inequality, for this fails to account for the forms of exclusion in state socialist societies.

> Rather than stretching the conception of property and capital to fit positional, credential, cultural, and Communist Party exclusion, it would be better to begin with more general concepts. I suggest that bureaucratization and formal rationalization are appropriate general concepts for this task, and that contemporary positional, credential, cultural property, and Communist Party exclusion

are particular forms and special cases of these two more general phenomena. (1988: 175)

This particular emphasis is not to be found in Mann (1993) or Savage et al. (1992), but it certainly is not at odds with their stances. But of direct relevance to the present theme is Murphy's other emphasis; namely that Parkin (1979: 54, 58) is wrong to attribute the same importance to cultural capital as to property. Now it might be claimed that Murphy had misread Parkin at this point, and that what Parkin meant was that it is their importance to his theory that is equal, not their practical importance in society. But while Parkin certainly does mean this, it is quite clear that Murphy's reading is correct, for the rather curious reason that *Parkin does not actually theorize the middle class*. Although Parkin provides the basis for others to do this, as can be seen from the work of Savage et al. (1992) and Witz (1992), his own position is that:

> property ownership ... [and] credentialism ... may thus be thought of as the core components of *the* dominant class under modern capitalism. . . . [There are] common class interests fostered by private property and credentials ... (1979: 48) (emphasis added)

Murphy is right to prise these two apart, and to describe 'positional property' and 'cultural capital' as metaphors, but his next point, that 'Credentials are better conceived of as derivative and contingent forms of exclusion than as a principal form' (1988: 162) needs further consideration, especially because in other statments of this point (Murphy, 1988: 173, 1990: 71) he adds the term 'subordinate'. This seems to imply that the middle class, far from being part of the bourgeoisie as Parkin would have it, have an almost illusory grasp on their exploitationary 'assets'. Murphy certainly does not go as far as this – which would take him into a Marxian position, which he clearly does not hold: but on the other hand, he might not agree with the line taken in the present work, that the credential, cultural and other assets of the middle class do give them a real exploitationary power, a power inferior to that of property, but not *subordinate* in the sense of being 'under the direction of'. His view that the legally established credentialled professions – law, medicine, accountancy etc., – are in a markedly different position from, say chemical engineers, fits in with the present treatment, as does the lesser power he ascribes to the 'mediative professions' (cf. Johnson, 1972).

Any divergence in the two accounts lies in the interpretation of the data on which the nature of the middle class, and professions in particular, are based. It comes down to a question of the degree of independence that cultural capital can be said to have, and the degree of jurisdiction that its possessors have over it. My view is that the possessors of such an asset have an advantage over non-possessors that amounts to exploitation. The fact that wielders of ecomomic power can alter the nature of that asset renders their advantage contingent, but in the case of the 'legally established' professions, it is not clear what would constitute an empirical example of such an event. And while the job of the chemical engineer may be in the gift of the board of directors, a chemical plant is not going to be run by someone whose terminal age of education was 16.

This has been a somewhat selective review of work on social closure, but then it is not intended to be an exhaustive examination of the topic; rather it is aimed at showing the utility of this concept, in that at the societal level it is integrated into one version of Weber's master concept of 'rationalization', at the level of class formation it can be viewed as the means by which members and segments of society make use of their 'assets', while at the level of individual and family status and identity it is the mechanism by which social and psychological rewards are obtained. Finally, it is an important key to understanding empirical cases of the professional project.

Social stratification and the professional project

The main themes outlined in the preceding sections enable the sociologist to get to grips with the long-debated problems of the middle class, including the professions. All these treatments draw on the insights (and problems!) generated by the founding theorists, and on the commentaries of Parkin (1979) and Wright (1985) and others, and the following synthesis is an attempt to theorize the location of such groups in the system of inequality.

1   Mann (1993) provides a theory of society and social development that is closely woven in with the historical data of Western society. It takes a dynamic, diachronic view of the social world that emphasizes its messy pluralistic nature: in particular it rejects the idea of 'great classes' in dialectical struggle, in favour of the notion of a varying number of classes whose self-consciousness and potentiality for action depends on a number of factors, not necessarily connected with class, such as the existence of what he terms 'segments'. This allows for the theorizing, not only of the middle class *sui generis*, but also of sections within it, such as professions.
2   The actual means that enables a class or sub-class to appear on the socio-historical stage is theorized by Savage et al.'s (1992) concept of 'social assets'. Members of the old regime, the bourgeoisie, the middle class and so on have greater or less possession or control of economic and cultural assets and of organization, which enable them to exploit (directly or indirectly) those members of society who have fewer assets, or none.
3   The strategies that the possessors of assets employ to exert and secure their exploitative power are social closure and usurpation; and these can be brought into play at different levels, and in different modes – as has been demonstrated by Beshers (1962) and Murphy (1988).

The only serious lack of fit between these three theoretical schemes emerges at this point, for Murphy is emphatic that one of the most important middle class assets – knowledge and credentials – is contingent upon the owners of economic assets, the capitalists, whereas the view of Savage et al. is that it exists in its own right. The present work takes the Savage position, with the proviso that no asset gives its possessor complete freedom of action, which must always be circumscribed by competitors, the market, public opinion and the state (cf. Johnson, 1980: 379).

The advantages of this general theoretical stance are that:

1   The middle class(es) have a real existence and do not have to be explained as 'contradictory' or 'ambiguous': nor is it necessary to have to search for evidence that they are in the process of withering away or being absorbed by some other class.
2   They also have a real history, and as modern society emerged in its various forms, they can be seen to have coalesced into bourgeoisie (*grande* and *petite*), professionals, *bildungsbergertum*, state functionaries, careerists and so on. Such groups developed, merged and waned as capitalism and the state developed and changed. As European states staked out their nineteenth-century empires, a whole sub-set of the middle class appeared to staff their administration, to maintain order and defend boundaries, to exploit their markets and to build their infrastructure.
3   It follows that the middle class is not homogenous. There have always been differences, initially between the landed gentry and their urban connections in banking, shipping and colonial exploitation,[5] and later between entrepreneurs, civil servants, the military, professions, managers etc. It is the great achievement of Savage et al. to have shown how consistent these differences are at the present time and how they have their roots in the historical development of capitalist, market society.

None the less, Savage et al. feel that, in spite of the strength of their argument, in which the concept of class formation is placed centre stage (1992: 226), problems remain in sorting out the rival theoretical claims of 'structuration' (Giddens, 1973), 'class formation' and 'class structure' (Goldthorpe, 1980; Marshall et al., 1988; Poulantzas, 1975; Wright, 1985). The nub of the matter, they seem to be saying, is that class theory is multi-stranded. It aims to deal with a whole collection of processes whereby individuals move into class positions, classes are formed, become social collectivities and causal powers, while at the same time constituting the structure of exploitation and the background from which new generations emerge to reproduce and modify that structure. The only way to comprehend such complexity is to give priority to diachronic, historical analysis of class dynamics, and even that involves abandoning some of the strands in the theory (Savage et al., 1992: 228). To adopt other tactics 'leads to a mode of class analysis in which the structure of class positions is taken as given and is not itself subject to inquiry' (Marshall et al., 1988: 84); and E.P. Thompson is quoted as denying the possibility of being able to 'stop the clock' in order to analyse class structure: 'if we stop history at a given point, then there are no classes but simply a mass of individuals' (1963: 11).

The appropriateness of Savage et al.'s line of thought for the present purpose becomes particularly clear at this point, for they put forward the study of the professions as an illustration of viability of their notion of dynamic class formation. They do not elaborate this illustration at length, getting no further than quoting Johnson's programmatic statement that 'A profession is not then an occupation, but a means of controlling an occupation'; that is, the question is not who is in which occupational position or how is that position to be defined, but *how is the group controlled, and how are claims to privileged positions developed and sustained* (1992: 229)? in short, the professional project.

The professional project is carried forward at three levels – the individual, the practice or the firm, and the professional association. All these, in various ways, bring their assets to bear in pursuit of the project.

Economic assets are not the most important for professionals, because there is no great investment in buildings, plant or machinery. On the other hand, professional practices need working capital, to pay the rent and any employees until fees start to come in; and they may not come in very promptly, because the gentlemanly standards of professionals inhibit them from chasing their debtors too vigorously. There is also the need to display a certain level of 'respectability', in the location of premises, the standard of furnishing, the personal appearance of staff and so on. A practice cannot be started on a shoestring; a certain amount of capital or credit is needed.

These considerations also apply to the professional organization. The profession has to be administered and regulated and some central facilities – library, council chamber and so on – have to be provided and the greater part of the business of closure, credentialling and so on is conducted at this level. When setting up their headquarters, British professional bodies have almost invariably taken the opportunity to obtain a building that proclaims their status in its size, construction, location and so on: and as such things do not come cheap, they are also making a statement about their financial soundness (more of this in Chapter 7).

Secondly, there are **organizational assets**. 'Isn't it the case that most credentialling bodies are organizations?' ask Savage et al. (1992: 15). Indeed they are, and while they are on nothing like the same scale as the huge bureaucracies of government, industry or commerce, they do actually belong to the members and serve their interests directly, providing an important means for the preservation and transmission of assets. But professionals have, since the mid-twentieth century, been turning their professional partnerships into organizations. Accountants are the most notable example, for the largest half-dozen or so are international organizations with tens of thousands of professional members (employees and partners). Lawyers are not far behind, especially in the USA, and the biggest architects' practices are also sizeable. Doctors, who fifty years ago were often sole practitioners, now work in group practices, whose range of activities is still expanding, while hospital doctors and surgeons are clearly beneficiaries of organizational assets. The fact that many professionals now work in state or private bureaucracies should be seen not as a sign that they are being proletarianized (because they are subject to bureaucratic rules), but rather that it makes them, to an extent, beneficiaries of organizational assets.

Cultural assets are the most important, for the professional project is above all aimed at achieving social closure in the realm of knowledge, credentialled skill and respectability. At all three of the levels mentioned above, professions and their members work diligently at these tasks. Individuals strive, more or less consciously, more or less overtly, to distinguish themselves from their friends and competitors; presenting themselves as having the standing, the knowledge, the skill, the demeanour appropriate to a vet, a midwife, a barrister or a dentist. Firms of professionals work even more systematically at the same task, but at a public level, as well as doing some of the work of developing, protecting and passing on the knowledge and skills of the profession: and in the very act of carrying on their professional business they are helping to maintain the professional monopoly. The professional body likewise pursues all these objectives, but at the same time promotes the professional image and consciousness and advances the collective interest *vis-à-vis* the public, other professions and the state. Merely to describe these activities is to show how closely related the groups' cultural assets are to their economic advantage, and therefore to their capacity for exploitation.

A more detailed examination of the deployment of 'assets' by professionals will be included in Chapter 7, when the concept of the professional project will be given explicit empirical shape.

The dynamics of class formation

The study of the professional project can provide a valuable insight into the changes that have occurred in stratification during the history of modern society: but this can only be achieved if the discussion of collective social mobility is set in the context of the stratification of the period in which it occurred. But this exercise is confronted with the problem that *the social order, including social stratification, was going through a process of change of which the emergence of the groups in question was itself part.* The development of the accountancy profession is a case in point, because enormous changes occurred in the social structure during the period of its emergence, from 1800, when there seem to have been about a dozen people in London calling themselves 'accountant', to 1880, when the

Institute of Chartered Accountants in England and Wales, with a membership of 1200, was granted a Royal Charter.

In 1800 Britain was already industrializing, producing 10 million tons of coal and importing 50 million pounds of cotton, but many aspects of the old order still prevailed. Modern social classes were no doubt beginning to form, but historians such as Perkin emphasize that two-thirds of the population still lived in the countryside and that many of the pre-steam factories 'were conscious examples of paternal benevolence and discipline, ideal examples of the old society in miniature' (1972: 178). This was in some respects still a 'status society', with one major horizontal cleavage between 'gentleman' and 'common people'. Above and below this divide

> was a finely graded hierarchy of great subtlety and discrimination, in which men were acutely aware of their, exact relation to those immediately above and below them, but only vaguely conscious except at the very top of their connections with those of their own level.

This continuum was held together by patronage in a great variety of forms and which crossed the major cleavage.

Within thirty or forty years the dramatic changes of rapidly, advancing industrialism had made themselves felt. The working class had taken on its characteristic form (Thompson, 1963) and contemporary sociological models of class can usefully be applied (Foster, 1974; Neale, 1972). However, two important observations must be noted before assuming that the system of social stratification into which British professions emerged was essentially modern. The first is made by Neale (1972), who argues that a five class model, which he derives from Dahrendorf's (1959) ideas, should be employed, rather than a model of present-day stratification.

The five classes are made up as follows.

1 **Upper class**: aristocrat, landholding, authoritarian, exclusive.
2 **Middle class**: industrial and commercial property-owners, senior military and professional men; aspiring to acceptance by the upper class.
3 **Middling class**: *petit bourgeois*, aspiring professional men, other literates and artisans; individuated or privatized like the middle class but collectively less deferential and more in favour of radical change.
4 **Working class A**: Industrial proletariat in factory areas, workers in domestic industries; collectivist and non-deferential.
5 **Working class B**: agricultural labourers, domestic servants, urban poor; deferential and dependent.

The important point for the study of the professions is the distinction between the **middle** and the **middling** classes, the former traditional and deferential and still adhering to the values of Perkins's 'old society', the latter aspiring and privatized (cf. Goldthorpe et al., 1969). It seems likely from Foster's (1974) study of the emergent bourgeoisie of Lancashire that only a small minority of this group allied themselves with the 'county' people or voted Tory; the greater part stayed closer to their radical origins, voted Whig and saw themselves as part of the national, urban bourgeoisie.[6]

Stratification in Britain at the start of the nineteenth century is still characterized by the fine gradations of the traditional status system. The class system emerges as one where the landed elite are still prominent and where both the middle and the working classes have traditional and radical elements. In this general picture it is the division of the middle class that is of particular relevance to study of the emerging professions. Capitalist industrialization and commerce provided opportunities for aspiring professionals by means of the increased division of labour they generated. The case of accountants is a clear example of the provision of openings by reason of 'global capital's' need for 'control agents', to use the Marxian terminology of Johnson and Caygill (1978). Scottish and English accountants were fortunate beneficiaries of Britain's leading position in industrialization, which enabled them to lead the development of accountancy across the world, including the USA.

But British accountants, like other emergent professions, tended to draw their members from Neale's 'middling class', and such groups had to work out strategies which would ensure their acceptance in society. The more radical members would no doubt have preferred to see the system and its values change, so that their work would be recognized on its own merits: the USA provided an example of this, and as will be seen in Chapter 4, the establishment of professional acceptability on the basis of 'modern' criteria was a long hard road. British professions, however, preferred to exploit the traditionalism that still strongly persisted in midnineteenth-century society, as will be demonstrated in the examples of the professional project presented in Chapter 7. It is worth noting here the case of Scottish accountants, whose (successful) petitions to the Privy Council for Royal Charters emphasize their *respectability* far more than their education, training or usefulness to society, thus relying on an appeal to traditional, status values, rather than 'modern' criteria. In all respects they fit Neale's model of the aspirant 'middling' class (Macdonald, 1984).

This account of professional and class formation and collective social mobility has no direct counterpart in the treatment of this topic by Savage et al., which emphasizes the point made earlier that the origins of the modern middle class date to an early stage of modern society and have relative independence from the 'old regime'. On the other hand there is nothing in Savage et al. that conflicts with the thesis advanced here. Savage's view is that:

> The crucial changes evident in the nineteenth century did not involve the novel formation of professions, but rather they created the structural links between professionalism and cultural capital, educational credentials, gender segregation and the state which came to mark out the singularity of British middle class

formation. They marked the development of a close association between cultural assets and professionalism: an association of far-reaching historical significance. (1992: 38)

What the present analysis adds is the particularly British way in which the professional project combined the symbols of the 'old regime' with modern knowledge, credentials and meritocratic criteria; as well as incorporating 'old' middle class personnel, often the bearers of those symbols.

What should be noted in relation to professional/class formation is that aspirant groups engaged in collective upward social mobility pulled themselves up both by their own bootstraps *and* by the coat-tails of those above them.

Professions, bureaucracy and proletarianization

Organizations are, it has been argued above, a potential source of middle class assets; but there has long been a school of thought that sees bureaucratization as antithetical to professionalism. One version can be found in Hall (1968, 1975), whose studies of professionals working in organizational settings lead him to conclude that there are many circumstances in which organization rules drive out professional criteria, diminishing professional power and prestige. Another aspect of this idea is that bureaucracies are not merely systems of rules, they are also means of handling knowledge and therefore the threat that they pose to the professional ideal is the systematization of professional knowledge in a manner that will remove professional judgement, 'indeterminacy' and ultimately professional power, by rationalizing the corpus of knowledge into bureaucratic procedures and division of labour (Jamous and Peloille, 1970). A further view is that the division of labour in the form of bureaucratic specialization is just one element in a three-pronged assault on professionalism, the other two being 'paraprofessionalism' (new groupings of skills that arise from the demands of a more discerning and better educated clientele), and the advent of widespread information technology (Haug, 1973). Finally there is the 'deskilling' hypothesis of Braverman (1974) and his followers, of which deprofessionalization could be seen as part.

Now, there is some truth in all these observations, and in the case of the last-mentioned there is the long-standing prediction of Marx, based on his theory of capitalist development, which his devotees revere, with all the conviction of chiliasts awaiting the Second Coming. But Braverman's hypothesis and its endorsement by many sociologists has probably contributed significantly to the decline of Marxian theory in recent decades, because it stimulated a plethora of research, the greater part of which disconfirmed the hypothesis. While it is true that many aspects of work have become 'deskilled' in the sense that old crafts and shop-floor know-how have been displaced, the overall composition of the workforce is more, not less, skilled (Littler, 1982; Penn, 1985; Wood, 1982, 1989).

The more particular issue of the proletarianization of the professions depends on the answers to three questions: (1) What are the consequences for professionals of their employment in bureaucratic settings? (2) What ensues from the introduction of IT? (3) Is the appearance of 'paraprofessionals' a real innovation or is it merely the normal functioning of the 'system of the professions'? Let us look at each in turn.

(1) Even the data of Hall (1968), who is one of the first to float this idea, throw up a number of consequences of the bureaucratic setting for professionals, and his mature conclusions (1975: 135) emphasize the variety of professional work situations rather than regarding any as 'de-professionalized'. In fact the conclusion that would flow from the view of Savage et al. is that professionals in organizations might well have added organizational assets to their class advantages. Chartered Accountants moving from private practice into organizational employment do not normally disadvantage themselves thereby; any diminution in professional autonomy is often soon offset by managerial privileges and sometimes by promotion to the highest levels. There has certainly been one leading British company with six Chartered Accountants on the board.[7] Likewise, one gets no sense that doctors employed by the Department of Health have jeopardized their class assets.

(2) The advent of artificial intelligence and publicly available technical data bases conjures up the visions, on the one hand, of the general practitioner reduced to a key-board operator, typing the patient's responses and getting out a computer diagnosis; and on the other, of a lay individual going down to the public library to get legal advice on the law of tort from an interactive consultation program. Neither seems plausible. The state will never relax the law on medicines to the point where a pharmacist will accept a prescription, or a consultant a referral, or an advocate a brief, from a machine. It seems much more probable that the existing professions will be able to incorporate new technology into their existing practice, by one or other of the strategies that they have successfully used to cope with social and technical change in the past. In fact some doctors have computerized patient records, which actually gives them more control over the consultation, for they have all the facts about the patient immediately available, without having to sort through a bulky file or rely on the patient's memory. Where such technology is more likely to advantage the lay person is in dealing with civil service departments, such as Social Security or Inland Revenue.

(3) Changes in the jurisdiction and market of a profession may well throw up challenges to the existing arrangements, but the views of Haug (1973) and Oppenheimer (1973) that there is a sea-change of such magnitude in technology or lay demand can only have seemed plausible in the heady 'counter-cultural' atmosphere of the late 1960s and early 1970s

(cf. Roszak, 1969). That is indeed the era of Haug's (1973) 'deprofessional-ism' paper, and of Oppenheimer's (1973) article on 'proletarianization'. Today, the evidence for these hypotheses seems to be essentially part of the ebb and flow of professional jurisdictions so clearly charted by Abbott (1988). Some of such challenges to existing practice may succeed, but they are far more likely to be deflected or absorbed by the existing occupations, and if successful, there is a good chance that they are mounted by a specialist group within an existing profession (cf. Halpern (1988), on the case of paediatrics in the USA). In fact, it seems that Haug (1988) is the only sociologist with any faith in the deprofessionalization hypothesis. She admits that there is insufficient evidence to retain it, but then continues, 'But certainly there is no evidence favouring rejecting it either' (1988: 54). By this she means that her hypothesis was a prediction – as indeed it was (1973: 208) – and that its non-fulfilment after fifteen years does not mean that it will not happen in the future: another chiliast!

The conclusion to this brief review of the possibility of the 'proletar-ianization' of the professions and the reduction in their class advantages by the forces of bureaucracy must be that the position of the established professions in Britain and probably in the rest of the Western world is not seriously threatened. Even if one acknowledges the force of Murphy's (1988) arguments, that their knowledge base and indeed their whole situation is contingent on the owners of capital assets, there still seems little doubt that their existing class advantages are such that they can not only resist the challenges of social and technical change, but very often they can turn them to their advantage. The greatest danger to their position is perhaps the state, which in recent decades has attempted to increase both regulation and market competition in relation to professions (Savage et al., 1992: 73); but they seem to have been able to accommodate to these pressures. The occupations which have lost some of their class advantage are those that Johnson (1972) terms 'mediative professions', that is, those who are dependent on public sector provision of the service that gives them employment – school teachers, nurses, social workers and so on.

Conclusion

The professional project is intended to secure for its members economic and social advantage, thus achieving upward social mobility. It is therefore essential to relate this conceptual tool to the social stratification of the society in which the project is pursued. Not only would this place the project in context, it should also widen our understanding of class formation and the working of the structure of inequality as a whole.

The notion of 'project' is by definition part of an action approach to sociology and is something that must be studied over time (although it could also be used in comparative synchronic studies); it follows that the conception of stratification that is used to contextualize it must also have these characteristics. Such a theoretical approach was found in the work first of all of Michael Mann, whose wide-ranging study of the historical development of networks of social power provides a theorization of social class with which the concept of professional project is entirely compatible. The important features of a diachronic approach and the explicit theorizing of the middle class, present in Mann, were also to be found in the work of Savage et al., together with a conceptualization of the basis of middle class power and the kind of exploitative advantages it conferred. The work of Murphy provided the theoretical analysis of that mechanism essential to the professional project, social closure. These authors explicitly modify and develop the Weberian tradition.

The bringing together of these conceptual strands provided a theoretical context for the professional project and an elaboration of the assets on which a profession can base its particular closure and usurpation strategies, thereby enhancing our understanding of professions. At the same time it is hoped that this combination of theoretical themes will shed some light on social class formation and especially the way in which class positions are, on one dimension at least, attained by the action of class members, rather than being the inevitable outcome of some 'law' of capitalist development.

A conceptualization of social class was thus developed that explicitly theorized the middle class and middle class formation, against a societal background of historical development and change; and which provided insight into the capacities of the middle class people to establish their new positions in a modernizing society, to achieve individual and collective upward social mobility and to attain the position of a 'causal power'.

In reviewing these conceptualizations of stratification, the middle class and the professions, there were a number of junctures at which the state appeared an important condition, or even the *sine qua non* of class or professional formation, and all the sources referred to in developing the theoretical perspective of this chapter devote considerable attention to this feature. We shall revert to this topic in Chapter 4, after a consideration of the diversity of professional formations to be found in different cultures (Chapter 3).

Notes

1 Those who argue that Marx should not be seen as 'determinist' should note how often such words as 'indispensable', 'definite' and of course 'determine' occur in his Preface to *A Contribution to the Critique of Political Economy*.

2 I do not know who, if anybody, actually said this, but what Marx wrote was 'My own dialectical method is not only fundamentally different from the Hegelian dialectical method, but it is its direct opposite' (Bottomore and Rubel, 1963: 23).

3 Engels's footnote to the 1888 English edition seems to disagree with me, but it is too vague to be sure.

4   One may note that Mann is a sociologist with a profound understanding of history and that Savage is a historian turned sociologist.

5   Jane Austen's *Mansfield Park* contains the classic example of Sir Thomas Bertram, who is a cultivated gentleman at home and (even if Jane Austen does not realize it) a slave-owning entrepreneur in the West Indies.

6   Another point to note about the system of stratification in the nineteenth century, as modern professions emerged, is the way in which the aristocratic elite survived, contrary to the accepted view that after the Reform Act of 1832 this is the century of the industrial and commercial bourgeoisie. In fact, both wealth and power remained very much in the hands of the landed aristocracy. The work of Arnstein (1973) and Rubenstein (1977) show that the really wealthy were to be found not in manufacturing, but in commerce and that they tended to be associated with the land-owners, who not only remained extremely wealthy, but who continued to dominate politics. In the sixty years following the Great Reform Act only two cabinets contained less than 50 per cent aristocrats, both Gladstone's – 47 per cent in 1868 and 41 per cent in 1892. Likewise, in the first half of the century 96 per cent of millionaires were land-owners, while in the last two decades of the century the figure fell to 39 per cent.

7   Grand Metropolitan Hotels in the late 1970s.

3

The cultural context of professions

'The professional project', as outlined in Chapter 1, is a conceptualization that some sociologists have found of value in the study of the professions, while others have either damned it with faint praise or acted as if it did not exist; yet others, more tellingly, have argued that it is so firmly based in British/American culture that its ethnocentricity undermines any potential it might have as a concept in general sociology. More particularly, it is claimed that the study of other societies shows that the state can act in ways that almost vitiate the capacity of knowledge-based occupations to act independently in pursuit of the professional project (Burrage, 1990; Collins, 1990; Torstendahl, 1990).

In order to evaluate these criticisms, this chapter compares the projects pursued by the professions of law and medicine in four different societies, as they moved into the age of industrial capitalism – Britain (or more specifically England), the USA, France and Germany. These projects are seen as being undertaken in interaction with the state, which is conceptualized in terms of 'crystallizations' of state structures (Mann, 1993).

It is concluded that, while there are empirical cases in which the actions of the professions are seriously circumscribed, these constitute one end of a range of freedom of action rather than an invalidation of the concept of the professional project.

Professions and the state

As noted in the conclusion to the previous chapter, professions aim for a monopoly of the provision of services of a particular kind; monopolies can only be granted by the state, and therefore professions have a distinctive relationship with the state. In order to discuss this relationship it is necessary to characterize the state; and since the emphasis on the 'professional project' is essentially a diachronic, historical one, I propose to turn to the work of historical sociologists for a model from which such a characterization can be drawn.

The works of Hall (1985), Gellner (1988), Tilly (1990), Corrigan and Sayer (1985), and Mann (1986, 1993), are all concerned with the empirical problems of the development of modern society and its institutions, and in general write in terms of social actors – states, classes, elites, the church etc. – rather than within the framework of a theory of *society per se*. In this they follow in Weber's footsteps and Mann and Hall, in particular, differ from earlier theorists in that instead of having 'society' as their master concept (Hall, 1985: 29; Mann, 1986: 2),[1] they start from the notion that human activities generate networks of power – economic, ideological, military and political. While the last of these, in modern Western (especially nineteenth-century European) society, has largely been in the hands of a state, which centralized administrative control over a defined geographical area, such control has rarely been total and unified, and has invariably been intertwined with certain aspects of the other three power networks. What is required for the present purpose is a model of the state that provides the means for the delineation of the emergent forms of the state with which professions have had to deal; and this can be found in Mann (1993). The components of his definition provide the basis for a consideration of the ways in which the modern state may vary, and the theoretical guidelines for a study of the way empirical historical circumstances have led to the particular manifestations of the modern state, in which professions have emerged in a variety of forms.

The full version of Mann's definition (1993: 55), 'much influenced by Weber', is:

1 The state is a differentiated set of institutions and personnel
2 embodying centrality, in the sense that political relations radiate to and from a centre, to cover a
3 territorially demarcated area over which it exercises
4 some degree of authoritative, binding rule-making, backed up by some degree of organized physical force.

But of great sociological importance are the additional observations that the modern state *penetrates* territories with both law and administration; and conversely, 'citizens' and 'parties' also penetrate the state (1993: 56–7): and that a distinction must be drawn between *despotic power* exercised by state elites over civil society; and the *infrastructural power* of a central state, whether despotic or not, to penetrate civil society. 'Far from being singular and centralized, modern states are polymorphous power networks stretching between centre and territories' (1993: 75). The task he then addresses is to chart the variety of ways in which states have 'crystallized', and it is this analysis that provides a basis for considering the different state/profession relationships.

This approach is in line with Mann's view that social existence is not only complex but 'messy' (1986: 4); the key to understanding the mess is the concept of power networks, but these are inevitably intertwined. Mann's theory of the modern state aims to provide a guide to the complexity of their development and an understanding of the particular crystallizations that were to be found in about 1914. 'Crystallizations' is a metaphor from chemistry, by which Mann (1993: 75) intends to convey the notion that the state in different societies took on different forms in relation to various aspects of political and other power networks. This is not the place to recapitulate these in full, interesting and valuable though they are: it is sufficient for the present purpose to pick up his conclusion that, at the extensive level, crystallizations can be discerned occurring on four broad tracks: towards the maturation of capitalist economic relations, towards greater representation, towards greater national centralization, and professionalizing and bureaucratizing state militarism.

It must be noted that in concentrating on these four, Mann acknowledges that he is leaving aside the moral-ideological crystallization (which relates the political with the ideological power network), because at this period it became less significant in its own right and became intertwined with representational and national crystallizations. But this dimension also became significantly intertwined with a sixth crystallization, the state as patriarchal, and this too he does not consider in its own right; this appears to be because his focus is on states and parties. This is a shortcoming for a study of professions, but is not too much of a handicap, for as will appear below, patriarchy is very much tied up with representation.

Capitalism is a feature that characterizes all modern Western states, one which met no serious challenge until after 1914. Although its particular crystallization varied according to the speed and timing of the move from feudalism, Mann agrees with the *Communist Manifesto* that 'The executive of the modern state is but a committee for managing the common affairs of the whole bourgeoisie'; except, that is, for the 'but', because he sees the state as doing a great deal more than this. On the other hand there is no reason to suppose that all states carried out this function in the same manner, although capitalism did generate classes and class conflict, which brings us to representation.

Representation in this period 'can be arranged along a continuum running from despotic monarchy to full party democracy, along which my countries [France, Great Britain, Austria, Prussia-Germany and the USA] moved unevenly' (1993: 83). Mann sees representation as having two aspects, contestation and participation: contestation started as a struggle by the newly emerging classes against monarchical despotism, and is concerned to establish the legitimacy of opposition, while participation is concerned with which classes and which ethnic, religious and linguistic communities should be entitled to the vote, to hold public office and to have access to state educational credentials. This is a point at which the state/patriarchy crystallization becomes significant, because in all these representational issues women were discriminated against.

The nation is likewise linked to the previous crystallization, for much domestic controversy was concerned with the question of *where* to participate: how centralized, how uniform and how 'national' should the state be? The issue of centralization versus confederalism provoked civil war, most famously in the United States of America, but also in Germany, Italy and the Hapsburg lands. It also materialized, less violently, in debates on how far the state should foster 'national' religious or educational systems. Infrastructures might be expanded in the form of local-regional government, as in the USA in its early years, or centralized, as in post-revolutionary France. The crystallization of nationhood also manifested itself externally, in the questions of how nationalistic, how territorial and how aggressive foreign policy should be.

Militarism is once again connected to the previous crystallization, because aggressive nationalism and geopolitics can only be successfully pursued in the modern world when backed by a bureaucratized and professional military; but it is also linked to the matter of representation, because an elite bent on restricting this requires a means of repression. Once again, the USA represents one end of the range of possibilities, with its low level of militarism, not only in the nineteenth century, but even, by European standards, up to the outbreak of the Second World War – although their capacity to conscript millions of men within months of the attack on Pearl Harbor might argue against this view. In Germany, the special position of the military as almost a constitutional part of the state represents the other end of the continuum.

Although I have given only a précis of the more relevant aspects of Mann's theory, it might be thought that this is still an overelaborate conceptualization for the necessarily simplified task of cross-cultural comparison envisaged here. But simplified though it may be, the reality is in fact complex (and indeed 'messy'), and I suggest that the state crystallizations outlined here enable one to get a realistic grasp of the variety of ways in which the state has developed and in which it functions in modern societies.

This point may be illustrated by a brief comparison with the framework employed by Joppke (1992), who undertakes a cross-cultural comparison of the way in which anti-nuclear protest movements have fared in different societies. It comprises the following elements.

1 **State structures**, which shape the actions of members of 'civil society'. These may be characterized in various ways, and Joppke quotes Badie and Birnbaum (1983), who distinguish between states that attempt to run the social system through a powerful bureaucracy and those that are much weaker and where civil society runs itself. Birnbaum (1988) contrasts the nineteenth-century French state (highly differentiated) with the German (fused with the dominant class), and with the British (undifferentiated and invisible) (Joppke, 1992: 313).

2 **Political culture**, which may be defined as 'the set of attitudes, beliefs and sentiments which give order and meaning to a political process and which provide the underlying assumptions and rules that govern behaviour in the political system' (Pye, 1968: 218).

3 **Temporal opportunity**, which is the second factor which mediates between state structures and collective action. In the case of professions for example, Burrage (1988) has argued that the social and

political revolutions of England (1642), America (1776) and France (1789) were crucial formative events in the development of the legal professions of those societies.

The first of Joppke's concepts bears a family resemblance to Mann's conceptualization of the state; in it, ideas similar to some of Mann's can be discerned, although expressed in much more general terms. The second, however, political culture, is a rather different idea from those to be found in Mann, and seems at first glance to introduce a useful amplification of the latter's approach, as it characterizes the framework within which political actors would operate: it seems to expose a shortcoming in Mann's apparently structural theory. But Mann describes his framework as a 'partly institutional, partly functional, polymorphous theory' and it is based on the notion of networks of power. These, in effect, incorporate the normative order, which means that 'culture' is part of the conceptualization of state, parties, elites, classes etc. who are the actors in the political power network. This is exemplified by the way in which he sees widely held political orientations as concomitants of particular political situations. American populism goes hand in hand with the lack of a cultured aristocratic elite and professions and a large civil service (1993: 573), nationalism in France was stimulated by military expansion (p. 579), while racism in Britain grew with the need to control the empire (p. 581). Likewise, in his account of the emergence of the post-colonial United States, the ideologies of tradition, liberalism and populism take second place to the political and material interests of the contending groups (pp. 159–62).

While at first glance it appears from Mann's approach that 'culture' is redundant as a separate concept, it is in fact incorporated into his account by means of a more detailed treatment of participants' interests than can be found in Joppke's treatment. The latter's theory is constructed in a way that makes 'culture' a necessary concomitant, largely because 'state structures' are presented in such general terms as strong versus anti-statism (1992: 315, 316), which themselves gloss over the refinements of infrastructural power, despotic power, state/civil society interpenetration and representation. But having said all that, 'culture' will be employed, since the material presented in this and the next chapter does have more in common with Joppke's than with Mann's, in that it deals with smaller scale social actors than states, classes and parties; and at this level 'culture' does have an expository and explanatory value.

Finally, 'temporal opportunity', when compared with the rigour of Mann's theory, seems a rather common-sensical notion; for in the interplay of multiple power actors, temporal opportunities are constantly occurring, and the more dramatic ones are merely the consequences of the weakness or failure of other power actors. For example, the success of the Bolsheviks in Russia in 1917 occurred in the temporal opportunity provided by military defeat; but on the other hand, in geopolitical terms, it was occasioned by the relative success of Germany, in national terms by the failure of the state and the miliary, and in the context of classes and parties, by the failure of the Mensheviks.

The problem of ethnocentrism

With these conceptual tools, the task of this chapter can be addressed – which is, as stated above, to assess the view that the notion of a 'professional project' is too close to its (admittedly) Anglo-American origins to further the study of this aspect of modern society. Critics who take this view have felt that this emphasis so distorts the study of the professions that it is necessary to reformulate the theoretical approach developed in Britain and America. Torstendahl (1990: 59), for example, argues that the very terms 'professionalism' and 'professionalization' are so bound into the English language as to seriously undermine their validity and interest. Another view is that existing frameworks are too circumscribed to cope with the comparative social history that the sociology of the professions now requires (Burrage et al., 1990). In this case the remedy is seen to be the development of an 'actor-based framework' which widens the scope of analysis by including the state, the users and the universities as equal participants on the theoretical stage (although specifically excluding Abbott's (1988) important emphasis on other professionals). Another attempt to deal with the supposed parochiality of current theory is that of Collins (1990: 15), who suggests that 'there are two principal models of this wondrous occupation we are tracking down: (1) the Anglo-America, . . . and (2) the Continental'. Such a proposal is not without its value for attention must certainly be paid to cross-cultural variation, but the outlining of 'ideal types', which is Collins's purpose, seems to be merely programmatic and, in the absence of any empirical material, generates no real advance.

So, to evaluate this critique, this chapter will review briefly the development of law and medicine in four different modern societies, with differing state crystallizations; England (not Britain, because Scotland is not covered), the USA, France and Germany. The focus is not so much on the details of the professions *per se* as on the features of the social and cultural context which formed their background, so that the extent to which it fostered or hindered their growth may be assessed. The concluding section of the chapter will consider whether the concepts introduced in the analysis of knowledge-based occupations are valid across cultures, and in substantive terms it will assess how far, in the modern cultural environment where knowledge is autonomous and markets are free, the possessors of specialist knowledge wished and were able to pursue the professional project, and what were the freedoms and constraints that they experienced in different societies.

At the same time, however, this discussion will help to deal with another problem; for in the past, sociologists of the professions have tended to ignore the effect of different cultures on the development of such occupational groups. Carr-Saunders and Wilson (1933), for example, write about the professions as if their remarks had universal applicability, whereas in fact their material is almost entirely English, with occasional references to Scotland. Johnson (1972) refers in his opening sentence to 'industrial societies' but he draws almost exclusively on American and British authors, without distinguishing between these two quite different cultures, and making no allusion at all to other industrial societies. Bias of this kind is understandable, or at least explicable, because in Britain and the USA professions have flourished as in no other cultural context, and by the same token other societies show different patterns of development.

But before embarking on this cross-cultural comparison, there is one crucial historical observation to be made, which is the contrast between the modern societies under review and all earlier, traditional, agrarian societies. *It is only in modern societies, where knowledge is a unified, autonomous realm (Gellner, 1988) and where free markets in goods and services exist (Weber, 1978), that the opportunity for professions to emerge has occurred.* This freedom and autonomy is part of the 'rationalization' of modern society in which new modes of cognition arose, distinct from the traditional 'status-cultural' knowledge (Murphy, 1988: 246) that preceded it; and in which traditional constraints on economic activity are dismantled. But the exercise of this freedom is then constrained by the reaction of a society, and more particularly of the state, to the initiatives of the professional groups. It follows that the various forms taken by the state are going to play a part in shaping the nature of that reaction, the openings that present themselves to knowledge-based occupations and the motivations of their members.

England

From the fifteenth century or earlier England was characterized by political unity and institutional pluralism. The success of the barons in maintaining their rights *vis-à-vis* the Crown was counter-balanced by the Crown's success in imposing a unified political order. This in turn relied, in part, on the support of the towns, who were rewarded by charters which gave them a measure of autonomy. This balance of institutions was the basis of a culture in which occupations were able to achieve a measure of self-government, and, in contrast to more centralized and autocratic regimes elsewhere in Europe, were able to defend their independence and carry it through to the modern period, so providing the antecedents for contemporary professions. Some of these connections may now appear somewhat remote, but in the case of law, descent can be traced directly.

Law

> We have heard the chimes at midnight, Master Shallow ... I do remember him at Clement's Inn.

> (Sir John Falstaff, *Henry IV*, part 2 Act III, scene ii)

Shakespeare's play is set in 1403–13 and occupies nine historic days and three extra 'Falstaffian' days: the latter are in effect Elizabethan and not two hundred years earlier (as may be seen from a reference to Tudor coinage). In the scene Falstaff and Shallow are talking about what were in effect their student days (fifty-five years earlier according to Justice Silence) in Clement's Inn. This was an Inn of Chancery, and one of ten or so Inns which acted as preparatory law schools from which students could proceed to apprenticeship in an Inn of Court and eventual membership of the Bar. (Clement's Inn and Clifford's Inn were linked to the Inner Temple.) But many of the students would become attorneys (the forerunners of solicitors) and for not a few it was an alternative education to a university. For Shallow and Falstaff and many more it would have provided the grounding for a country gentleman or county justice. Falstaff, in fact, although apparently enrolled in Clement's Inn, was also a page to Thomas Mowbray, Duke of Norfolk.

The purpose of this historico-literary digression is to illustrate the flourishing independence of the Inns of Court and of Chancery in the early modern period of English history. The means by which society was provided with judges, advocates and attorneys as well as those mainstays of local administration, the gentlemen JPs, were essentially independent of the state. Having been licensed or chartered in the distant past, they were effectively self-regulating, controlling entry, education, training and licensing. It can also be seen how the gentry – that crucial class for the development of modern England – were by this means linked to certain aspects of the decentralized state, providing the basis of local administration, the functioning of the legal system, the membership of the judiciary, and a recruiting ground for ministers of state. (In 1597, for example, Francis Bacon was both Lord Chancellor of England and Treasurer of Gray's Inn.) The legal profession was thus both autonomous and linked to the state through overlapping memberships, thereby exemplifying Birnbaum's characterization of the English state as 'undifferentiated and invisible' (quoted above).

At the end of the Tudor period, power in English society can be seen as a kind of symbiosis of monarch, Parliament and (what Charles II termed) 'lesser governments'. In other words there was a sharing of power with a variety of agencies – cities, boroughs, universities, trading companies and collegial associations of traders (Livery Companies) and professionals (Inns, Colleges etc.). But this is the period of the absolutist states: Spain, well established and now joined with Austria/Hungary in the Hapsburg Empire; France, a unified territory from the accession of Henry IV (of Navarre) in 1589; and, further afield, the Muscovite and Ottoman

Empires. With these examples before it, the English (or now more realistically British) monarchy tried to achieve a similar dominance, resulting in the well-known struggle with Parliament in the Civil War (1642–51); less well known are its consequences for the legal profession and the battle with the 'lesser governments'.

This upheaval is one of three societal revolutions examined by Burrage (1988), to show the cultural variation in the development of the state/ profession relationship as exemplified by law. The other two are the USA and France, and I shall draw quite heavily on his work in what follows.

It is not relevant to rehearse how Charles I claimed a divine right of kings and how Parliament demonstrated that the supposed embodiment of that right was only too mortal, except perhaps to note that the Parliamentarians got into a profound muddle in trying to provide a legal basis for their actions. On the other hand it is noteworthy that as soon as Charles called the Parliament that was to be his undoing nine years later, it set about reforming those legal institutions which it saw as the instruments of arbitrary monarchical power (the Star Chamber, for example). But because they saw themselves as *restoring* the proper legal order, Parliament did not have any plan for reform and certainly no explicit ideology on which such a plan could be based. But at the same time there were plenty of grievances against the legal system and a small flood of pamphlets and tracts appeared, which have survived thanks to the diligence of a bookseller near St Paul's who decided to collect every published document on the topic.

Many pamphleteers wanted a laification of the law in one way or another, but the dominant theme was an attack on the legal profession, their vested interest in complex and obscure law and legal proceedings, and the Inns of Court themselves. During the Commonwealth, three major attempts were made to reform the law so as to deal with such abuses; by the Hales Commission (1651–2), the Barebones Parliament (1653) and the Lord Protector Cromwell himself (1654–56). All failed.

The reason for failure seems to have been the strength of the lawyers themselves, which rested on two main factors. First, the lawyers stood for the *status quo*, and that was what Parliament itself claimed its position to be – its objective was to remove what were seen as illicit monarchical innovations; and secondly, the cohesion of the lawyers. The collegial spirit, generated by the very institutions, the Inns, which some legislators wished to abolish, provided the base for a solidarity which withstood all attempts at reform. Once again the ideological weakness of the reforming Parliamentarians put them at a disadvantage. They had nothing to offer in that respect which would induce a lawyer to abandon his collegial loyalty.

The restoration of Charles II renewed the tripartite distribution of power referred to above, but while Charles hankered for an absolutism like that being established in France by Louis XIV, his conviction that 'I am too old to go again to my travels' (he was only 30 when he said this!) led him to proceed with caution in rebuilding monarchical power. But that was his objective when in 1683 he issued writs of *quo warranto*, challenging the charters of municipal bodies, livery companies and others including the Royal College of Physicians – but excluding the Inns of Court. This was intended as just the first step in regaining control of 'the lesser governments', which would have had led to further steps that would no doubt have included collectivities of lawyers and eventually Parliament. But Charles died in 1685 and his less cautious brother, James II, soon caused serious opposition to this policy, opposition which was certainly a significant part of that general antagonism triggered into revolution by the birth of his son (because it was thought that this ensured a Catholic heir to the throne, and that was the final straw). The radical shift of power to Parliament in the constitutional monarchy that followed the Glorious Revolution of 1688 left the charter-holders' power intact and even enhanced and provided an institutionalization of the principle of 'lesser governments' which still flourishes in contemporary Britain.

It is perhaps something of a historical puzzle why the professional bodies were left with their power intact, because they were not objects of universal approval. Lawyers in particular have been the targets of playwrights, poets and novelists such as Shaw, Coleridge and Dickens; but some satirical lines from *The Beggars' Opera* (John Gay, 1728) provide a clue to the answer to this puzzle:

The priest calls the lawyer a cheat,
The lawyer beknaves the divine,
And the statesman because he's so great
Thinks his trade as honest as mine.

These are the words of the highwayman, MacHeath!

What these lines bring to mind is that the statesman, the lawyer and the priest are all part of the same class, the landed gentry. This is the class which provided many Members of Parliament and whose younger sons, who did not succeed to family estates, found employment in the professions or the military: a state of affairs which persisted from Tudor times to the late nineteenth century. A considerable proportion of Members of Parliament were therefore probably reluctant to turn a critical or regulatory eye on the professions. With minor exceptions in the nineteenth and twentieth centuries lawyers, especially the barristers, have retained control of their own affairs. Solicitors have been subject to more regulation and to them we must now turn.

In all Western societies there is some division of legal labour, but the distinctive formality of this in all parts of Britain tends to be overlooked. The absence of the barrister/solicitor distinction in the USA tends to be seen as an interesting cultural variation of no great significance. In fact, it is part of a societal divergence which undermines many glib generalizations about the professions.

The monopoly of the Inns of Court in England was a monopoly of pleading in the High Court and, by association with that institution, of

places on the bench (i.e. judges). They distinguished themselves successfully by various exclusionary practices from other legal practitioners now
called solicitors. Solicitors were technically 'officers of the court' and from
being experts in procedure and documentation came to be the exclusive
gate-keepers to the legal process and to the barristers. As such, the state
was concerned to control them and in 1825 the Solicitors Act was passed
and the solicitors' professional body, The Law Society, established.
Although the barristers' exclusionary practices had established their own
status as superior to that of solicitors, the latter worked away steadily,
especially during the nineteenth century, to build their monopoly and their
own social status. It is their success in this regard that led them to a
position of near equality with the bar (there is, for example, no great
difference in the social background of the two groups) and to the point
that when merger was mooted in the mid 1980s, the solicitors eventually
turned away from it. Their monopoly and its social and economic rewards
were secure and the uniformity of training and qualification provided
secure membership for even the small-town sole practitioner. In a unified
profession the big successful London practices of barristers and solicitors
would merge and create a stratified profession, where the small and
isolated practitioners would clearly be second-class members. The rank
and file decided that the uncertainties of a scramble for work in a unified
profession would more than offset any gains. Both branches of the
profession and the government backed off.

The legal profession in Britain is thus the epitome of that telling
seventeenth-century phrase 'lesser governments'. Its members have control over their own affairs in every respect and their power over the
functioning of the legal and judicial system is extensive. More than any
other profession they are an extension of the state; and the state's
acceptance of this position could not be shown more clearly than by
the action in 1948 of a Labour government in handing over practically the
whole responsibility (including financial) for the administration of
the Legal Aid Scheme. (Faced with steeply rising costs, the state reclaimed
financial administration in 1987.)

An analysis of the legal profession can provide a key to understanding
the nature of knowledge-based occupations in Britain and how they fit
into British culture and society.

1 The legal profession's organizations epitomize the notion of 'lesser
   governments'.
2 It is linked to the state directly by constituting the personnel who enact
   the judicial processes and who provide the judges.
3 It has been and to an extent still is in a more general way, by kinship
   (literal and metaphoric) linked with the members of the legislature;
   both lawyers and legislators have been likewise linked to other
   professionals.

For these reasons the legitimacy of 'lesser governments' has tended not to be questioned and the principle has been extended. The close affinity between professions and the class of the gentry explains the keenness of aspirant professional groups in Britain to emphasize their members' respectability and 'gentlemanliness'.

Medicine

The medical profession also displays those aspects of British society and culture which appear so clearly in the case of the law, especially the plurality of powers and association with the gentry.

Although the state played a crucial role in the official founding of the medical profession by granting a royal charter and passing an Act of Parliament in the early sixteenth century, the stimulus for this action seems to have come from the eminent scholar and physician Linacre (who was also a priest, head of an Oxford College and tutor to Prince Arthur, elder brother of Henry VIII). The system for the control of the medical profession which developed involved both the class aspect and the dispersion of power, for the membership was restricted to graduates of Oxford and Cambridge and certification was in the hands of the Church. Over the centuries other groups emerged in the profession, so that by the time the state finally took a step towards regulation by passing the Apothecaries Act in 1815, there were physicians, surgeons, apothecaries and the doubly qualified apothecary-surgeons.

Any further will to reform on the part of the state seems to have been lacking and the initiatives for change which led to forty years of internecine struggle and to eventual unification under the Medical Act of 1858 were the work of individuals and professional groups. Outstanding among these was Thomas Wakely, apothecary-surgeon, politician and founder editor of *The Lancet*. Not only did the state leave the initiative to reformers and professionals, but the regulative mechanisms set up by the Medical Act were dominated, not by state officials as they would have been on the Continent, but by the professionals themselves.

From the power-base thus achieved the medical profession was able to dominate paramedical occupations (Larkin, 1983) and to mount a major confrontation with the government over the public provision of health care when the first health insurance scheme was introduced in 1910. Although this battle was eventually lost, the doctors' organization, the British Medical Association, was able to withstand the government in 1945 and to secure considerable alterations to the original proposals (Parry and Parry, 1976).

The state's lack of interest in controlling medicine and health can also be seen in its failure to play any significant part in the development of hospitals, once again in contrast to France and Germany for instance. While this meant that this aspect of medicine remained relatively underdeveloped, it also resulted in the hospitals falling under the control of the doctors. A corresponding lack of state interest in higher education led to a relative weakness in medicine in the universities which allowed the hospital doctors to secure a dominant position in medical education, which they retained when the teaching hospitals became incorporated into the universities. This hegemony was exercised to an important extent through the Royal Colleges (especially of Physicians and Surgeons) who controlled all post-qualifying exams.

Summary

Britain, in the modern period, is characterized by a low level of despotic power, an early development of infrastructural power and by considerable penetration of the state by civil society. These features, in a quite unique way, go back to the feudal period, and even to William the Conqueror's remarkable amalgam of Norman feudalism and Saxon self-regulation combined with a degree of bureaucracy that his contemporaries saw as alien to both (Corrigan and Sayer, 1985: 15). The checks on despotic power that were developed in later centuries survived into the Tudor period and at that critical stage in the development of modern society the merging of the old regime with the rising bourgeoisie that is such a striking feature of British society throughout the modern period was already in evidence. The attempt in the seventeenth century to turn the state into a despotism failed, and Britain's long revolution – 1642 to 1688 – so clearly reinforced existing trends that some historians (Corrigan and Sayer, 1985; Thompson, 1978) suggest the possibility at least that if Charles I had chosen compromise instead of confrontation, the same outcome would have been achieved without a 'revolution'.[2]

In spite of such events as the rebellions of 1715 and 1745, the Gordon riots, the naval mutinies of the 1790s, the following century saw the legitimation of these political structures. While the centre of power was in the hands of a landed elite, *participation and representation* were extended to the gentry and the bourgeoisie: equally important were the relative lack of class exclusivity on the part of the elite (Earle, 1989), and the continuation of the use of these groups as the means of running what had been, for pre-modern society, an extensive political infrastructure. It was this (relatively) widespread participation in political, administrative and judicial power which accounted for the lack of serious challenge to the old regime. By the same token, the regulation of capitalism and its concomitant – 'formally rational, abstract, utilitarian knowledge' – was not systematically pursued by the state; and in the case of the latter, when regulation of its practitioners could not be avoided, resort was made to the customary methods of control; that is, statutory or chartered powers were bestowed on groups to regulate themselves, with minimum supervision by the state. This was fertile ground for the professional project.

Medicine, law and indeed most professional occupations in Britain have been able to regulate their own education and training, which is a very important part of control over entry to the professions. On the other hand, there is some validity in the conception of the professions as an 'articulation' of the modern capitalist state (Johnson, 1980). This can be seen to have particular relevance in the case of law (Johnson, 1982) which is, after all, in the nature of things linked to the judicial function and thus to the state in any society with a centralized polity. The extension of state power over the institutions of civil society has occurred relatively late in Britain and in a way that has preserved much of the pluralism of the pre-modern period. This means that although the legal profession is clearly linked to the state, there is considerable autonomy for their organizations, which retain forms and practices that go back to the Middle Ages, and which are not subordinate to civil servants or academics. Absence of control by the latter is another consequence of the relatively low level of state intervention; the universities have until recently been allowed a large measure of self-government, but this has left them with little control over professional education.

The United States of America

English-speaking writers on the sociology of the professions seem to have conspired to blur the cultural differences between Britain and America and, until the 1980s to have ignored continental models. The first crack in this ethnocentrism came, to his credit, from Eliot Freidson (1983: 22) apparently as a result of a visiting fellowship at CNRS in France. In that paper he emphasizes the distinctive European professionalism but continues to write of 'Anglo-American' institutions. In this section, therefore, I want to prise apart 'Anglo' and 'American' and look at the distinctive features of American professions, especially law.

Law

The American colonies, in the period before the War of Independence (1775–83), contained several cultural themes. For example, many colonists had left Britain because of their dissatisfaction with the political and/or religious state of affairs and they took with them a strong antipathy to monarchy, aristocracy, established religion and elitism in all its forms. On the other hand there was a sizeable proportion whose aim was literally to colonize the New World and to exploit its natural resources – especially land – for their own benefit and that of families at home. So while pre-revolutionary American society had a distinctive cast of its own – democratic and anti-elitist – it had none the less developed into a clearly stratified society with a wealthy elite, orientated to British and European values. The sons of this elite were often sent to Britain for professional education, producing a stratum of lawyers trained in the Inns of Court and doctors from Edinburgh (Larson, 1977: 111). At the same time, the preference of the well-to-do of Philadelphia for having their offspring taught Latin (Bridenhaugh and Bridenhaugh, 1962: 3) was the despair of Benjamin Franklin. Not surprisingly lawyers and doctors with such a background formed exclusive professional groups. In many cases, however, these groups were not formalized and Burrage (1988: 244) notes that in the mid-eighteenth century only in three colonies, New York, Rhode Island and Massachusetts, are there known to have been groups with formal rules of association, although there is some evidence of corporate solidarity in Pennsylvania and Virginia. In Charleston, South Carolina, twenty-four of the thirty lawyers had been trained in London, and it may be supposed that they formed no association because they regarded themselves as members of their Inn.

With such a low level of organization among lawyers it is not surprising that there was little direct action for reform of the profession by revolutionary governments, certainly as compared with the French revolutionaries a few years later. The lack of reform must also have been due in part to the lack of a centralized legal system, which reforms might attack, and indeed the picture is one of slow and piecemeal change. In the post-revolutionary era as the values of populism gained in influence, many of the Tory elite departed for Britain or Canada and their organizations declined or disappeared. But the rate of change, as compared with what came later, was not dramatic. George Washington was after all from a well-established family with aristocratic connections, a plantation- and slave-owner from Virginia who ordered his clothes from London. His successors as President, apart from John Adams of Massachussetts, constitute what has been called the Virginian Dynasty (1801–1825) of Jefferson, Madison and Monroe, all of whom came from similar backgrounds.

None the less, protest against the legal profession was voiced in some states, primarily in Massachussetts, but also in Pennsylvania, New Hampshire, Vermont, Connecticut, New York and New Jersey. However it was in the newly admitted state of Ohio that in 1802 formal requirements and qualifications for legal practice as a counsellor-at-law were abolished. This lead was followed by Georgia (1806), Tennessee (1809) and South Carolina (1812).

But this legislative assault on the profession did not stop the formation of voluntary associations of lawyers, in fact one might suppose that it fostered it and, until 1820, there was an 'efflorescence' of such associations (Halliday, 1987: 61). But then social change seemed to come into line with legislative change, and from 1830 until a decade after the end of the Civil War 'bar meetings and bar associations gradually, and then entirely, collapsed . . . Only the Law Association of Philadelphia and a rare isolated exception elsewhere, survived' (Halliday, 1987: 61–2). The question of why this trend should have occurred in the USA is raised by both Burrage and Halliday, and from a list of possible explanations comprising the Revolution, the frontier, industrialization and Jacksonian democracy, Burrage chooses the first and Halliday the last. Burrage, pleading lack of space, offers five lines of reasons for his choice; Halliday offers none. In fact, both are right. For the Revolution and Jacksonian democracy are equally manifestations of the radical egalitarianism that Lipset (1964: 77) describes so eloquently. The 'radical temper' is articulated more clearly by the Jeffersonians than by the Federalists and they in turn are upstaged by Andrew Jackson and his followers from 1830 onwards. This party in their turn were subject to radical attack by the Whigs who tried to pour scorn on 'King' Jackson, lay charges of aristocratic origins and voluptuous extravagance at the door of his successor, Van Buren, and to promote their presidential candidate, General Tyler, under the symbols of the Log Cabin and the Common Man (Lipset, 1964: 83).

Halliday (1987: 61) points out that Jacksonian democracy looked askance at the idea of a profession, claiming for itself a special status, and goes on to quote Roscoe Pound (1977, 228–9):

> To dignify any one calling by styling it a profession seemed undemocratic and un-American. Distrust of things English, pioneer distrust of specialists, led to the general rejection of a common-law idea of an organized, responsible, self-regulating profession.

Likewise Richard Hofstadter (1962: 155–6):

> [the Jacksonian movement's] distrust of expertise, its dislike for centralization, its desire to uproot the entrenched classes, and its doctrine that important functions are simple enough to be performed by anyone, amounted to a repudiation not only of the system of government by gentlemen which the nation had inherited from the eighteenth century but also the special value of the educated classes in civic life.

Americans proclaimed their right to 'life, liberty and quackery' (Shyrock 1947: 262).

But to attribute the assault on the professions and their consequent retreat to 'Jacksonian democracy', or indeed to the Revolution, is to mistake particular manifestations for the underlying current. A better understanding is obtained by following Lipset's analysis: 'Two themes, equality and achievement, emerged from the interplay between the Puritan tradition and the Revolutionary ethos in the early formation of America's institutions' (1964: 101). From 1800 to 1870 these themes were pushed to their logical extremes as not only the law but medicine, religion and engineering were made open to all, at least in theory: (in fact, practitioners were white males, the vast majority of whom were Protestants with British antecedents). This logic even included the rejection of qualifications because, as noted above, qualifications were only available to the elite, and in the early years were obtained from British institutions with their 'aristocratic' connections.

The opening of knowledge-based occupations to all may well conform to the American ethos but the problem remains for practitioners: how do they persuade their clients or patients that they have the skills they claim? Qualification or credentials are the means such occupations normally employ, but when the means of attaining them are tainted and the culture emphasizes achievement, then the soi-disant professional is thrown back on what he can make of the methods of the tradesman or the huckster. At the same time a market opportunity is created for educationalists and it is on the foundation of 'modern', practical knowledge (Larson, 1977: 61) that American professions slowly begin to build. Learning by doing, in a law office, a consulting room or on a civil engineering project, took a firm root during the decades of professional decline, but the schools of law, medicine and engineering gradually outgrew their blatantly commercial inception and established *their* reputations on which practitioners could in turn rely. But this development was slow. In 1830 there were only six law schools and such establishments did not become numerous until the end of the century, by which time Harvard Law School had established a model for others to follow.

Medicine

The American Medical Association is often seen as one of the most powerful professional organizations in the world, but, in comparison with many Old World bodies, it is of late foundation (1847), only achieved large-scale membership in the 1920s and still only has about half the American medical profession as members. As with law, this state of affairs has its roots in America's colonial and revolutionary past. In colonial times, doctors were trained in Europe for the most part and it was not until 1751 that the first hospital was founded (in Philadelphia) and not until the 1760s that medical colleges were established in Philadelphia and New York. These innovations gave rise to conflict between the Medical Societies who issued licences to practise to those who had served an apprenticeship, and the medical colleges and their diplomates. In the early nineteenth century the medical societies had been successful in persuading state legislatures to restrict practice to their members, but it now became in the interests of the medical colleges to urge the repeal of this legislation. They were supported by the 'health sects' that arose between 1810 and 1830, such as botanic medicine (Thomsonism), eclecticism, vegetarianism and most importantly homeopathy. These movements had the advantage that scientific medicine had a very slender knowledge base and tended to use 'heroic' (that is, savage) remedies, while the alternative approaches, while having even less in the way of reliable knowledge, very often did their patients less harm. Possibly more significant was the fact that the medical profession could be successfully labelled by the medical sectarians as 'experts', protected by a legal monopoly, as associated with traditional elites and with the wealthy classes who employed them – even though this was far from the whole truth.

Alternative medicine, on the other hand, presented itself as the appropriate concomitant to democracy, populism and American modernity; indeed, Thomson, the eponymous leader of one of the groups, was an ardent adherent of Jacksonian radicalism (Larson, 1977: 128–30). In the prevailing populist climate and in response to these pressures state legislatures deprived the medical societies of their licensing powers and American medicine was reduced to a condition of factional disorganization.

Medical orthodoxy was eventually restored by the survival of the medical colleges. In the mid-nineteenth century many medical schools were established, but they were all commercial enterprises; many were short-lived and few were associated with universities. Their more volatile existence was due to the underlying problem of the paucity of medical knowledge and the opportunity for innovative therapies to challenge the existing orthodoxy, thus threatening established medicine and inducing schisms and dissension in medical schools. Even within orthodox medicine controversies raged: as late as 1849 there were fiercely divided opinions about how to deal with the cholera epidemic in New York. However the rise of the public health movement in the post-Civil War period and the development of bacteriology at the end of the nineteenth century enabled orthodox medicine to establish its claim to superiority and the American Medical Association became the acknowledged organization for doctors, especially after its reorganization in the early 1900s.

Summary

The contrast with Britain is striking, where orthodox medicine was firmly based in 'aristocratic' institutions and 'gentlemanly' values and was able to achieve a secure state-licensed basis in the 1850s, even though its knowledge base was as fragile as that of the American profession and less robust than the French or German.

In America, the lack, or at least the impotence of professional organization, must have also been affected by geographical dispersion and by rapid social change. One should note the following features.

1 The huge area over which Americans were spread even by 1800; the contrasts between North and South, and 'the frontier'.
2 Changing and growing metropolitan centres (not just one as in Britain and France). In 1776 Philadelphia was the second largest 'English' city after London, only to be overtaken by New York and in due course Chicago, where both the ABA and the AMA headquarters are located.
3 The political and judicial structure of the United States which has given rise, especially in law and medicine, to district associations for metropolis or county, state and nation (for example, Chicago, Illinois and American Bar Associations).

But whatever the contribution of such factors to the weakness of American professional associations up to the mid-nineteenth century, there is no doubt of the significance of state crystallizations. Lipset (1964) labels America as *The First New Nation* – which indeed it was – but at the same time there was no other new nation quite like it. Britain was unique in that it modernized quite unconsciously and unpurposefully; but America was equally unique in that, being composed to a significant extent of people who had rejected Britain, it deliberately created itself on the basis of values at variance with those dominant in the erstwhile mother-country. The revolutionaries created a state that, while formally defined, was neither strong nor centralized and that was so completely penetrated by civil society that representation and participation gave the electorate the right to appoint almost every official from the President of the Federal Government to the local dog-catcher. The potentiality for despotic power was nullified and infrastructural power was, in the early decades of the new republic, in the hands of the constituent states. By giving every citizen the right to bear arms, the state did not even attempt to monopolize physical force. The emphasis on the rights of the individual was part of the most thorough-going crystallization of participation to be found in any modern state. Its counterpart was a conscious abstention from interference by the state in economic/capitalist activity, which was interpreted as the duty to prevent any group within society doing likewise – hence the steady elimination, in the early nineteenth century, of professional associations, which would have prohibited ordinary unqualified citizens from exercising the right to pursue any economic activity they saw fit.

Deprived of an organizational base and consequently having no appeal to traditional values, professions had to rely on their expert knowledge as the basis for their claim to special recognition. But lack of an organization meant that they had no means of controlling and passing on their knowledge, which was in the hands of universities and colleges. It was in this way that as professional bodies reappeared after 1870 the chief bases of their professional project were their modern knowledge and the institution in which it was lodged, the university.

America, like Britain, had a pluralistic culture, both politically and otherwise, but in stark contrast, indeed in direct opposition to Britain, American institutions turned not to the values of tradition but to the ideal of the 'common man' or populism. As in Britain *laissez-faire* prevailed, but it was the individual citizen who benefited. At the same time everything aristocratic and traditional, especially their manifestation in organized groups, was swept away by the 'radical temper', leaving every practitioner of a knowledge-based occupation to establish his own reputation and to compete with any lay person who wished to enter the market for services.

Although there is a tendency to refer to the Anglo-American world, in connection with the professions, it cannot be emphasized enough that the two state crystallizations present striking differences. While in both societies professions pursued their projects, they did so in very different

contexts which presented them with dissimilar problems and opportunities, and with their own culturally provided means of facing them.

France

France emerged from feudalism by a somewhat different route from that
followed by England and with a balance between bourgeoisie, gentry,
nobles and monarch that allowed the last-named much greater scope for
centralization and absolutism. The tactics of the Stuarts in England can be
seen as an (unsuccessful) attempt to emulate the achievements of the
French monarchy, and more particularly its succession of talented ministers – Richelieu, Mazarin and Colbert (1624 to 1680). So at the key time
when constitutional monarchy was established in Britain (1688), absolutism was triumphant in France. The three loci of power referred to above
in the case of Britain existed likewise in France but the balance was quite
different owing to the overwhelming power of the Crown. In such
circumstances the 'lesser governments' of the professional bodies were
much more dependent on the state and probably had less real autonomy
than their British counterparts. Both law and medicine were divided into
a number of professional organizations of varying status, with some of
those in medicine linked to the Church. Opinions differ as to the degree of
autonomy enjoyed by professionals. Abbott, who gives attention to
medicine as well as law, refers to the interventionist approach of the Old
Regime, which from the seventeenth century has graded and regulated
occupations with areas of work creating an architectonic structure (1988:
158); thus achieving far greater authority over the professions than the
English or American state. Burrage (1988: 232), on the other hand, sees
the pre-revolutionary legal profession as having achieved the goals of the
professional project, including a large measure of self-government. He
even cites their inclusion in a hierarchical status structure of law leading
up to judges and culminating in the Crown as an advantage, rather than a
limitation.

But whatever the balance of control between Crown and profession
under the old regime, there is no doubt that the state in revolutionary
France and in subsequent monarchical, republican and imperial manifestations, retained the centralized power of absolutism, tempered of course by
varying forms of democracy; furthermore, it used that power to reform
and control professional occupations to an extent unknown in the Anglo-
American world.

Law

The revolutionary Constituent Assembly (August 1789) launched a
thorough-going attack on the existing judicial system and its corporate
institutions. These formed an interlinked hierarchy reflecting the legal
division of labour. The provincial magisterial bodies (*parlements*) and the

judges (*parlementaires*) stood at the summit; next came the *avocats* (equivalent to English barristers) followed by *procureurs* (solicitors) and then by lower orders of notaries, ushers and recorders, each with their own organizations. The Assembly rapidly came to take it for granted that these organizations would be abolished, and when in 1790 the new legal system was inaugurated they indeed had no place in the new courts and judicial procedures, which emphasized lay participation without the intervention of legal specialists. In contrast to the English barristers in 1649, the French *avocats* in 1789 gave no support to their own institutions, which for all their autonomy were none the less seen both by members and outsiders as inextricably bound up in the absolute monarchical power and its manifold abuses. There were over two hundred *avocats* in the Constituent Assembly: only one spoke up in favour of the lawyers' organizations.

The new system reduced significantly the role of the professional lawyers and in this there was no doubt a parallel to the populist style of democracy displayed in America. But in addition there was the principle, still prominent in French society, that groups which interpose themselves between the individual and the democratic state frustrate the functioning of the 'General Will' – an important concept in the thought of Jean-Jacques Rousseau, one of the main ideologues of the Revolution (Russell, 1946: 725). The professional organizations were not only disbanded, they were forbidden: *avoués*, who replaced *procureurs*, were expressly prohibited from creating an association and they and the *avocats* acted as independent individuals, in so far as they were required – for the purpose of the reformers was to reconstitute the law so that it could function effectively in the hands of the laity. 'By 1794 there was effectively no legal profession, no protected professional jurisdictions and no orders of advocates' (Burrage, 1988: 234).

But law in a modern society cannot long remain in the hands of the laity, because not only must the law in the nature of things be as complex as the society itself, but the Napoleonic reforms, reviving principles of Roman law and founded on the notion of 'positive law' effectively raised law to a level of abstraction and subtlety that would soon convince a lay person acting alone that specialist assistance was needed. Napoleon was none the less opposed to such a revival and it was only some years after he had instituted a new system of courts, and restored the law schools (making their diploma a prerequisite for the office of judge, prosecutor or *avoué*) that he allowed the *avocats* to resurrect their professional bodies. What is significant for the nature of French professional institutions is that these bodies of lawyers were under the control and supervision of the state (Ministry of Justice) and that the law schools, the gateway to the profession, were likewise state institutions. This example of state-provided elite education is the first of several which, as will appear, is very significant for the position of the professions in French society.

With the defeat of Napoleon by Britain and Prussia in 1815 and the end of his particular blend of Republic and Empire, France went through a series of political changes until 1871 when the Third Republic was established. The restored monarchy had lasted until 1848 when Napoleon's nephew, Louis Napoleon, introduced the Second Republic, which very soon became the Second Empire, and which lasted until the defeat of the Franco-Prussian war (1870–71). Throughout this period the *avocats* worked hard to re-establish the self-government of their order. Progress was made in the 1820s, and in 1830 the king restored their rights of self-government in full, although in the two decades that followed judges and Crown legal officers successfully challenged these powers. Louis Napoleon, however, restricted their autonomy once again, and it was not until 1870 that an imperial decree restored them to the position of 1830. This, however, was one in which their professional control was restricted in a number of respects. With the restoration of the Republic in 1871 the dramatic changes and the confrontations ceased and, until its reform in 1971, the profession worked away at its collective objectives in an unobtrusive way. But the revolutionary changes had left their mark and had created the social and cultural circumstances in which law and the professions still function in France.

First of all the *avocats* did not have a monopoly of their jurisdiction. *Avoués* and *notaires* and other legal experts were able to plead in court and the *avocats* could not achieve control of this chaotic situation. Secondly their self-government was seriously flawed. The *ministère publique* successfully claimed disciplinary authority over the orders, and although resisted collectively, this stance was undermined by individuals who would appeal to the courts against the disciplinary rulings of their own order. Lastly there were the far-reaching consequences of the actions of revolutionary and post-revolutionary governments to give a central position to state-provided tertiary education. Not only are modern universities creations of the state (notably by the reforms of 1896) but the state has, since the time of Napoleon, been concerned to produce well-qualified recruits for the civil service and for other elite positions by means of the *Grandes Ecoles*. The law schools ranked below these and the lawyers were therefore consigned to a lower status than many state officials in the Ministry of Justice etc. In a status system which was very much state-orientated this disability could not be overcome. In addition to this general disadvantage, the repeated setbacks suffered by the professional organizations at the hands of state authority in various guises left them with seriously diminished prestige. But the state educational system provided yet another problem for the professional autonomy of law by giving to the professors of the law schools more control over the diploma which provided entry to the profession than to the order of advocates, thus depriving them of a key element in professional closure. The professors were also seen as the appropriate sources of legal and legislative advice for the civil service, rather than the *avocats*, thus giving lower prestige to the practitioner as compared with the academic.

Medicine

The French medical profession also displays the consequences of its cultural environment and the powerful position of the state. Pre-revolutionary France enjoyed (or suffered) an abundant variety of medical practitioners – physicians, surgeons, pharmacists, 'empirics', 'operators', *spagiristes* and, above all, members of the clergy, especially the rural *curées* and the sisters who staffed French hospitals. This competition continued into the nineteenth century with various bonesetters and empirical healers contesting rural medical work with the *curées* and the *officiers de santé* (Abbott, 1988: 157–8). Like English professions, the higher status groups attempted to secure their jurisdiction, but whereas the former secured regulation by legislation or charter which established their organization, in France it was a matter of aligning professional groups with the state, so surgeons' organizations were brought into a system of regulation headed by the King's Surgeon, which distinguished them from physicians and provided protection against the inroads of charlatans.

This state-dominated structure of organizations and division of pro-fessional labour was reformed after the Revolution, by the creation of a simplified system with two strata, *médecins* and *officiers de santé* each with officially defined functions. The state control of professional education in the nineteenth century also reduced professional power as compared with Britain. A degree in medicine was the starting point but the syllabus and examinations were in the hands of the professors, not the professional bodies. For the doctors, the universities were more the site of a battle with *officiers de santé* and pharmacists than an aid to professional prestige and expertise.

This relative weakness *vis-à-vis* the state seems to have provided the opportunity for a number of bodies to emerge who represented the medical profession. First there is *L'Ordre des Médecins*, the 'professional' body; then there is *L'Association Génerale des Médecins de France* which is a merger of local organizations; and finally there are professional trades unions which emerged in the period of the syndicalism in France in the late nineteenth century, such as the *Confédération des Syndicats Médicaux Français*. In contrast to the USA in particular, where the AMA can act on behalf of the whole medical profession, the attempts to deal with the greater power of the state have resulted in separate organizations to handle professional control, professional support and economic bargaining with the state.

Summary

French culture during the period in which the professions developed shared some characteristics with British society and some with American, but differed strikingly in that its old regime political system was a centralized, absolutist monarchy. The post-revolutionary state was demo-cratic and absolutist by turns, but certainly remained centralized, despite the efforts of, for example, the Girondistes to the contrary. A major change, however, was that infrastructural power, whose decay provided some of the revolutionary motivation, was established, firmly and effectively. The characteristically French form of participation, while encouraging direct participation in the political process, at the same time restricted the autonomy of the institutions of civil society (such as the professions) *vis-à-vis* the strongly articulated and centralized state structure. In addition to these salient features, the following points should be noted.

1 French society demonstrated a degree of pluralism because institutions such as professional bodies were founded before the period of absolutism. The older professions such as law and medicine developed a division of labour and a hierarchy of specialisms, but as the centralized monarchy grew more powerful these were subordinated to state officials.
2 The revolutionary Assemblies reformed and simplified professional organizations, but retained centralized control; despite a number of changes during the nineteenth century, state control remained in place.
3 The revolution also brought in a populist ideology based on the writings of Jean-Jacques Rousseau which challenged not only the elitism inherent in professionalism, but the very existence of such institutions, since they could be considered to interfere with functioning of the General Will.
4 Greater state power, as compared with Britain and the USA, was accompanied by a greater sense of state responsibility. The state, therefore, took initiatives in health and education, which from a technical point of view benefited the professions. On the other hand it both consolidated the influence of the state and allowed academics a measure of control over training and entry qualifications.
5 State sponsorship of higher education resulted in the *grandes écoles*, providing the middle class with an affiliation that carried greater cachet and higher status than professional membership.

Germany

Germany, conceived of as a geographical area, goes back, like France (Gaul), to Roman times. But unlike France, Germany did not emerge from the feudal period as a unified entity but remained a jumble of principalities and powers until the nineteenth century when the Prussian-dominated North German Federation emerged, to be succeeded in 1871 by the German Empire (*Kaiserreich*).

In so far as professions emerge in interaction with the state, this means that German professions tended to be as weak as the various principalities (etc.) in which their members lived. Those in the territories of the larger entities (Austria-Hungary, Prussia and Bavaria) were faced with powerful, absolute monarchical states. But while knowledge-based occupations found the culture infertile, knowledge itself flourished in the German university system.

In 1648, at the end of the Thirty Years War, Germany was divided into 234 distinct territorial units, fifty-one free cities and innumerable estates of Imperial Knights. Austria was the only sizeable entity and even this was composed of an Archduchy, a Kingdom, a Margravate and several Duchies. Geographical divisions were complicated by rulers' allegiances to either the Papacy or the Holy Roman Emperor and by Catholic and Protestant religious affiliations.

Political power in this myriad of states was basically autocratic and the bulk of the population was – nominally at least and often in reality – in a condition of serfdom. There was practically no evidence of the 'lesser governments' so characteristic of Britain nor of the diffusion of power among the gentry and civic corporations. Another difference from Britain and from France was the absence of a metropolis to compare with London or Paris, and with these geo-political features went (as one might expect) a comparative lack of commercialism. Although the notion of 'Ruritania' was not coined until the very end of the nineteenth century, in many ways it captures the feeling of Germany in the eighteenth century as it emerges into the modern period.[3]

One feature of German society, however, not evident in Ruritania, was the university. At the time of the Reformation (1520s) there were sixteen German universities and in the next 200 years thirteen Protestant and three Catholic universities were founded. Some universities ceased to exist in the Napoleonic Wars, but four more were founded between 1800 and 1818. So at a date when Britain had six universities, Germany had nearly thirty. These foundations were in part the outcome of rivalry and competition and status-striving between rulers and cities, and part of that rivalry was rooted in religion. But for a ruler, they served the important function of turning out educated people to staff the administrative system, people who in the absence of a tradition of administration by the aristocracy or the gentry, moved into positions of considerable power.

German universities, therefore, had considerable significance in their society because of their association with the state and with the administrative elite, because of their relative importance in social and cultural terms in the absence of a metropolis, and because of their large numbers. This significance was enhanced by the reforms to pedagogy and philosophy initiated by Humboldt, Schiller and others from the 1790s onwards, based on neo-humanism and a neo-classicism that emphasized the virtues of ancient republican Greece. The values of good citizenship and an opposition to commercialism provided a vital reinforcement of certain existing trends and underpinned the ideology of the *Bildungsburgertum* or 'the educated middle class' (Jarauch, 1990; Kocka, 1990; Turner, 1980). Throughout the nineteenth and early twentieth centuries, these cultural features provided the basis for a complete structuring of middle-class life and values, in which the relationship between the *Bildungsburgertum* and the state left little or no room for independent professional bodies, and knowledge-based work was aligned with the civil service rather than the market.

Law

The history of the legal profession in Germany demonstrates the domination of the state over knowledge-based occupations, which leads Siegrist (1990: 46) and many others to talk of 'professionalization from above'. It was a situation so different from that obtaining in the British and American cases that the terminology used in English is not strictly applicable; the translators of Siegrist (1990) use the terms 'attorney' and 'lawyer' in ways that seem less than exact, and although they write of 'the bar', there is no mention of barristers or advocates.

The multiplicity of German states displayed a variety of circumstances in which lawyers functioned but there was widespread acceptance of the notion that the lawyer was a free agent representing a client. However, as the authoritarian bureaucratic state emerged in the late eighteenth century, notably in Prussia, but also in Bavaria and the Hapsburg Empire, the position of lawyers was increasingly regulated. In the 1780s attorneys with the title 'assistant counsel' were declared to be employees of the state, and a few years later the Prussian attorney was defined as a 'commissar of justice' and the bar to which he belonged came under state control. This subordination appears to be all the more oppressive in that lawyers did not receive salaries or pensions, in spite of being regarded as civil servants. Although the smaller German states were slower to follow this path, the larger autocratic states discouraged lawyers from regarding themselves as representatives of private clients, especially those with 'improper' interests, and rather emphasized their role of 'officers of the court', and thus as official servants of justice. Attempts were also made to curtail their participation in and influence on legal proceedings by extending the authority of judges. In the competition for influence and status between the various groups within the law – legal bureaucrats, judges, law professors and attorneys – the latter had undoubtedly come off worst at the start of the nineteenth century.

In Germany, however, as elsewhere in Europe, movements of liberal reform were under way and the autocratic powers showed signs of yielding in some respects. None the less, arbitrary state power was well entrenched and lawyers had to fight not only for the right to act as free professionals, but even for the arena in which to perform their advocacy, because the public oral legal process was not the norm. This legal institution, a feature of the British system for centuries, was established in the 1830s giving lawyers not only increased rights but the means to enhance their status and prestige by public performance of their skills. But gains such as these were counterbalanced by the clearer articulation of state authority over the lawyers, ensuring the rigid exclusion of lay participation from the legal process and the even greater control over legal education by legal academics. Lawyers were thus denied the means whereby they could develop and control their rewards and prestige, for everything from training to the scale of fees to the award of honours remained in the hands of the state.

The unification of the German Empire might well have reinforced state control but other influences were at work. The rapidly growing German economy enhanced the influence of civil society *vis-à-vis* the state and together with the movement towards liberalism in politics (and other areas) created a much more market-orientated society. When a new Lawyer Code (RAO) came into force in 1879, to regulate a unified profession in the new empire, it gave lawyers more freedom of action and autonomy, although their influence over legal education remained weak and many still believed that only affiliation with the state apparatus could bestow prestige. Bar associations were founded from 1860 onwards, but never attained the prestige and independence that characterized the British, American or even the French bar.

Industrialization and economic growth created a new demand for legal experts, and the legal profession in the late nineteenth century grew relatively (to the total employed), as well as absolutely. Greater size gave legal associations more influence, and lawyers provided many political leaders up to the 1930s. But in a society with a tradition of centralized bureaucratic authority and a value-system which emphasized *Bildungsbur-gertum* rather than professional prestige, lawyers in Germany never moved far from the position of being unofficial civil servants. When the Nazi takeover occurred in 1933, the professions, law among them, were no more able to halt the shift to Fascism than any other part of German civil society.

None the less, this relative weakness of the German legal profession should not be taken as evidence of its lack of motivation as regards a 'professional project'. Siegrist (1990: 63) writes:

> The bureaucratic model [of profession] understates the early traces of a professional identity that later became more clearly defined. Although the rise of the German bar was initiated by the state, attorneys themselves later developed a genuine professionalization resembling the English or American practice.

Medicine

German doctors in the eighteenth century were, like doctors everywhere, handicapped in their pursuit of professionalism by lack of effective medical knowledge and by their dependence on the wealthy for patronage. In common with other professionals, their dispersion over numerous small political units gave them little opportunity to form associations capable of bargaining with the state. In these circumstances doctors, too, were inclined to emphasize their membership of the 'educated middle-class' rather than their distinctive professionalism.

As medical knowledge and skills advanced during the nineteenth century, doctors were handicapped in their attempts to take advantage of this by their wide dispersal and lack of organization. The state was able to retain the initiative that it already possessed by virtue of controlling and financing the institutions in which medical education took place. Even before the gains in medical knowledge of the nineteenth century, the Prussian administration had started to push doctors from their largely unscientific approach to medicine by requiring practical treatment of two hospital patients for a month as part of the examination.

State registration of doctors and control of their education continued during the nineteenth century and, in contrast to Britain, professional organizations only constituted one, relatively minor, element in the development of medicine. As in France, state interest in public health took the form of sponsorship of hospitals which gave doctors a base both professionally and scientifically. On the other hand, it gave the state the interest and means to maintain control over medicine and medical education.

Another feature of health and medicine in Germany which was also both an advantage and a constraint for doctors was the system of health insurance, which grew steadily during the nineteenth century providing health care for a far larger proportion of the population than in Britain or the USA. This considerably extended the doctors' clientele, emancipating them from dependence on wealthy patients, but at the same time allowing first employers and later insurance companies to intervene between doctor and patient. The question of choice of doctor became a matter of bitter contention between doctors' associations and insurance companies, with the former using strike action in some instances. The dispute came to an acrimonious impasse which, interesting to note, was resolved by state legislative action. The doctors' associations were thus successful in a sense, but for much of the nineteenth century were restricted in their actions by the legislation controlling trade associations, and even when this constraint was removed their position *vis-à-vis* the state left them unable to achieve anything like the power and autonomy of British professional bodies.

As with lawyers, state control of professional activity led doctors into conflicts which they could not really win. As a result, says Huerkamp (1990: 82), 'doctors' status anxieties were promoted, which turned out to be one of the most important influences in the extraordinarily rapid political and ideological integration of physicians into the Nazi state after 1933'. On the other hand, although emphasizing the slowness of professional development in German medicine, Huerkamp also refers to doctors' 'rigorous campaign for material and professional goals' (1990: 81).

Summary

1   During the nineteenth century the autocratic states of Germany, led by Prussia, worked towards unification and in 1871 emerged as the *Kaiserreich* or German Empire. The state in this society was clearly the strongest of those considered in this chapter.
2   State involvement in public health and higher education, as in France, gave the professions practical advantages in terms of their knowledge base, but deprived them of control over important aspects of training and qualifications, subordinating them to civil servants and academics.
3   There was no strong populist sentiment in Germany as there was in France and America. Liberal reform came slowly and did not run deep enough to counter the penetration of the state into every aspect of civil society.
4   The university system, however, was long established and vigorous and, even more than in France, offered a focus for middle-class aspirations. As a result, high status accrued to members of the *Bildungsburgertum* or 'educated middle class' and this was more strongly associated with the civil service and academia than with the professions.
5   The German state structure was clearly the most strongly developed of those reviewed here. Like other modern states it emerged from an alliance of the old regime and the bourgeoisie, but one in which the old despotism was not only modernized, but was joined by a third partner, the military. In this context the bourgeoisie was content not to further the penetration of the state by civil society, partly for fear that this would only result in power for working class parties and trade unions. Instead they relied, quite correctly as it turned out, on the state to provide the means for capitalist development; a course which proved quite as successful as that taken by their counterparts in Britain and France. At the same time there was a status system that valued education and public office above public professional practice. None the less, lawyers and doctors strove for autonomy and independence: their relative lack of success should be seen as evidence of the forces ranged against them rather than the lack of a 'professional project'.

Professional project and cultural context

The objective in this chapter has been to assess the criticism of ethnocentrism that has been levelled at the professional project as a sociological concept. 'The professional project', as a theoretical approach, has not been subjected to a thorough-going critique by any sociologist. It has been found wanting in various respects by a number of writers, but for the most part this has tended to take the form of 'guilt by association' with other parts of Larson's (1977) account of the rise of professionalism, rather than the conceptual core of her thesis. So issue is taken with the latter, quasi-Marxian part of her book (Halliday, 1983), with a perceived overemphasis on monopoly (Halliday, 1987) or on social mobility (Abbott, 1988). Alternatively, criticism is implicit rather than specified, in that writers such as Collins (1990) put forward schemes for the study of the professions that aim to be fundamental revisions of the study of the professions, without stating who is being consigned to the dustbin.

A rather different case is that of Burrage (1990) and Burrage et al. (1990). The first of these compares the development of professions and manual occupational associations, such as trade unions in three cultures – France, the USA and Britain (in fact England). Burrage adduces convincing evidence to show that the patterns of development of the two kinds of occupational organization are sufficiently similar to suggest that they were affected by the same conditions and that these were cultural and political rather than economic. At the outset, Burrage (1990: 153) refers in passing to the 'professional project' and in his conclusions, he clearly refers to occupational organizations as actors (pp. 172–3). On the other hand, he also refers to 'determinants' and to 'dependent and independent variables' and places a greater emphasis on political events – namely revolutions – rather than political culture. The professional project could well form the linchpin of the analysis of these data, but it is clear from Burrage et al. (1990) that they prefer a different emphasis; one which sees the social position of knowledge-based occupations as the outcome of a multi-dimensional interplay of actors. In one sense this is no more than a truism of action theory, in so far as the concept of a social actor implies the existence of others. On the other hand, this approach underemphasizes or even ignores the *purposefulness* that the notion of 'project' entails, and to give four actors equal weight, as if they were sitting down at the bridge table together, loses much of the insight of action theory. Even Abbott's (1988) view that there is a fifth actor – other professions – is put to one side, which would seem to leave a considerable hiatus in the model.

So although Burrage's empirical work seems to fit pretty well with the notion of a 'professional project', his more theoretical piece seems to shift the emphasis away from the core of this concept, which tends to confirm the impression that many sociologists fail to perceive the real value of Larson's ideas and to 'talk past' her, rather than actively disagree. But if theoretical criticism of the concept lacks a cutting edge, there is still the question of how adequately it reflects the reality of professions, past and present, and in particular its generalizability to cultures other than the Anglo-American.

The nub of the case against using the 'professional project' as the key concept for understanding knowledge-based occupations is that it is ethnocentric; that is, it refers to a specifically Anglo-American phenomenon, and is so laden with the values of that culture as to render it unviable in the analysis of any other society. In the case of France it might be said to have some utility, although loss of control of certain aspects of professional activity to the state and to other agencies might cast doubt on this. Germany, however, presents a case where the state has always been more powerful, the universities have secured more control over the knowledge base than the practitioners, and social prestige is allocated differently. Professional organizations have thus always been weaker and, given the different cultural context, it could be argued that they have never had either the aims or the cultural base that the 'professional project' assumes. By extension it could be supposed that other societies which have a history of a dominant state and came late to industrialization would likewise have knowledge-based occupations that would be unamenable to analysis in terms of the 'professional project'. Eastern Europe and Russia would be examples, and in societies that had gone through a fascist period – Spain, Italy and Japan – it might be particularly true.

State crystallizations

Before drawing a definite conclusion, the conceptual elements set out in the early sections must be reviewed in the light of the empirical data. I have suggested that the most salient features of the context in which the professional project is pursued are probably the four crystallizations of the state, that Mann (1993) sees as most important: of these (capitalism, representation, nation and militarism) the first two are probably the most significant for professions. Equally important, however, are the characteristics that Mann appends to his definition of the state (see p. 66 above), namely (a) the extent that the state penetrates its territories; and conversely (b) the degree to which 'citizens' and 'parties' also penetrate the state; (c) the distinction between despotic power exercised by elites over civil society, and the infrastructural power of the state, whether despotic or not, to penetrate civil society.

Basically, the professional project seems best able to prosper where civil society penetrates the state, which in consequence is pluralistic or decentralized. In these circumstances the state is willing to hand over important functions to those in society who are interested in them, given certain safeguards (the regulative bargain). In a society such as Britain, which retains strong elements of tradition in its culture and institutions, one set of recipients of this handover are organizations of professionals who can show themselves to be allied with established and 'respectable' structures in society. In the United States of America, on the other hand, the decentralized state is clearly based in a legal-rational order, with a written constitution. Its commitment is to democratically responsible institutions and it was therefore at the outset opposed to professional bodies and to their professional project, as being elitist, monopolistic and anti-populist. The later divergence from this stance was legitimated by emphasis of professional bodies' modern rational knowledge, and the use of the universities as their institutional base. Control of knowledge-based practitioners was at all periods in the hands of the constituent states of the Union.

France and Germany were characterized, at the formative periods for professions, by centralized states, and while the various revolutions that these societies have experienced have changed their political institutions, they have not altered their centralization nor the notion of state responsibility for the public control, and even provision, of knowledge-based services. France differed from Germany in that it threw off its despotism, but the ensuing participation and representation was not of a kind to allow much penetration of the state by civil society. In consequence, knowledge-based services have remained in the ambit of the state, restricting the success of the professional project.

The moral-ideological crystallizations allow the state to function in particular ways. Thus in Britain the notion of 'lesser governments' is accepted and endorsed as the means by which much regulation and provision of services should be carried out; and further, it accepts, as appropriate appointees, collectivities which bear the stamp of tradition and respectability. In the USA, while the principle of devolution of powers is accepted, the last criterion for choosing an appropriate recipient would be tradition. In the past the individual was seen as able to handle all powers not arrogated by the state (the populist element), but from the mid-nineteenth century onwards the 'modern' criterion of formal rational knowledge has been applied, resulting in the allocation of power to those with educational qualifications, the organizations that educated them and the organizations they founded themselves to market their knowledge. Thus political ideology in America is a compound of rationalism, liberalism and populism, while in Britain traditionalism replaces populism and colours the other two components.

In France and Germany these elements are also to be found, but in different proportions and with the important addition of a centralized state, less penetrated by civil society. French political ideology retains some elements of tradition, but these tend to derive from the Napoleonic era rather than the *ancien régime*, so there is little cultural support for such devolution of powers as existed in pre-revolutionary France. So rationalism and liberalism are coloured by a statism that derives primarily from the Revolution and is imbued with the notion that the state is the embodiment of the 'General Will', and that allocation of powers to 'lesser governments' would undermine the operation of democracy. Germany displays similar elements, but here the statism is much stronger and derives in part from a traditional source, in that the modern German state was created by the Prussian autocracy and showed itself in 1932 fatally ready to mutate into dictatorship. This traumatic lapse has itself left an indelible print on German political culture, which now contains a resolute democraticism.

The ways in which groups in these various societies achieve social closure is bound to have some fairly direct connection with the institutional and cultural features just outlined. Thus, in Britain and the USA, status groups are free to form round their own activities and features, while in France and Germany the tendency is for members of society to use the state structures and its off-shoots such as the universities as the basis for status group formation and for social closure. The most interesting comparison is perhaps between Britain and Germany, for in the former groups have had the greatest freedom to achieve social closure on the basis of their professional activities, whereas in the latter, the 'statist' institutions of civil service and university form the means of socially enclosing a much larger number of people in the *Bildungsburgertum*.

But it must be recalled that even in the strongly statist culture of Germany, with its 'professionalization from above', evidence was adduced which shows the desire of members of knowledge-based occupations to achieve autonomy and to embark on a professional project.

Conclusion

The following arguments can be advanced in favour of the 'professional project'.

1 It has proven utility in dealing with Britain and the USA.
2 It has been shown above that professional groups have existed and striven for professional autonomy in France and Germany; even 'professionalization from above', which is sometimes said to characterize the latter, does not remove the features of market society that permit occupational groups to pursue their project (Siegrist, 1990). Various contributions allow one to see how it could be applied to most northern European societies (see Burrage and Torstendahl, 1990; Torstendahl and Burrage, 1990).
3 The erstwhile communist societies (USSR etc.) are examples in which knowledge-based services may be provided and regulated entirely by the state, but this is no reason to abandon the concept of 'project'. It merely provides the other end of a continuum from a society like Britain, where to all intents and purposes certain aspects of the legal system are in private hands. In Mann's terms, the state penetrated civil society in a thorough-going manner, while representation occurred only by means of institutions controlled by the Communist Party and the state.

In addition it should be noted that the use of the 'professional project' as a tool of analysis has a number of other advantages, amongst which one may cite the following.

1 It provides the means for prising apart the components of 'Anglo-American' institutions and showing that while they have common

roots, in American society those roots have been nourished by an ideology which deliberately opposed the traditional ethos of British society and have blossomed into forms that are quite distinct.

2 It reminds us that social stratification is not something that is a natural by-product of the economic structure or 'the relations of production'. While these provide the bases of economic rewards and must therefore be of great significance, position in society is also the outcome of interpersonal evaluation and thus something that individuals and groups *have to work at*. No group puts more into such efforts than a professional body, even if, as in statist societies, their achievements are relatively modest.

Notes

1 'There is no one master concept or basic unit of "society". It may seem an odd position for a sociologist to adopt, but if I could, I would abolish the concept of "society" altogether' (Mann, 1986: 2).

'Our sense of society, derived from Durkheim and Weber, . . . is quite useless when seeking to understand modern societies and perhaps even more so when seeking to understand agrarian civilizations' (Hall, 1985: 29).

2 On the other hand, there is the existentialist-marxist view of such events; namely that it is only contestation that makes people aware of their oppression and deprivation, and gives them the motivation to do something about it; cf. Marcuse (1964).

3 Ruritania occurs in Anthony Hope's novel *The Prisoner of Zenda* (1894), and my point is confirmed by the observation that the last factual location mentioned before entering that fictional country is Dresden.

4

Professions and the state

... close corporations are only justifiable if there is great good to be performed or a great evil to be remedied ... This is the old mediaeval ... guild system coming back again.

(The Marquis of Salisbury (opposing the Professional Accountants Bill), House of Lords Debates 15.7.1909, vol. 2(45): 572)

We have new regulatory responsibilities under the Insolvency Act. We shall be acquiring others through the Financial Services Act and ... because of the Eighth Directive [of the EC].

(Institute of Chartered Accountants in England and Wales, Annual Report, 1986, p. 3)

These opening quotations provide an example of how the attitude of the British state to the professions (as represented by accountancy) has changed during the twentieth century – from a reluctance to grant them a special position in the economic order, to the use of them as an instrument of regulation. This chapter will show that, in addition to the cross-cultural variations in the state/profession relation discussed in Chapter 3, it has varied over time (as the above quotations suggest) and has varied between different aspects of the state at the same time.

The cross-cultural comparison of the pursuit of the professional project was based on the conception of the state developed by Mann (1993) and, in order to cover the necessary material, was couched in fairly broad terms. Mann, of course, emphasizes the complexity and the messiness of society and therefore of an entity such as the state, whose power, even when despotic, may at different times and in varying circumstances be exercised by a monarch, his ministers, their administrators, by other elites such as the military, and so on. The same is true of other social actors, such as parties – or professions – whose policies and strategies are not pursued in a consistently purposeful way. Historians and sociologists, including myself in the previous chapter, are obliged to make things appear more orderly than they are in fact, and the present chapter will attempt to put matters right by looking at the messy reality of the interactions between the British state and the professions.

A profession's relation with the state, while latent for much of the time, is fundamental. Occupations that attempt to secure for themselves the two dimensions of professionalism – market control and social mobility – 'generally seek to establish a *legal monopoly* through licensure by the state' (Parkin, 1979: 57–8). The importance of this aspect is not reflected in sociological writing on the professions which varies in the extent to which it takes cognizance of state/profession interactions. Freidson (1986: 187–8) for example has little to say on this topic, while Larson (1977) refers to the state more frequently, but treats it very much as a background factor. Other socio-historical accounts (such as Berlant, 1975; Parry and Parry, 1976) do give the state more prominence.

However, there are some writers who tackle the state/professions relationship directly (cf. Macdonald and Ritzer, 1988). For example, Portwood and Fielding (1981), in their investigation of the sources of professional prestige, make numerous references to the profession/state relationship, and make specific reference (*inter alia*) to accountants, who are the subject of the greater part of the empirical material in this chapter, while their earlier paper (1980) is directly concerned with professions and the state (although, unlike this chapter, the concern is with 'personal service' professions). Halliday's work on the professions also deals with the state, particularly the character of the power, *vis-à-vis* the state and society, that a profession can derive from the nature of its knowledge base (Halliday, 1985). In a later work (1987), the state comes into focus in a different way when he examines the particular character of the legal profession, in that it not merely relates to the state but directly performs some of its functions, and can in some respects be considered part of the state.

State formation and professional autonomy

The state/profession relationship is also to be found in the work of Johnson, although approached from a quite different angle. It is central to 'The State and the Professions: the peculiarities of the British' (1982), while his paper of 1980 has a direct, and that of 1977 a limited bearing on the topic. The merit of these papers is that they bring together empirical data about the state and the professions and discuss them from a theoretical point of view. This is also true of Fielding and Portwood, and Halliday, but while these authors draw on both Marxian and Weberian concepts (for example, Fielding and Portwood, 1980: 50 and Halliday, 1983: 321), Johnson's theoretical stance is much more explicitly Marxian. In the first of the papers cited (1982), it is noticeable that he contrasts the 'Weberian tradition' (in quotes) with the Marxian alternative (no quotes). However, Johnson keeps the interplay of social actors at centre-stage, and his general characterization of this problem gives a specifically historical dimension to the relationship between state and professions, and therefore makes a useful starting point for this chapter.

Johnson shares the view of British state and society put forward in Chapter 3; that is, that state, elites and civil society were remarkably close-knit during the development of modernity, a view that he expresses as follows:

> The transition to capitalism in England was not marked by a separation of economic and political institutions, but by an historically unique articulation which involved the interrelated processes of state formation and profession-alisation.
>
> [T]he processes ... of professionalisation are integral to the process of state formation. ... The history of this relationship is not one of original separation followed by intervention or resistance to intervention. (Johnson, 1982: 188, 190)

Johnson's argument, which these passages introduce, is that the state was actively instrumental in the development of the professions in the nineteenth century, and that there is no evidence to support 'the common theme of intervention'. That is, 'that the existence of some external repressive public authority has the consequence of transforming pro-fessionals into functionaries and their associations into outposts of corporate organization' (1982: 187). No reference is made to anyone who actually holds this view, so it may be assumed that it is a straw man to be knocked down by his own view, with its supporting data, 'of the profession/state relationship in which, as a historical process, *the pro-fessions are emergent as an aspect of state formation and state formation is a major condition of professional autonomy* – where such exists' (p. 189; emphasis in the original). The corollary of this view is that either the state achieves its purposes by professional formation, or that the outcome is an inevitable consequence of 'the historical process' (p. 190).

Johnson's material covers two areas; first the reform of the English legal system in the 1830s and 1840s, and the part played by the profession of law; and secondly the relations between the state and professional bodies in the context of the British Empire.

There are two aspect of reform under the first heading – the county courts and land registration – both of which Johnson sees as part of the commodification of land during the development of full-blown capitalism. The decentralization of justice involved in setting up the county courts was intimately connected with property, because in the main these courts dealt with cases involving debt, which was more often than not secured on property. The pressure for reform came from the provincial bourgeoisie and attorneys, who had to use the centralized system of justice and to employ London legal agents to act for them; this cumbersome system was so expensive that the cost of obtaining a judgment averaged four times the amount in dispute. The outcome, in the shape of the County Courts Act of 1846, was both a victory and a defeat for the reformers: a victory, because cases could now be dealt with locally, quickly and cheaply; a defeat because attorneys did not succeed in obtaining the right to plead in these courts, which remained in the hands of the barristers. The division of the English legal profession was made more secure than ever, and the antagonism between provinces and metropolis was reinforced.

However, the attorneys and solicitors were far from dissatisfied with this division of legal labour, because it confirmed the monopoly in conveyancing that they had been granted in 1803; and this lay behind their opposition of the establishment of a land registry, which is Johnson's next example of the state/profession relationship. The central registration of titles to land is, one would have thought, an example of rational bureaucratic administration that would be of advantage to everyone, including the state. But, as Johnson recounts, the English legal profession successfully resisted this reform in the mid-nineteenth century. Johnson gives as the reasons for this, first, the unity of the profession – barristers and solicitors, London and the provinces – in opposing it as the existing system provided them all with easy money; and secondly, the failure of the modern idea of free trade to penetrate the market in land, due to the satisfaction of the aristocracy with the existing legal framework, and the desire of the bourgeoisie to leave the traditional status elements in land holding intact so that they might benefit from them themselves in due course.

The second area that Johnson covers is the involvement of the professions with the British imperial state between the mid-nineteenth and mid-twentieth centuries, looking particularly at medicine, architecture and accountancy. He shows clearly that the imperial state acted much more purposefully and successfully in establishing an infrastructure of regulation of these professions and their practice, than the home government. The metropolitan professions were willing to cooperate with, and provide a service for, the state, because they were able thereby to extend their influence and increase their membership. '[T]he degree of autonomy which a number of the British professions have enjoyed – particularly in the arena of qualification and entry – arises out of their involvement in empire and their relations with the imperial state' (1982: 206).

However, there are one or two points to be made about Johnson's treatment. First of all, Mann's model of multiple social actors would lead to the specific recognition of the bourgeoisie as a social actor in these events, and their ability to influence the outcome of state initiatives by reason of the 'participation' that they had achieved. Particularly significant is the observation that there were a disproportionate number of lawyers in Parliament, which appears as almost a throw-away line. Secondly, cognizance must be taken of Halliday's (1987) point that the law is by definition an arm of the state, despite the degree of independence it achieved in nineteenth-century Britain. Furthermore, while altruism seems to be at a pretty low level in the developments outlined above, there are occasions when their position does lead lawyers to act in a public spirited way, and that they do look 'beyond monopoly' as Halliday says. So, for example, the establishment of the system of county courts *was* a good thing.

Although land registration would appear to be equally desirable, in this instance the legal profession was united in its opposition to the reforms proposed in the wake of the County Courts Act, for the self-seeking reasons that Johnson describes. But the impression that he gives of a reform movement that went away is misleading. In the first place, land registration was a widely accepted instrument of modern bureaucracy. It was present in America from the earliest settlement, France instituted it in 1790, relatively backward Austria-Hungary had it in place early in the nineteenth century, while it had existed in Bohemia, of all places, for at least 200 years before that. So it is not surprising that in England, the first of modern societies, a statute requiring land registration was passed in the reign of Henry VIII. This turned out to be unenforceable, but many attempts were made to secure the same result in succeeding centuries: and furthermore, such efforts were not abandoned in the mid-nineteenth century, as Johnson implies, but continued unceasingly until an Act was eventually passed in 1897. Lastly, no evidence is offered for the class motivation that is claimed to underlie the failure to reform.

There is a similar lack of support for the view that the profession/state relationship was 'significantly affected' by the involvement of professional bodies in the administration of empire, and this conclusion seems to be based on things which did not happen – a connection which is difficult to substantiate.

But these are matters of detail, which do not detract from the value of this paper as a whole. Two impressions, that are at odds with each other, emerge. One is of several levels of conflict – between the state, classes, professions and between sections of professions – in which the state is not always able to prevail; and the other is of a general model of the 'process of state formation'. Admittedly, this impression is heightened by the recollection of the more explicitly Marxian tone of his earlier papers (Johnson, 1977, 1980), and a mature assessment must be that the stance of this paper is not dissimilar from that adopted in this book, but is obscured by the continued use of terminology of a theoretical position now abandoned. But this is a problem that can be by-passed, at a theoretical level, by adopting a conception of the state derived from Mann (1993), and on the empirical side by looking in more detail at specific series of events and at the actors participating in them.

Johnson clearly demonstrates in this, as in his other papers, a wide knowledge of the history of professionalization, but he cannot in the space available provide more than an outline of events, and one objective of this chapter is to provide specific data on some of the 'processes' he refers to, and to shed light on the nature of the 'articulation' within which they took place.[1] It should be noted at the outset, however, that these terms used by Johnson do not reflect the emphasis on social action that is inherent in the concept of the professional project: on the contrary, they are metaphors that tend to imply the priority, and even the inevitability, of structures and their immanent developments, rather than the interplay of agents and its outcome. Indeed, a closer look at the actual events in which professions and state interact will call in question the whole concept of 'process'.

Instead, professional bodies and state representatives will, in the accounts which follow, be presented acting purposefully to achieve particular ends, and if any metaphor is apt it is that of a gladiatorial arena. The protagonists find their purposes attract opponents and allies of various kinds. These purposes and (most importantly) those of the state, do not remain constant; there is a variety of outcomes of these struggles – a word used by participants (ICAEW, 1966: 16).[2]

As in the previous chapter, these social actors will be seen in relation to the conceptualization employed by Mann (1993), whose metaphor of 'crystallization', while probably aiming to capture much the same phenomenon as 'articulation', is spelt out in more detail. Furthermore, it allows for the development of Johnson's treatment, when combined with a closer look at the empirical details of the professions' search for 'a legal monopoly based on licensure by the state'.

In addition, the data presented will throw light on what can happen in the course of the pursuit of monopoly, and how successful it has been; they will also be relevant both to the sociological problems of the state/profession interface and to studies of inter- and intra-professional conflict (see Macdonald and Ritzer, 1988). Most importantly, however, this account will unpack some of the complexities embraced by the term 'the state', and will show how its various crystallizations have varied in importance for its relations with the professions.

Three groups of data will be presented.

1   A recapitulation of attempts by three professions – medicine, (Berlant, 1975; Kronus, 1976; Larson, 1977; Parry and Parry, 1976), architecture (Kaye, 1960) and accountancy (Garrett, 1961; ICAEW, 1966; Macdonald, 1984, 1985a; Stacey, 1954; plus primary sources), to secure statutory registration and thereby achieve social closure.
2   A more detailed consideration of the efforts of accountants to obtain registration in the years preceding the First World War.
3   A comparison of certain state/professional interactions at different points in time.

Accountancy will be examined in more detail, because its attempts at registration (and hence legal monopoly, closure etc.) extending over seventy years were in fact never successful. What may be regarded as the climacteric of this sequence (1907–11) has been investigated particularly closely.

Three cases of professional formation

Medicine

For medicine in England at the end of the eighteenth century, there were twenty-two licensing bodies – including universities, medical guilds, corporations and even the Archbishop of Canterbury (T.H. Huxley quoted in Berlant 1975: 158), while *The Medical Register* was a private venture published by a Dr S.F. Simmons (Clark, 1964: 602). The transition from this state of *laissez-faire* to the Medical Registration Act of 1858 took over fifty years to achieve, for it was in 1806 that the Royal College of Physicians first put forward a proposal to extend its powers of control over all types of medical practice in England and Wales (Parry and Parry, 1976: 110). No legislation followed from this proposal but the Apothecaries Act of 1815 started the movement of reform which was taken up in the 1820s by Thomas Wakeley, surgeon, medical reformer, founder of *The Lancet* (1823) and, from 1835 to 1852, an MP.

The details of the struggles of this period are recounted elsewhere (Berlant, 1975; Parry and Parry, 1976), and there is no need to recapitulate them here. The essential feature was the desire of those who felt that they occupied a position of status and market control not to dilute their privilege by admitting to a register those in an inferior position to themselves.[3] The contestants were the professional bodies of the physicians, the surgeons and the apothecaries as well as various medical associations, especially the Provincial Medical and Surgical Association which subsequently became the British Medical Association. But in addition to this internecine strife, the ideologues of *laissez-faire* also opposed the drive for reform as constituting a monopoly. This opposition led to a shift in position of the reformers who had to concede some state control of their affairs before Parliament would allow monopoly. The outcome was a curious mixture of self-control and state control embodied in the General Medical Council and the existence of a register for all qualified doctors, but no prohibition of practice by the unqualified. The resulting position is summed up by Berlant:

> the clash between the liberals and the medical profession was resolved in 1858 by the Medical Act, which provided for a number of institutional changes not strictly in keeping with the profession's traditional monopolization strategy of legally privileged restriction and professional autonomy. A new monopolization strategy was apparently constructed, using state administrative devices to give the profession a number of competitive advantages in the market as well as to stabilize the profession's internal institutional arrangements. The new strategy disarmed the attacks of the liberals not only by claiming exemption from liberal theory (through ideological appeals to the liberals), but also by finding loopholes in liberal theory and constructing institutions to fit through those loopholes. (1975: 167)

During the latter half of the nineteenth century the state became gradually more involved with the practice of medicine, but chiefly in a piecemeal fashion through the operation of the Poor Law Board and the Public Health Act of 1872. More significant was the abolition of the General Board of Health in 1854: this meant that until the establishment of the Ministry of Health in 1919 there was no central state agency dealing with health. On the other hand the position of doctors was strengthened by their majority presence on the statutory General Medical Council and by their domination of the hospitals, which grew dramatically in numbers and importance during this period.

In the first decade of the present century, however, the reforming wing of the Liberal Party became dominant in party policy and in 1911 the first real measure of the Welfare State, the National Insurance Act, became law. Its provisions divided the doctors, with the BMA strenuously opposing it. Support for the BMA position dwindled, however, in the face of an increased offer of the capitation fee from the government and the rank and file finally accepted it.

From this date onwards the doctors were clearly involved in a state medical service, but the bargain was one which guaranteed a market for doctors in the sector of the population that had hitherto been unavailable to medicine for reasons of poverty. Furthermore, although under the control of the state, to the extent of their involvement, doctors were none the less in a powerful position because the Ministry of Health had to rely on advice from doctors in conducting its affairs, in the absence of specialists of its own (Berlant, 1975: 172). This state of affairs was carried a stage further by the inauguration of the National Health Service in 1946. Changing positions of doctors (previously isolationist) and state (at one time non-interventionist) have not altered the profession's pursuit of its interests.

> While everyday practice may or may not be different under these systems, they have not changed the fundamental strategy by which the profession has tended to pursue its interests since the mid-nineteenth century. The profession has simply developed more effective tactics and administrative relationships to make use of the increased potential for interest satisfaction in its relationship to the state. In retrospect, the liberal threat to the existence of the medical profession ironically resulted in institutional changes which, though unanticipated, improved the interest position of the profession once the state began to play a significant role in distributing services to the nation. (Berlant, 1975: 174)

Architecture

From the late eighteenth century onwards architects have founded numerous associations. The early ones were social or study societies, starting with the Architects Club (1791) and followed by the London Architectural Society (1806) and the Architectural Society (1831). The Institute of British Architects was founded in 1834 'for facilitating the acquirement of architectural knowledge, for the promotion of the different branches of science connected with it, and for establishing an uniformity and respectability of practice in the profession' (quoted in Carr-Saunders and Wilson 1933: 178). This statement was actually made at the official opening meeting of the Institute in June 1835, twelve months after the initial 'foundation', which was itself the outcome of six months of meetings and changes of name, in the course of which the architects dissociated themselves from the surveyors who had originally been involved as well.

The Institute obtained a Royal Charter two years later, as a result of the efforts of their first President Earl de Grey and in 1866, by Royal Command, became the Royal Institute of British Architects. The earlier bodies either became defunct or were absorbed into the RIBA, but by 1847 younger architects were already feeling themselves excluded from the RIBA and some of them formed the Architectural Association. These two bodies existed in a state of rivalry for many years, although the AA came to have a more educational function as time went on and a *modus vivendi* was reached. The Institute moved only slowly towards control of members by examination and towards the idea of state registration – too slow in fact for some, who in 1884 broke away to form the Society of Architects. Throughout the 1880s and 1890s the Society drafted bills seeking statutory registration of architects which were introduced into Parliament, but only to have them blocked by the RIBA. This occurred in 1886, 1889 and 1891. On the last of these occasions a memorial explaining the reasons for opposition was drawn up and published in *The Times* (3 March 1891) over the names of twenty-four members of the RIBA, twenty-two architects who were not members of the RIBA (including such leading lights as Champney, Lethaby, Gilbert Scott, Norman Shaw and Webb!), and twenty-four non-architects, who included many leading painters of the time.

The Memorialists having failed to reach agreement with the RIBA on holding a meeting, went on to publish a collection of thirteen essays opposing registration chiefly on the basis that architecture is an art. The controversy died down over the next decade but when further registration bills were introduced – in 1892, 1900 and 1903 – the RIBA petitioned against them. However, by 1904 the Council set up a committee to consider the whole matter and a Bill was drafted to reform the Institute (and in fact to rename it the Royal College of Architecture); in 1906 this bill and another rival registration bill were before Parliament simultaneously. Both failed.

By this time the two parties were coming together, and after the RIBA had obtained a supplemental charter, which provided for reform such as the Society wanted, the two bodies attempted to amalgamate. This proved so constitutionally difficult that it was not actually achieved until 1925. Two years later a registration bill was introduced, referred to a Select Committee and ultimately shelved. It was re-introduced in 1928 only to meet the same fate: after another re-introduction in 1930 it was referred to a standing committee and finally passed in a diluted form in 1931. Dilution occurred in that registration was made voluntary, while at the same time the organization and representation provided by the Act in its greatly amended form was complex and unwieldy. Worst of all, there was little in the public mind to distinguish between a 'registered architect' and an architect; and with voluntary registration, there might be no difference! This particular problem was removed by the Architects (Registration) Act of 1938, but the constitution of the Registration Council, with a multitude of professional bodies represented on it but with a controlling majority in the hands of the RIBA, has ensured that the Balkanization of architecture which has bedevilled the occupation from the outset has continued until the present day.

Accountancy

Accountancy has never achieved the statutory registration that Parkin (1979: 57) emphasizes, although the Chartered Institutes of England and Wales and of Scotland (ICAEW and ICAS) have achieved a virtual monopoly of public practice (Macdonald, 1985a). The failure to achieve statutory regulation, which was not for want of trying, was related to a number of factors: while these apply in some measure to all professions, they came together in a particular form in the case of accountancy. They were:

1 The nature of accountancy practice, which
2 combined with a conflict of objectives within the membership and hence produced
3 an inability to circumscribe effectively either the practice or the membership of accountancy; and lastly
4 the attitude and objectives of the state.

These points are set out in some detail in Chapter 7, so for the purpose of this chapter it will be sufficient to trace only the general outline of the history of accountancy registration, in order to focus on what now appears to be a turning point in that history.

Accountancy only began to organize itself as an occupation about a century after the onset of industrialization, but that surprising observation is really a consequence of the fact that joint stock companies with limited liability only became generally possible with the passing of the first Companies Act of 1855. Early accountancy practice was in fact dominated by bankruptcy work and it was the advent of new legislation in that field that provided an important impetus for the founding of accountancy bodies in Edinburgh and Glasgow and the granting of Royal Charters in 1854 and 1855 respectively. In 1870 the first local societies of accountants were formed in England; two years later they amalgamated into a national body and formed the Institute of Accountants in England but by this time there was another national body of accountants in existence, the Society of Accountants.

In 1878 a draft bill was published which would have provided for the incorporation of accountants by statute and presumably their registration – although none of the secondary sources (Carr-Saunders and Wilson, 1933; ICAEW, 1966; Stacey, 1954) is specific on this matter. The bill was greeted by a lack of unanimity within the Institute and downright opposition by the Society of Accountants. After a year of vigorous negotiation a revised bill was drafted only to be met by government rejection, in the shape of advice from the Duke of Richmond, Lord President of the Council, that the government was not prepared to find parliamentary time for the bill, and suggesting that an application for a Royal Charter was likely to be successful. This reaction from a Conservative government contrasted with the response of the Liberal administration ten years earlier, when G.J. Goschen, President of the Poor Law Board (why him?!) had advised that the Privy Council had for the previous two years declined to grant charters and suggested incorporation under the Companies Act.

The opening chapter of the history of English accounting thus contains the three elements which are to be found in all subsequent efforts to achieve statutory registration – internal dissent, external challenge and government indifference.

In the period between 1879 and the First World War something of the order of twenty-six bills were drafted on the registration of accountants or on protecting the designation 'Chartered Accountant'.

The ICAEW's attempts to secure legislation went through a number of phases during the thirty-five years preceding the First World War, namely:

1 1878–80: initial attempt at registration followed by grant of Royal Charter;
2 1891–92: attempts to obtain statutory protection of the title 'Chartered Accountant';
3 1893–1900: ICAEW, ISAA, ICAS and others drafted numerous registration bills, some of which were introduced in Parliament, but got no further than a first reading;
4 1904–06: ICAEW reverts to attempt to protect the 'Chartered' title;
5 1907–14: continued attempts to obtain statutory registration: second reading in the House of Lords and promise of a Joint Parliamentary Committee.

With the outbreak of war, these efforts were abandoned and not resumed, for reasons that will be discussed below. In the last of these periods, however, the joint efforts of ICAEW and ISAA came closest to realizing their goal and it is therefore logical to look at this period for evidence of 'interaction' and 'articulation' of state and profession. A contrast will then be drawn between these years and those after the First World War.

Drafting the bill   The Professional Accountants Bill was first debated on 15 July 1909, but that event was preceded by two years of drafting, negotiation and redrafting. The first mention of it in the ICAEW Council Minutes in October 1907, when the President reported on a conference with the ISAA, gives no reason why the matter should have become important again. The level of interest in registration among accountants may be gauged by the number of items a year on the topic appearing in *The Accountant*. It appears to have been an important topic in the period up to the granting of the charter in 1880 and again in 1893, when both the Institute and the Society sponsored bills. In 1896/7, when five bills were drafted, interest reached a peak, but slumped again after the joint propsals of these two bodies were rejected by their members. While the pages of *The Accountant* show that the topic never disappeared from view entirely, there is a marked upswing of interest from 1905 onwards. It is possible that the circumstances of other professions stimulated the interest of accountants. Architects had had a registration bill defeated in 1903, and had set up a special committee to consider the matter in 1904; and in 1906 there were actually two rival bills before Parliament (Carr-Saunders and Wilson 1933: 181; Kaye, 1960: 147–8). It was in 1906 also that dentists became aware that their Registration Act was an inadequate protection against competition from dental companies (Carr-Saunders and Wilson, 1933: 112).

Not only are the motives of the Council of the ICAEW not apparent, the details of their deliberations and negotiations are also unavailable because their records for this period consist purely of council and committee minute books which record only documents tabled, actions taken and resolutions passed. The reports they received and the letters they wrote have not been preserved. The organ of the State with which they interacted (the Board of Trade) has left even less. The Public Records Office contains no material'at all that relates to accountants at this period.

However, it is clear that the ICAEW and the ISAA negotiated steadily and successfully until June 1908 when they sent their draft bill to the Board of Trade and had a meeting with the Parliamentary Secretary. The matter was put before the President of the Board of Trade (Winston Churchill) who wrote in January 1909 on the subject of admitting women to the ICAEW and ISAA. A matter of judicial procedure was sorted out with the Lord Chancellor and a letter was received from the Comptroller of Companies which led them rather belatedly to consult the Scottish and Irish Institutes of Chartered Accountants. The latter replied but it seems that these bodies were not really brought into the scheme proposed, which is astonishing considering the difficulties experienced in this respect in earlier legislative attempts. In April 1909 the bill and an explanatory memorandum was circulated to members and letters of support were received from local societies. In May a sub-committee was set up (somewhat belatedly) to deal specifically with the bill, while the Central Association of Accountants (a small, recently formed body) wrote asking for a meeting to discuss the Bill. Correspondence continued with the Scottish and Irish Institutes and a meeting was held with representatives of the latter only ten days before the second reading in the House of Lords.

The legislative process   The impression, given by the council minutes, that a number of matters relating to the bill were unresolved is confirmed by what transpired in the House of Lords on 15 July 1909, when the bill received its second reading. There is no account available of how the Earl of Chichester came to be the sponsor, except that a remark in his speech indicates that he had some City experience. On the other hand, it appears that at the age of 39 he was not a particularly adept parliamentarian. His speech made it clear that matters relating to Scottish and Irish accountants had not been resolved to their satisfaction and even admitted that one clause 'had been very badly drafted, and I believe a new clause has already been drawn up' (HoL, 1909, vol. 2 (45): 566). This enabled the peers who had been briefed by those bodies to come down heavily on that issue. Chichester was probably unfortunate in that the immediately preceding debate had been on the Smallholdings and Allotments (Scotland) Bill which meant that Scottish peers were over-represented in the House and included the Secretary of State for Scotland. The opposition came largely from them and the Irish peers ('I do not remember ever having read such a selfish measure', HoL, vol. 2 (45): 570). Strong support came only from a peer representing the Board of Trade who said that it was 'an important measure', and that the Board of Trade thought that 'it is probably desirable that some such machinery should be set up'. However, even he, as a Scottish peer, 'would not be found consenting to any injustice being done to our fellow countrymen'.

It was not until the end of the debate that the heavy guns of traditional Conservatism were brought to bear in the form of Lord Salisbury. 'Close corporations are only justifiable if there is great good to be performed or a great evil to be remedied . . . is it the case that there are a great number of accountants who ought not to be accountants. Is there any evidence of the fact?' (HoL, vol. 2, 45: 572). When the House divided, there were fourteen votes on each side – doubly inconclusive because it showed that the House was inquorate! When the debate was resumed four days later the motion was agreed to and adjourned *sine die*; in other words, dropped. Three peers had spoken for the bill and six against.

After this debacle the Board of Trade felt sufficiently concerned to set up meetings between the ICAEW, ICAS and ICAI. Discussions undoubtedly took place and the ICAEW's sub-committee for the bill received a report that it had been introduced into the House of Commons in June 1910, but apparently never achieved a second reading. Re-drafting continued until the end of 1910 and in January 1911 a bill approved by all three Institutes and the Society was sent to the Board of Trade. With the Board's approval, it was introduced into the House of Lords by a much better prepared Lord Chichester. The Scottish and Irish objections had been met, one member expressed the approval of the London Chamber of Commerce, the government's view was 'warmer and more cordial than on the last occasion' and even Lord Salisbury had mellowed to the point where he was 'able to reckon himself one of the supporters of the . . . Bill'. Seven peers spoke in favour and none against. The bill was then referred to a joint committee of both Houses of Parliament, but when it reached the Lower House this was ruled to be an inadmissible way of by-passing debate in the Commons and was ruled out of order.

Activity by the professional bodies, starting in 1909, again stimulated *The Accountant's* interest, but although the parliamentary efforts continued, the members concern for the matter flagged, so that by the time a bill actually passed its second reading in the Lords in 1911, the annual level of items in the journal had fallen to only a quarter of that of 1909.

Thereafter the ICAEW continued to discuss legislative plans rather than take action. In March 1912 the President reported to Council that re-introduction of the bill was proposed, but three months later the sub-committee postponed a decision until January 1913 when it was decided to let the matter stand over. In July that year their attention was directed instead to yet another bill to protect the title 'Chartered Accountant' by means of a public register; in April 1914 that too was abandoned when the Registration sub-committee reported that it was unable to agree. In the pages of *The Accountant* the number of items on registration slipped from six in 1912 to two in 1913, to none in 1914: in fact the topic does not occur again until 1923.

The state initiative   The interest in registration, judging by items in *The Accountant*, had a passing upsurge in 1922–23 and then increased rapidly to a peak in 1929 and 1930. The reason for the first of these rises is not clear but the second coincides with the setting up of a Board of Trade Departmental Committee on the Registration of Accountants.

In the 1920s the problem of the proliferation of small accountancy bodies, grudgingly acknowledged in 1911, made itself felt on the legislators themselves. They found that, with a steady flow of Municipal Authority bills to deal with, they were continually having to decide on the eligibility as auditors of members of minor bodies, and in 1929 the Select Committee on Local Legislation recommended that the profession be put on a unified basis to avoid the tedious business of repeatedly deciding who was to be a local auditor. The proceedings of the Departmental Committee are documented in the literature (ICAEW, 1966; Stacey, 1954) and need not be recapitulated here. Suffice it to say that seventeen accountancy bodies and eighteen non-accountancy bodies gave evidence; broadly speaking, only the minor, non-chartered accountancy bodies wanted registration of accountants. The issue has only been raised once since then, in the late 1940s: but with the specific naming in the 1948 Companies Act of the chief accountancy bodies as the only auditors of all but the smallest limited companies, their monopoly was complete in practical terms and the statutory register became, for most accountants, an irrelevance.

The state, professions and historical change

> ... the transition to capitalism in England was not marked by a separation of economic and political institutions but an historically unique articulation which involved the inter-related processes of state formation and professionalisation.

> (Johnson, 1982: 188)

This statement, which sums up the main thrust of Johnson's argument (see also Johnson, 1980), holds true only at the most general level. In his final paragraph Johnson settles for the 'claim that modern professions are a product of state formation', but adds the qualification that the degree of autonomy attained was confined to the imperial period, was 'peculiarly British' and should not be taken 'as the classical and potentially universal form' (1982: 208). But from the cases set out above (cases used by Johnson himself) one gets some idea of the complexity and untidiness of this so-called 'process'; and Johnson himself says immediately before the passages just quoted, 'The view that professionalization is not a single process with a given end-state also suggests that the relationship with changing state forms was also in flux.'

The history of 'modern' professions covers the past two hundred years and during that time significant changes have occurred in professional practice of all kinds, and in the state. To refer to what has occurred as 'an historically unique articulation' is to encourage us to overlook sociologically significant changes. It would, therefore, be worthwhile to consider, in light of the data presented, both here and by Johnson, what can be said about the state, the professions and intra-professional conflict.

To look first at the state, Johnson (1982: 206) refers to 'the emergent forms of the liberal-bourgeois state and the later construction of an imperial state apparatus', and it is reasonable to accept the existence, probably contemporaneously, of a liberal-bourgeois state – or alternatively 'liberal-democratic' (p. 196) – and an imperial state. But in addition, theorists of the state such as Poggi (1978: 122) argue that during the twentieth century a significant shift has occurred in the location of the state/society divide. Poggi avoids attaching labels to the modern state, but he specifies the ways in which the state has advanced its influence in welfare, warfare and economic regulation. Certainly the terms 'welfare state' and 'corporatist state' have been used to characterize the third and fourth quarters of the twentieth century and these variants, it could be argued, have involved real and significant changes in the state/profession relationship.

The remarkably erratic development of the profession/state relationship in Britain can be rendered more intelligible if the state is characterized in the terms of Mann's theory, rather than hoping that the conceptual flotsam left behind by the high tide of Marxism can provide an explanatory structure. This can be done by considering some of the crystallizations of the state, and some of the political institutions that form the main framework of his conceptualization (see Chapter 3).

(1) **Capitalism**. Although Britain was the cradle of capitalism, the British state was one of the last of Western societies to crystallize in this respect. As Mann (1993: 480–1) points out: 'The Victorian state was capitalist, [but] many Victorians distinguished between commercial matters, on which the state should merely assist capitalist self regulation, and social questions, which were legitimate matters of state intervention.' He goes on to quote Lord Macaulay: 'the principle of non-interference is one which cannot be applied . . . where the public health or the public morality are concerned'.

The professions, even that of medicine, did not fall under this rubric, and so the liberal state made no effort to bring the various branches of medicine into line in the decades leading up to the Medical Act of 1858. Their eventual unity was largely the work of the indefatigable reformer Thomas Wakely. The state took no steps to regulate the professions of architecture or accountancy in Britain before the First World War, limiting itself to responding to their initiatives, maintaining a 'cool and correct' attitude, ready to promote great good or remedy great evil, but not to take any positive action (except to ensure that if there were a register of accountants, it would include women).

In the last third of the twentieth century, the corporatist state[4] emerged in Britain (Goldthorpe, 1985; Winkler, 1977) and received a particular impetus from Thatcherism. The actions of the state in this phase appear to be directed at control chiefly of the economy, but also of other institutions such as education, by means of existing agencies. The 'regulative bargain' remains at the basis of the state/profession relationship but the profession is used as a channel for state action, especially controls. The best example is probably accountants and their status as a 'recognized professional body' under the Financial Services Act 1988. Cooper et al. (1988: 4) not only discuss this example but regard the current position as one in which the state, in the form of the DTI, is actually a *sponsor* of bodies such as the ICAEW. The corporatist state, in its Thatcherite form, is also suspicious of monopoly and has therefore taken steps to ensure that consumers are more aware of the variety of services and practitioners among whom they may choose, and to promote competition between practitioners. Professional monopolies are thus less watertight and the terms of the 'regulative bargain' have shifted somewhat.[5]

(2) **Geopolitics**. Mann has always argued strongly that state theory has neglected diplomacy and military power, pointing out that agrarian states raised at least three-quarters of their revenue to make war (1993: 69): and while Britain did little to regulate capitalism, it was so successful in the pursuit of war and geopolitics that by the end of the Napoleonic wars, it had established something approaching a world hegemony, in which British capitalism could operate unhindered. The British state could not

afford to be 'liberal' in running its empire and so one finds a very different ethos obtaining there from that which prevailed at home. In India particularly, but probably elsewhere, medicine was drawn into the administrative apparatus; colonial regimes in South Africa and Australia were far more ready to legislate for the registration of accountants and architects, as shown by Johnson (1982) and as can be readily perceived from the pages of *The Accountant* of the pre-1914 period.

So the end of the nineteenth century and the first quarter of the twentieth sees a much more extensive state power, modelled in certain ways upon the Roman Imperium, but which does not affect the metropolis, except in relation to the ambiguous, problematic case of Ireland. Many social institutions therefore have two sets of relationships with the state at this period, one in its imperial mode and the other in its domestic mode, which moves from traditional liberalism towards intevention and welfare. The two modes are not entirely discrete and professional bodies in Britain were certainly involved in colonial and dominion regulation and legislation.

But in addition to the imperial state, the demands of geopolitics have twice in the present century obliged Britain to become what might be called a 'warfare state', when it had to adopt a centralized regime of a pervasiveness comparable to that of a totalitarian state. Many professionals – especially medics, but also lawyers, clergy and others – were sucked into the military apparatus; but others, notably accountants, became important in various sectors and at a variety of levels of the civil administration. To give just two examples: in the First World War many Chartered Accountants were placed in positions of seniority and no less than seven were knighted for their services. In the Second World War accountancy firms were responsible for monitoring such things as meat rationing, price regulation and government supply contracts (Loft, 1986). As Garrett (1961: 231) puts it: 'To take the profit out of war ... accountability and independent certification at a thousand and one points was called for by Government departments.'

(3) The **moral-ideological crystallization** of the modern British state developed slowly, continuing to be limited to the control of the worst exploitative excesses of capitalism, and to an increasing awareness of public health matters, such as the provision of clean water supply and sewage systems. The need for education and health provision as part of an infrastructure to support the capitalist and military crystallizations took much longer to dawn on the British elite than on those of her European neighbours. Legislative provision for education occurred in the last third of the nineteenth century, but the 'welfare' state does not emerge until 1911 with the National Insurance Act. This measure brought a profession, medicine, into direct contact and conflict with the state as never before and provoked serious internal dissension within medicine. The outcome involved decidedly more than any 'regulative bargain' (Cooper et al., 1988: 9) that existed up to that time because the doctors were now actually

involved in a state-run system and could see that it was in their financial and iatric interest. The extensions to this system were minor until the inauguration of the NHS in 1946, which has given rise to the most clear-cut example of the mutually advantageous inter-relationship of state and profession. Its introduction involved a major clash of wills between the Health Minister and the BMA, with the latter emerging successful although many, both then and later, regarded it as a pyrrhic victory.

It is medicine, para-medicine and other personal service professions which have become particularly involved in state organization and who, according to Fielding and Portwood (1980), derive distinct advantages from being 'bureaucratic'.

Like the state, professions also change, although one might argue that the ideas and activities of, for example, the Royal College of Surgeons when it was founded in 1800 are possibly closer to their contemporary counterparts than those of the state at the time of Pitt's administration are to those of the modern state. In other words, the RCS had embarked on its professional project, using modern criteria for admission and committed to the active development of a scientific knowledge base, while the state, though rapidly being forced into the adoption of modern methods of administration, was in most respects still in the grip of 'Old Corruption'.[6]

First of all there has been a shift in the emphases that professions have given to the bases on which they claim to be special. Particularly in their early days, professional bodies have emphasized their respectability and 'gentlemanly' character (Macdonald, 1984). Doctors were keen to show they did not engage in trade (Parry and Parry, 1976); architects emphasized that they were not builders (Kaye, 1960). Accountants insisted they did not act as auctioneers (ICAEW, 1966). This ploy had a double value as it underpinned both the claim to high status, and the warrant for a monopoly – because as high status persons they could be trusted to charge a fair price and could not be expected to engage in cut-throat commercial competition. This reliance on traditional values provided professionals with starting points (Johnson, 1977; Macdonald, 1984; Portwood and Fielding, 1981): once on course the emphasis has shifted to high educational attainment and technical expertise – the modern rational legitimation (Larson, 1977: 68). Once that had been achieved, professionals have ventured back towards entrepreneurialism, for example, primary health care in the USA, and consultancy and investment advice by accountants everywhere. This kind of change has therefore two aspects.

1 The general aspect of an early reliance on traditional values in establishing occupational distinctiveness, which has diminished, relatively at least, as knowledge and other modern sources of prestige have assumed greater importance (Larson, 1977: 68).

2 The particular aspect of the disengagement from entrepreneurialism which was clearly established by the nineteenth-century professions. In

the late twentieth century, by contrast, professionals have modified their position so as to fit in with the increased emphasis on commercialism as a social value – always more prevalent in the USA. Not only are there lucrative opportunities for doctors, lawyers, accountants etc., but the latter two at least may now advertise.

Secondly, the knowledge base of professions has changed over the past two centuries and hence, following Halliday (1985), their power *vis-à-vis* the state. The way in which different kinds of knowledge may affect the power relations of professions with both the state and civil society, together with the details of Halliday's categories of professional knowledge, will be discussed in Chapter 6, but the following may be noted.

1 Medical knowledge really only achieved a wide scientific base in the late nineteenth century. Such things as the inordinate proportion of medical training devoted to anatomy (mere description) and the problems of the AMA in competing with 'snake- oil' doctors in the western territories and states bear witness to this. In the twentieth century biochemistry, pharmacology etc. have transformed medical knowledge. In addition, all the medically related professions now rely heavily on high technology.
2 Legal and technical knowledge has also proliferated considerably in the fields of law, accountancy, architecture etc. Mastery of this knowledge has likewise become much more salient, although as with medicine, information technology now offers a way of handling these knowledge bases which in certain respects poses a threat to the professions.

Thirdly, in addition to the changes discussed above that have clearly occurred in both the state and the professions, the positions of professions have varied due to conflict; internal conflict between members of the profession and external conflict between the profession and other occupational groups, the state and even the public.

The professional/state relationship in Britain, especially as concerns the striking of the 'regulative bargain', has been more influenced by internal conflict within the occupation at certain periods than by anything else. This is clearly to be seen in all the cases described above, particularly in the case of accountants, who seem to have been unable to learn the lessons of their past mistakes, so that they eventually failed altogether to secure registration. The chief cause of internal conflict is that members divide into (a) those who are content with their existing status and are not prepared to admit others who would dilute it and (b) those who feel that their position will continue to be threatened until a boundary is established which includes all those who constitute a real threat. This basic division may take particular forms based on region (doctors and accountants), discipline (radiographers; Larkin, 1983) or philosophy (architects). External conflict often arises because an emerging profession impinges on territory already staked out by another (Abbott, 1988; Freidson, 1986: 188) and this may modulate, over time, into bargaining over the extent and nature of the domination of the established profession over the new one. Conflicts with the state take many forms as the aims and philosophies of the two parties change.

Conflicts tend to get resolved in the long run, but at certain points in time dissension within an occupation seems to be more significant than anything else in determining the direction in which the state/profession relationship develops. The roots of discord lie in the forms of professional organization and in the nature of professional knowledge and practice, and as these are bound to change, internal or iternecine conflict may at any time re-emerge as the dominant influence on a profession's development, and thus on its relation with the state.

Conclusion

Whilst one can certainly argue that the professions were part and parcel of a 'process of state formation' it is also the case that those of their actions which involved or impinged on the state were carried out for motives and with objectives which had nothing to do, consciously, with state formation, and indeed often involved relationships with parties other than the state. On the contrary, professions perceived some of their actions as keeping the state (or 'officialism' as accountants termed it: ICAEW, 1966: 16) at bay. It is important to view these actions in the light of their overt objectives and the state's actual responses, at the time, and not to reinterpret such episodes to fit in with 'a secret history' (Marx, 1976: 176).

In this connection, the conclusion drawn by Fielding and Portwood should be noted:

> it is both possible and necessary to specify the form and extent of state heteronomy ... because it facilitates the analysis of profession–state relationships by placing them within the historical context of *the whole matrix of relationships* between a given profession, the state, other professions, occupations and interested bodies in related fields of employment and the clientele. (1980: 47–, emphasis added)

Whilst not denying that interaction with the state takes a certain priority – for instance, obtaining a Royal Charter – a professional body's conflicts, even in the course of trying to achieve legislative endorsement, are most importantly with other occupational groups, or even internal. It is the tripartite battle between surgeons, doctors and apothecaries, plus their internal divisions that caused a thirty-five year delay in medical registration: in the case of accountants the internal, internecine and inter-regional strife was so prolonged that the politically appropriate epoch actually passed without securing registration. If architects and surveyors and within the architects, educationalists and artists, had been able to agree, registration would not have been fifty years a-coming. At the same time, it must be acknowledged that those members, especially of the accountancy profession, who argued against registration on the grounds that it was unneccessary, seem to have had the right of it, because the failure to achieve it had little effect on closure or market control (Macdonald, 1985a).

It is important to specify the variety of ways in which the state acts and reacts at different periods in time, and the widely different stances it may adopt in relation to geopolitical as opposed to domestic policy. Johnson (1982: 207) is careful to note that 'the state [has] been transformed over time', but the various data quoted above need to be put in the context of a particular crystallization of the state, and the way that it has developed must be specified. Historically distinct forms must not be telescoped in the search for neat sociological aphorisms.

In the period of professionalization the state has changed considerably and the epithets 'liberal-bourgeois' and 'imperial' do not adequately characterize the changes of the past 200 years. The former term certainly describes the state until the first decade of this century but the political conflicts of 1906–14 were a prelude to a new shape of government that, as the century progressed, emerged as the corporatist state. The 'imperial' state was not some *fin de siècle* aberration but the forerunner, in its geopolitical crystallization, rather than its domestic, capitalist one, of the corporatist state of the 1970s and 1980s.[7]

The 'liberal bourgeois' state was definitely non-interventionist and was not proactive. All the legislative initiatives on occupational regulation come from the professional bodies. They certainly consulted with the Board of Trade, but the support they received from the government was no more than 'cool and correct' (HoL, 1909, vol. 2 (45): 573), even though the accountants, at any rate, attempted to support their case by reference to the legislation enacted by the 'imperial' state (HoL., 1909, vol. 2(45): 565). It is a nice historical irony that in July 1909 within days of the display of liberal non-intervention that greeted this legislative initiative by the ICAEW, Lloyd George adumbrated the Welfare State in his famous inflammatory Limehouse speech which not only shocked Conservatives but took the breath away of his Prime Minister, Asquith, and which foreshadowed the National Health Insurance Act of 1911 (Dangerfield, [1935] 1961: 21). That, of course, was the occasion on which Asquith threatened to swamp the House of Lords with Liberal Peers if the Lords insisted on exercising its prerogative. It is therefore not surprising that in such an atmosphere the Commons took exception to the way the Accountants Registration Bill had reached the Lower House.

The National Health Insurance Act was the first real step towards a Welfare State and brought the medical profession into head-on collision with the state. The First World War witnessed an enormous growth in state power, in line with the hypothesis of Mann (1986, 1993). These two forces, welfare and warfare, have been the occasion of a growth in state power of such dimensions that a different form of state must be distinguished from this period onwards. In this epoch the state in its new form engaged in different kinds of relationships with professional bodies. In the case of accountants, for the first time in seventy-five years of the existence of the chartered bodies, the Board of Trade set up a departmental committee to examine the position and to decide their future. Second World War and post-war governments again increased dramatically the intervention of the state in all aspects of civil society.

This leads to the final point to be made about the state–profession 'articulation'. 'Historically unique' is an inappropriate term, not only because of the long time span involved and the changes that occurred, but also because the contemporary interventionist/corporate state invades nearly all institutions, and there is nothing unique in the way in which it regulates, incorporates and makes use of professional organizations. That is the spirit of our times.

Professional bodies are certainly more closely interlinked with the state than formerly, but this characteristic is shared by almost every institution from the family, through charitable bodies to economic enterprises. This shift has not altered the basic characteristic of professional bodies, that each is based on 'a regulative bargain' with the state (Cooper et al., 1988: 9). As Portwood and Fielding (1981) point out, state heteronomy is not only necessary for the professions, it constitutes part of their legitimacy and their power.

Professions have arrived at their current position – by no means an end state (Macdonald and Ritzer, 1988) – by way of struggle and negotiation within and between their organizations, other groups and the state (Portwood and Fielding, 1981). During this century the state has changed from being, on the whole, disinterested (except where danger to life, or property is clearly an issue) to the proactive corporatist state. At the beginning of the century, in the terms of Mann's (1993) analysis, civil society penetrated the state to a considerable degree, and although representation still excluded women, its legislative system was certainly open to the initiatives of professional bodies. On the other hand the state crystallization in relation to capitalism had not advanced very far, and the legislature could not be persuaded to institute regulatory mechanisms that favoured the accountancy bodies. At the same period, however, the geopolitical crystallization of the state was well developed, and the state was willing to respond and even take the initiative where regulation of the Empire was concerned. The events of the century stimulated the state increasingly to penetrate civil society, but given the pre-existing involvement of civil society in the state, and the extent of representation, it preferred to use the existing structures of civil society – such as those provided by the professions – to extend its infrastructure and its regulatory mechanisms. Doctors and the Health Service, lawyers and Legal Aid, accountants and the Companies Acts are cases in point.

As the bases of social power continue to shift (Mann, 1986) and as technological innovation – especially of information and knowledge bases – advances, we can expect to see further changes in professions, the state and the relation between them.

Notes

1   A subsidiary aim is to consider the utility of the language that Johnson employs to describe and analyse the state/profession relationship and in particular the implications of terms such as 'articulation' and 'process'. Sociologists are in a sense condemned to the use of metaphor and 'articulation' is a particularly interesting example of such metaphoric terminology because it means both 'connected by joints' – like a lorry or a knee – *or* 'to speak distinctly': thus there is the irony that, in using a word metaphorically that can mean 'to speak clearly', it is not clear what is meant.

'Process' is also a problematic word in metaphor because of the variation in its literal use. 'Process' can refer, for example, to the brewing 'process', which includes the mashing 'process' and the fermentation 'process'. The first is a sequence of interrelated events which are the outcome of *human agency*, while the latter two are sequences which *occur naturally* by enzyme and bacterial action respectively in certain circumstances. So what exactly is a social 'process' in sociological metaphor? Johnson (1980: 361–7) in his last section gets quite carried away by 'process'. In just over 2000 words he uses it forty-two times in association with reproduction (e.g. of capital), class (e.g. formation), labour, production, ideological, social, political, occupational, surplus value, socialization, planning, or just plain 'process'. In his final page, every twenty-sixth word is 'process'. Such terminology might give rise to the view that a society, once it has adopted capitalism as the form of economic activity, is made up of a series of logically necessary events, interactions and consequences which follow with all the inevitability of the formation of the physical universe as a consequence of the Big Bang.

2   Abbreviations used in this chapter are:

ICAEW   Institute of Chartered Accountants in England and Wales
ICAS   Institute of Chartered Accountants in Scotland (used anachronistically) to refer to Scottish chartered accountants whose local societies only combined to form an Institute in 1954
ISAA   Incorporated Society of Accountants and Auditors
ICAI   Institute of Chartered Accountants in Ireland
DTI   Department of Trade and Industry

3   The niceties of status difference between physicians and apothecaries, and indeed between different phyisicians are frequently referred to in Trollope's novel *Dr Thorne*, which (coincidentally?) was published in 1858, the year of the Medical Registration Act. The main topic of the novel, it could be argued, is the sources of social prestige in mid-nineteenth-century England, although the social status of doctors does not attract the attention of the editor in her introduction to the Penguin edition (1991). However, here is a nice example:

'I remember when Bolus [an apothecary] was thought to be a very good sort of a doctor.'
'Is he—is he—' whispered Frank, 'is he by way of being a gentleman?'

4   'Corporatism. A form of social organization, in which the key economic political and social decisions are made by corporate groups, or these groups and the state jointly. Individuals have influence through their membership of corporate bodies. These include trade unions, professions, business corporations, political pressure groups and lobbies, and voluntary associations. Corporatism may be contrasted with decision-making via the market, in which individuals make their own private choices and collectively and cumulatively shape

society. At the political level, corporatism may also be contrasted with the traditional form of liberal democracy in which political decisions were taken only by governments representing the electorate directly' (Abercrombie et al., 1988: 53).

5   In a later version of this paper (Robson et al., 1994), the same empirical material is considered from the viewpoint of regulation as professional ideology, by means of an analysis of the discursive practices of professional bodies of accountants; which is rather different, but equally interesting.

6   'Corruption, the most infallible symptom of constitutional liberty', wrote Gibbon in *The Decline and Fall of the Roman Empire.* I do not think he was being ironic.

7   Interestingly enough the first state-owned enterprise was Imperial Airways.

5
Patriarchy and the professions

It is important for a profession, especially in its formative years, to demonstrate its respectability. This was essential to both aspects of the professional project, for, on the one hand, it was a means to upward social mobility, and on the other it was the key to monopoly, because those who could afford their services insisted on dealing with 'gentlemen'. The emphasis was on the first part of this word, for until the latter part of the nineteenth century, no one would have thought for a minute that such a person might be a woman. This expectation was part of the subordination of women which is usually termed 'patriarchy', although, as many writers on the topic observe, this is an unsatisfactory usage. Waters (1989: 194–5), for example, notes that its dictionary meaning is different from its meaning in feminism and sociology, that within these fields there is no agreement on the term's definition, and that it is 'ahistorical'. However, it continues in use, and in this chapter I shall follow Witz (1992: 11) and take it to refer 'to a societal-wide system of gender relations of male dominance and female subordination, ... [and] the ways in which male power is institutionalized within different sites in society'.

It has been brought very forcibly to the notice of sociologists that the conventional wisdom of their theories is seriously deficient in that it has nothing to say about this pervasive feature of society; and in consequence, many attempts have been made to remedy this by 'theorizing patriarchy'. Many insights have resulted from these efforts, but, as Acker (1989) concludes, they have failed to give sociology a sure grasp of the topic. The problem is something akin to the 'intangibility' of social class that was discussed in Chapter 2, although the reason for our failure to grasp it is rather different. Walby's (1989, 1990) theorizing of patriarchy provides a case in point when she writes:

> I think there are six main patriarchal structures which together constitute a system of patriarchy. These are: a patriarchal mode of production in which women's labour is expropriated by their husbands; patriarch relations within waged labour; the patriarchal state; male violence; patriarchal relations within sexuality; and patriarchal culture. (1989: 220)

These points certainly cover the main aspects or locations of male subordination of women, but it reads like a list, rather than a system; somehow the terminology does not seem to encompass the social reality we experience. I believe the reason for this is that 'patriarchy', like social class, is different from most of the raw material of sociology and therefore the terminology of structure and system do not really fit it.

Patriarchy is more like language than anything else. In primary socialization we learn how to be social, how to be moral and how to speak. These modes of behaviour are imprinted with near indelibility, and though capable of modification in secondary socialization, they will tend to come through in everything we do; we find them embodied in the institutions of society and are thereby enabled to cope with our social environment. Patriarchy runs through those elements of our primary socialization, like 'Brighton' through a stick of rock. It is for this reason that it is to be found embodied in social institutions (such as the state or the system of economic production), in culture, in social relationships and in language. It is, to change the metaphor, part of the grammar of society and social interaction: it is inherent in the structure of social existence, but unless our attention is drawn to it, we remain unconscious of it. But structure is not the whole picture, and like Walby (1989: 221) it must be seen as part of 'structuration' (Giddens, 1984), in which the complement to structure is reflexive human action. In consequence (once again following Walby), a vital level of analysis is patriarchal practices. These, in fact, will be prominent in the discussions of patriarchy in this chapter, and will therefore be closer to the approach of Witz (1992), who studies actors and their actions in the challenge to, and defence of, patriarchy; and whose conclusions are more to do with its pervasiveness, and where it is most vulnerable, rather than leading to a theory of the structure of patriarchy.

But patriarchy is not merely *like* language; in one respect, it *is* language. Not only has it been (and still is) possible for men and male groups to employ 'discursive strategies' to achieve and maintain their privileges, as will be illustrated later in this chapter, it is also the way in which words have values attached to them, reflecting and conveying a sense of male superiority. This is not the place to elaborate this by now well-established point, but it may be illustrated by considering the way in which the components of pairs of gendered nouns carry quite different meanings. For example, a gentlewoman is not just a gentleman in a skirt, nor is a heroine a hero without a moustache; a husband and wife are not merely two people with different genitalia. Each of these terms differs from its counterpart because it has its own penumbra of value and meaning. So a 'heroine' in, for example, a novel by Trollope is a young woman for whom everything comes right in the end as a result of 'feminine' virtues, chiefly patience and forbearance. A 'hero' displays quite different qualities, and usually some failings as well, but these are offset by his active pursuit of empirical ends in politics or the church in which his qualities bring him success – and very often a wife. One has to turn to more modern works to find a female hero, although they are still rare enough. Male heroines are found as frequently as hen's teeth.

But the social world contains not only lexical pairs, it contains relationships. Socialization provides us with a number of options of how to relate to other people, including models for relating to the opposite sex.

Atkinson and Delamont (1990: 101), drawing on the work of Reskin (1978) on women in science, suggest that:

> because people learn sex-role behaviours long before they learn scientific collegial ones, and the two systems of interpersonal relationships do not fit well together, problems arise when the two systems have to be merged into one. She points out that male scientists can forget gender and relate to women as scientists only, or forget the science and relate only as men to women, but more frequently they choose an intermediate position where 'they adapt conventional gender roles to the scientific setting to create a hybrid of gender and collegial roles that systematically introduces sex-role differentiation into the scientific community'. (Reskin, 1978: 10)

In science (and the professions are similar) there is a norm of collegiate egalitarianism, which is antithetical to the patterns of male–female role relations in western society.

> These ... include those based on kinship (father–daughter), on marriage, on romance (where the woman is reduced to the status of wife, girlfriend or mistress) or on quasi-scientific roles (where the woman is seen as lab technician or assistant). All these models impede the development of egalitarian colleague-ship for women – instead the woman is left in a position of structural dependence. (Atkinson and Delamount, 1990: 101)

This analysis of the position of women in science has clear parallels with the professions (and indeed in other work situations), and provides another illustration of the cultural pervasiveness that gives patriarchal practices their mask of legitimacy.

Women and modern society

It is possible to get the impression from some feminist writing that the oppression of women was more acute under early industrial capitalism than under any other form of society. While there is plenty of evidence from archaeology, history and ethnography to challenge such a view, it would be a difficult matter to resolve, and is of much less relevance to the study of the professions than the changes during the modern period. The position of women certainly changed as industrialism developed and while this was associated with capitalism, as Marxist feminists claim, it can be argued that a full understanding of what occurred requires an examination of the market and the division of labour on the one hand; and of the rise of the rational scientific spirit on the other. These are, of course, precisely the features of modern society that provided the seed-bed in which the professions could take root.

The important feature of the agrarian forms of society that preceded industrial society, from the point of view of assessing the relative status of women, was the comparative lack of differentiation of social institutions and organizations, a much lower level of the division of labour, and the concomitant distribution of knowledge throughout society. So, for example in a tribal society most aspects of social existence are subsumed under family and lineage and therefore social roles in economic, ritual, political and other activities are prescribed by that one institution, and the knowledge necessary to carry out those activities is bound up with the various roles and statuses. Likewise in an empire of antiquity or in feudal society, although the differentiation of institutions and roles is more pronounced, knowledge is embedded in the roles that go to make up those institutions (in fact knowledge and status are closely allied), and division of labour is not intensive. The crux of the matter for the present discussion is that many of these roles were occupied by women, and even if their statuses were almost always inferior to those of men, *their roles were part of the institutions of society and they therefore had some share in the knowledge of those societies* – even though it was not an equal share with men, and much of it was 'status knowledge', rather than rational empirical knowledge (Murphy, 1988).

The advent of modern capitalist market society, with its increasingly minute division of labour, and its rational scientific knowledge, began to change the position of women and the perception of the position of women. The main features of the upheaval involved and their consequences for women may be grouped as follows.

First, the increasingly numerous, diversified and large-scale economic activities mainly took place outside the home and were undertaken by men. Women's activities were thereby marginalized as domestic activities, or even abolished; and if they now took place in a factory, women only performed them as an adjunct to a machine. The status formerly attached to these activities – or the role of which they formed part – effectively disappeared, relegating much female economic activity to the sphere of an underclass. The possibility of women acting as proprietors or entrepreneurs, jointly with their husbands or on their own as widows, disappeared to a large extent (Earle, 1989: 160–74). Another aspect of the new economic order was that:

> capitalism led to an increase in the scale of business, with the result that fewer journeymen could afford to set up in business for themselves and so had to leave home each day to work on a master's premises where there was no place for their wives to work. (Earle, 1989: 163, quoting Clarke, 1919)

To attribute these changes to 'capitalism' is right in a sense, but it would perhaps be more accurate to ascribe them to the change to a market economy and to the advanced division of labour, which would have been just as necessary a part of the transformation if it had been impelled by cooperativism rather than capitalism.

Earle also draws on Clarke for the second reason why capitalism may have depressed the position of women.

> Capitalism also made the capitalists richer and placed them in a position where they could not only afford an idle wife but would positively want one as a sign of their rise in the world and a recognition of their newly genteel status – idleness and gentility being closely connected in the English mind ... 'The tradesman is foolishly vain of making his wife a gentlewoman, forsooth,'

complained Defoe. 'He will ever have her sit above in the parlour, and receive visits, and drink tea, and entertain her neighbours, or take a coach and go abroad; but as to the business, she shall not stoop to touch it.' (1989: 163)

Conspicuous consumption is the phenomenon that Earle has put his finger on, and it is by no means confined to the English, as Veblen (1970) makes clear. But it is true that the closeness of the bourgeoisie to the gentry and the relative openness of the latter make this development in England all the more likely (see Chapter 2).

Thirdly, the shift to a market economy opened up, as never before, the possibility of entrepreneurship on the basis of knowledge. The change from status knowledge to scientific knowledge, with nature rather than society as its referent, provided plentiful opportunities for the development of knowledge-based occupations. Knowledge was no longer enshrined in social institutions and their constituent statuses and roles, but a separate aspect of life, whose validity required that it should be independent and freely available to all, to acquire or to test or to extend.

This change had a number of consequences for women. First of all, it was an extension of the market principle, which benefited men at the expense of women, because men, with their superior position in society, were able to monopolize the new opportunities as they appeared. In the process, the second impact on women's positions occurred, which was that a number of hitherto female skills were drawn out of their traditional locations and into the market, thus depriving women of activities and the status that went with them. Many activities connected with illness and healing are examples of this. Examples of this kind lead on to the next aspect of change, which was that where these activities depended on the personal possession of esoteric knowledge and skills, they were drawn into occupational organizations, which as we have seen above, were impelled to emphasize their respectability, which was regarded as inhering above all in the concept of 'gentleman'. By calling on traditional values in this way they ensured not only respectability in a general sense, but also that such occupations were proof against any reduction in status, by reason of incursions by women. Furthermore, in the same way that the superior position of men allowed them to monopolize market opportunities, it also gave them the right to the new scientific rational knowledge, relegating traditional knowledge to the position, quite literally, of 'old wives tales'.

A fourth reason was that, in addition to combining with the market, the rational scientific approach to life acted against women in another respect also. Not only were they deprived of activities that had once been accorded status, but those residual roles now left to them were now to be judged by the harsh criteria of pragmatic rationalism, and were *ipso facto* downgraded. At the same time, the increasingly legal and statutory specification of rights and duties meant that women's disabilities became much more specific and hard to escape. It is in the age of Enlightenment that married women became *femmes coverts*, a change in status which, as Roxana[1] put it, meant 'giving up liberty, estate, authority, and every-thing to a man, and the woman was indeed, a meer woman ever after, that is to say a slave'. Roxana was hardly exaggerating. The legal position of married women in common law was based on the doctrine of conjugal unity, a doctrine neatly summarized by Blackstone[2] when he wrote that 'the husband and wife are one and the husband is that one'. (Earle, 1989: 158–9)

In the longer term, however, rationalism worked to the advantage of women, because *if* its criteria are applied to persons rather than to roles, then it becomes apparent that there are few socially valuable tasks in modern society that cannot be equally well performed by either gender. But it was a big *if*, because that invisible grammar of patriarchy has to be brought into consciousness, before rationality can make any impact.

One may conclude, therefore, that the position of women certainly suffered in the move to modern society, but this change cannot be extrapolated back into a trend that shows a decline from some golden age; a conception which has as little validity as the fall from innocence that Marx implies with his notion of the primitive communism of a bygone age. At the same time, the decline in the social position of women is better understood by a rather more detailed consideration of institutional change, rather than merely attributing it to capitalism *tout court*. Lastly, it is the spirit of modern rationalism that has provided an important weapon in the struggle to improve the position of women, and hopefully will continue to do so.

None the less, patriarchy has put up a stubborn resistance on many fronts. The professions have played an important role in this struggle and the following sections will discuss some aspects of this and look at the ways in which certain of their bastions have been attacked – and defended.

Social closure – the special case of patriarchy

The importance of social closure in the study of stratification has been examined in Chapter 2 and its particular relevance to the professions has been noted. What should also be observed is its value in explaining the operation of patriarchy in this context (even though this totally escaped the notice of the originator of the concept, Max Weber). Other theorists of social closure, such as Parkin (1979), Collins (1985) and Murphy (1988), make some use of it in relation to gender, but it is in the more empirically based work of Crompton and Sanderson (1989) and especially the important study by Witz (1992) that a full development of this approach can be found.

Before considering the application of Witz's elaboration of the social closure model to professions and patriarchy, it would be useful to consider a point to which Witz refers a number of times in her book, namely the importance of 'discursive strategies'. By 'discursive strategies' it is meant

that the 'discourse' of everyday interaction and especially the terms in
which those with power frame what they say and write, is often extremely
important in the maintenance of existing relations, such as those of gender.
Although Witz feels that she has underemphasized this point, once one
has been alerted to it it becomes apparent that the power position of, for
example, the medical profession in relation to women in the nineteenth
century, aspiring to become doctors, is reinforced, or even embedded in
the language they (and everybody else) speaks. A telling example is that
of midwifery, whose practice the medical profession contrived to define as
falling into two parts: the routinized nursing aspect and the 'interventionist' work. Nursing, in the discursive practices of the period, was
gendered as female which made it much easier for the doctors to take over
the interventionist side of midwifery practice (1992: 126–7).

Silence on a topic is an aspect of discourse, in the same way that doing
nothing is a kind of action, and there is an eloquence in the silence to be
found in work on the professions that antedates the women's movement.
Books that are widely quoted, such as Carr-Saunders and Wilson (1933)
and Millerson (1964), contain no references to women, except that the
members of certain professions such as nursing or midwifery are referred
to as 'she'. Perhaps women showed no great interest in entering
architecture or accountancy but the publications of Kaye (1960) and the
ICAEW (1966) likewise contain practically no references to women. The
latter in fact finds it '*amusing* to note that in 1865 the Society for the
Employment of Women advertised in the *Daily Telegraph*, offering
instruction to young women in commercial handwriting, arithmetic and
book-keeping . . .' (p. 65, emphasis added). While these authors rely on
silence and ignore both the efforts of women to enter professional
occupations and the defence of patriarchy to keep them out, another well-
known source, Lewis and Maude (1952), although going under the title
Professional People, has little to say about women, and that little is mainly
dismissive or hostile. For example, they write that the creation in 1870 of
a system of primary education 'as cheaply as possible . . . created another
great profession for women' (1952: 32); and again, they put forward the
view that the contemporary ethos of science and technology was 'not
without its effect on the younger professions. The young women who
flooded into them absorbed pseudo-science and jargon like sponges' (p.
51). No wonder that these authors imply that the most appropriate
occupation for an intelligent girl is 'to illuminate a home and a large family
with her intelligence' (p. 7).

Witz (1992: 7) suggests that 'discursive strategies' may usefully be seen
as a link between the concepts of ideology and closure practices, and the
cases she cites (of paramedical occupations) provide convincing examples.
These occupations, in their early days, were following the course of action
that Weber sees as normal when competition for livelihood develops: 'In
spite of their continued competition against one another, the jointly acting
competitors now form an "interest group" towards outsiders; there is a

growing tendency to set up some kind of association with rational regulations.' The next step is an attempt to 'establish a legal order that limits competition through formal monopolies' (Weber, 1978: 342). Witz's elaboration of the Weberian conceptualization of social closure to be found in Parkin (1979), Murphy (1988) and others, is a valuable contribution to research and theorizing about the professional project. This can best be introduced by considering her diagrammatic presentation of her model (Figure 5.1).

The left-hand side of this model is a representation of the use of the concept of social closure as it appears in the work of Parkin (1979) and Murphy (1988) and as applied to social stratification as a whole, except that the lower left quadrant is labelled 'inclusionary' rather than 'usurpationary' strategy as it would have been in Parkin's terminology. The right-hand side shows Witz's categories, which are elaborations of those on the left, but are sufficiently different to warrant separate treatment.

Exclusionary closure is the exercise of power by an occupational association in a downwards direction and is primarily concerned with the definition of the membership in such a way as to exclude those whom the professional body and its elite regard as 'ineligibles' (Parkin, 1979: 450) or 'outsiders' (Weber, 1978: 342). So an occupation embarking on a professional project, such as English accountants in the 1870s or British psychologists in the 1980s, will agree on definitions of membership for those already practising the occupational skills and frame these in a manner that is acceptable to the state; and it will also define the criteria to define future entrants to the professional body. The former is referred to

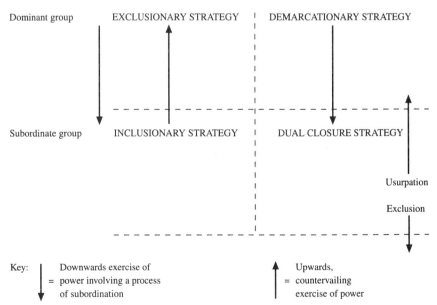

Figure 5.1 *Strategies of occupational closure: a conceptual model*
Source: Witz, 1992: 4

as a 'grandfather' clause (or more properly grandparent), while the latter will almost certainly involve the passing of examinations and/or the possession of degrees or diplomas of tertiary education. In addition, appropriate and inappropriate activities will be specified; so it is usual for advertising to be banned, while Chartered Accountants, for example, are not allowed to practise as auctioneers.

The term 'grandfather clause' exemplifies the gender dimension that Witz (1992) brings out in her discussion of this (and other) exclusionary strategies: for while the exclusionary criteria employed by professions are largely, on the face of it, to do with achievement, they are often in fact of a kind that are much more easily attained by those in a position of advantage already, and, in the past at least, this has effectively excluded women. So if the entry requirement is a university degree, and women are not admitted to university, then women are excluded from the occupation.

Demarcationary closure is an extension of the notion of exclusion, but rather than being simply the exercise of power to keep out ineligibles, it is the use of strategies to demarcate the boundaries between subordinate occupations, and if possible to maintain an advantage over practitioners in allied fields. The clearest examples are to be found in medicine, where doctors have played a crucial role in defining the areas of competence of paramedical groups, and have in effect been able to decide whether a skill shall be hived off to a subordinate group or whether it should become part of medical practice. There is clearly considerable overlap between this idea and Larkin's (1983) concept of 'occupational imperialism', as Witz (1992: 47) points out, and it can be applied, for example, to law and accountancy as well as medicine. But there are other examples of inter-occupational conflict, which do not fall into the category of 'occupational imperialism', such as that in Britain between barristers and solicitors, not to mention the numerous examples considered by Abbott (1988) under the rubric of 'jurisdictional' disputes.

But the 'imperialism' cases are important for Witz's (1992) concern with the gender dimension of these struggles: in many cases, for example midwifery and radiography (both of which are discussed below), the drawing of boundaries and the presence of women are inextricably tied up.

Inclusionary closure is the counterpart of exclusionary closure and has been developed by Witz (1992) from the work of Parkin (1979) and Murphy (1988), who draw on Weber's (1978) ideas. Weber did not really consider how those who were excluded by a dominant status group might react, but the notion of inclusionary strategy is used to cover the actions of such people, who attempt to make themselves eligible, either by devising ways to acquire the necessary characteristics or to force the professional body, or the credentialling educational establishments, or the state to change the rules which disadvantage them. Witz (1992) gives a graphic account of strategies adopted by women in the nineteenth century to gain entrance to the medical profession on equal terms with men, and the vigour with which the professional medical bodies deployed their forces to resist them. A rather different inclusionary path was followed by those accountants who were excluded from the Institute of Chartered Accountants on its formation in 1880. In 1885 they formed their own society, and steadily pursued a usurpationary strategy with such success that eventually, seventy-two years later, they achieved amalgamation with the Chartered Accountants.

Dual closure is the final quadrant of the diagram and deals with those occupations which having been successfully excluded by an occupation, strive to carve out their own occupational field, distinguishing it from that of other, probably dominant groups but establishing at the same time their own exclusionary practices. They do not emulate or aim for parity and eventual amalgamation with the dominant group in the manner of the Incorporated Accountants referred to above. This is the centre-piece of Witz's monograph, for she sees it as the means by which groups such as midwives and nurses undertook their gendered professional projects in the late nineteenth century. These are groups who found themselves on the receiving end of the demarcatory strategies of the medical profession and responded by, on the one hand, marking out the best territory they could in the face of the actions of the doctors, and on the other, by establishing their own exclusions of ineligibles and their own boundaries of practice.

The themes that Witz develops on the basis of her elaboration of the concept of social closure are, first, that the professional projects of the older professions in the nineteenth century were quite explicitly gendered, and when challenged, as the medical profession was, the project included a vigorous defence of their patriarchalism; and secondly, that the actions of the groups so excluded were themselves guided by a professional project.

Caring professions

The concepts involved in the notion of social closure, as applied to female professional projects, and that of 'gendered discourse' may be illustrated by contrasting the cases of 'caring' professions – such as nursing and midwifery – with those of professions that are not normally regarded as caring – accountancy or law, for example.

The paradigm cases of the caring professions, according to Abbott and Wallace (1990: 1), are nursing and social work, and they constitute a part of the 'personal service professions' (Halmos, 1973: 5), in contrast to the 'impersonal service professions' of law, accountancy etc. But Halmos is not concerned with the differentiation that exists within this group between the 'caring' professions and the doctors, dentists, priests and so on, not even the gross distinction that leaps to the eye today, that derives from patriarchy. Abbott and Wallace do concern themselves with this point, though not to the extent that one might expect: in addition they discuss a number of other important points that affect the position and the practice of these occupations. A discussion of these and allied topics will provide an introduction to further study of specific caring and uncaring professions in the sections that follow.

Mediation

The caring professions are for the most part those that Johnson (1972) terms 'mediative'; that is, they operate in conditions where 'the state attempts to remove from the producer or the consumer the authority to determine the content and subjects of practice' (p. 77), or where 'a third party mediates in the relation between producer and consumer, defining both the needs and the manner in which the needs are met' (p. 46). Social work, midwifery and health visiting all fall under the definitions of both 'caring' and 'mediative' professions; nursing comes into this category in the sense that nurses' opportunities for employment are mostly in the state-provided National Health Service, but the actual organizations in which they work may be semi-autonomous, while the medical profession is interposed between the nurses and the hospital on one hand, and the state on the other, by reason of their role in the regulation of the occupation. The most important mediative profession that falls outside the definition of caring is teaching. The caring professions can exist outside the ambit of the state, and rather more of their activities are carried out by private agencies in the USA than in Britain, but for the most part, in Britain, their activities are defined by the state – both the needs they are to deal with and the way in which those needs are to be met; and furthermore, their funds are provided by the state. These features of the caring professions, which are part of their condition as mediative professions, limit their power absolutely and in their dealings with other occupational groups, as well as putting them in a weak position to achieve economic rewards, which leads to the need to take, or to threaten to take industrial action, thus laying them open to the charge of acting 'unprofessionally' and jeopardizing their status still further.

Knowledge

The most important criterion for including an occupation within the scope of this book has been that its practice is based on a body of relatively esoteric knowledge. While practice is an essential part of any profession and its training, in the caring professions there is a considerable body of opinion that holds that practice is actually the more important aspect. This is particularly true of nursing, but there and elsewhere this notion has important consequences: first, it devalues the knowledge aspect of the occupation, thus casting doubt on its standing as a profession: and secondly, it emphasizes the caring part of the occupational task, and as caring is something that everyone undertakes in the context of the family, this again devalues the occupation. Mackay (1990: 34), reporting research on nurses conceptions of their occupation, found frequent rejection of the notion of the 'academic nurse', while other values, such as dedication to a vocation and to the patient, tended to foster a subservient attitude.

Indeterminacy

This concept will be dealt with more fully in Chapter 6, but it may be stated briefly here as the notion that the greater the element of judgement required in the exercise of professional knowledge, the less likely it is that the professional tasks will be open to routinization and inspection: such a situation will tend to enhance the power of the occupation. Both nursing and social work require considerable exercise of judgement in their practice, but the exercise of judgement in these cases is on the basis of knowledge that both the lay public and adjacent professions may not see as being sufficiently esoteric to take it into the true realm of 'indeterminacy'. Once again it may appear to be 'everyday', rather than professional knowledge.

In the case of nursing this occurs in two ways. The first derives from the nature of the knowledge base noted above, in that the judgements made by practitioners will appear to be quite mundane in many respects, especially to members of the superordinate medical profession and to those patients with long experience of hospitalization. The second is a consequence of the drives for managerial efficiency and clinical responsibility in hospitals, which tends to reduce judgement to rule-following wherever possible.

In social work the relative lack of indeterminacy is of a rather different kind and is rather less clear-cut. In part it stems from the change in the ethos of social work which occurred in the early 1970s, following the Seebohm Report (1968), which entailed abandoning the 'case work' approach with its quasi-psychiatric style in favour of the 'generic' way of working, with a broad, but ill-defined base in social science. This aspect of social work is discussed by Sheppard (1990), who regards this occupation as relatively high on indeterminacy for this reason and instances the multiplicity of mental health models on offer. But this is not really a case of indeterminacy because the judgement is being exercised by the practitioner on the knowledge base prior to the encounter with clients, not on the material presented by the client, in relation to a coherent theory. This is uncertainty, not indeterminacy. Sheppard also refers to the eclecticism of social work and the fact that 'social workers have also generated their own knowledge' (1990: 82). Once again this might be called 'indeterminacy', but is not what Jamous and Peloille (1970) were referring to in their seminal article on the this topic, for it once again merely reflects uncertainty in the knowledge base.

The ethos of social work, at least in the recent past, involves another feature that militates against its claim to indeterminacy and which was strongly advocated by the more radical members of the profession – and this was that they must not appear as professionals to their clients or they would merely establish a social distance between them that would interfere with the social worker's understanding of the client's problem and the client's willingness to accept the social worker's help. By some this notion was taken even further, to the point of denying the superiority of the social worker's knowledge, and the need to put themselves on a level of equality with the client in every respect, because genuine help cannot be based on a superior, patronizing position. The concept of indeterminacy cannot be applied to such a stance.

But in addition to these points there is the view that while the technical aspects of professional knowledge are open to all (in principle, if not in practice), indeterminacy is largely a masculine province. This notion has been put forward by Atkinson and Delamont (1990), drawing, as was noted earlier in this chapter, on work in the sociology of science as well as the professions. They link indeterminacy to Bourdieu's concept of habitus (1984), and to Freidson's 'clinical mentality'. They endorse Bourdieu's argument that mastery of the habitus is treated by the initiates as a matter of natural talent, of personality, of the 'virtuality' of practitioners. It follows that a central part of the essential performance skills of the occupation is never explicitly taught, but is believed to be innate, inborn and personal. Bourdieu and Passeron (1977) argued that in practice the French secondary and higher education systems examined qualities that were never explicitly taught; qualities which middle-class children had from their families but working-class pupils did not. They suggest that the notorious propensity of (professional) groups to self-recruit may be explained in the same way and that practitioners of a profession and those in its training schools share a sort of 'mythical charter' that the sons (and probably to a lesser extent daughters) of doctors acquire in family socialization.

To regard indeterminacy in this light leads to two conclusions. First is the general one that it helps to explain the difficulties experienced by women in what appears to be the straight-forward exercise of professional skills; that is, the technical aspect has to be applied in a manner that is largely a matter of male socialization. The second is the particular case of nursing, where the Nightingale movement attempted to achieve female control of the occupation by making its skills overwhelmingly 'indeterminate' – but embodying women's 'virtualities', not men's. This was an instance in which the professional project was pursued by means of a relatively unusual version of social closure tactic: instead of excluding women by making it impossible for them to acquire the technical aspects of the occupation, it excluded men by making the indeterminate aspects all-important and which were almost impossible for men to acquire. This tactic was in large measure successful, but at the cost of throwing away any chance of altering the traditional male/female role relationships that were discussed at the beginning of this chapter.

Objectivity

Another aspect of professional practice that is problematic for the caring professions is the expectation of objectivity. The assessment of a case, the definition of client's needs, the application of professional knowledge and the attainment of a solution or outcome must all be achieved without professional judgement being obscured by personal involvement or emotion. But when the overall objective and the means of achieving it involve *caring*, then a dilemma and a source of ambiguity appear. On one hand it is clear that nurses dealing with disease, trauma and death, and social workers faced with poverty, injustice, homelessness and abuse need to maintain objectivity in one sense, in order to avoid being emotionally overwhelmed and suffering 'burn-out'. On the other hand, the concept of 'vocation' and the expectation of dedication that goes with it require a degree of involvement that others who come into contact with the case may perceive as lack of objectivity.

Patriarchy and caring

Prejudice and inferior social position are normally found locked into a self-legitimating circle: for example, in the heyday of apartheid it was argued that the blacks were of lower intelligence than whites and therefore they did not need the same level of education; when blacks performed less well academically, this was taken as proof of the original premise. The self-legitimating logic of patriarchy is not only tied into a much more complex network of institutions, it also still has the support, sometimes unwitting and sometimes conscious, of many of its victims. The caring professions provide a classic example of the way the values of patriarchal society are built into institutions and practices, which many, if not most, of their members believe they have a vested interest in maintaining.

The reasons for this, and indeed many other features of the caring professions are to be found in their historical development. As noted above, the development of the market as an aspect of modern society is a crucial element in the explanation of the contemporary position of women in the professions, and it was a consequence of this phenomenon that one of the main areas in which women were able to enter the market, and indeed to professionalize, was that of health, caring and childbirth, but only into the residual activities left by the male professions with their claims to a scientific or esoteric knowledge base. These were tasks that were already socially defined as appropriate for women and it was really only by an elaboration of the feminine qualities of the work that women could achieve the first steps towards social closure.

From this underprivileged starting point, the logic of the development of the caring professions becomes clear. The caring tasks and routines of Florence Nightingale or (the fictional) Lady Bountiful, were the essence of the emergent professions of nursing and social work, and esoteric knowledge, especially in view of the relatively poor educational provision for women, was minimal. On this basis women were given some scope by patriarchal society to form occupational associations and to achieve some measure of autonomy over their work. But given that it was one in which knowledge was kept to a basic and practical level and 'probationership' was the means of acquiring occupational knowledge, it is not surprising that such professions came to devalue (relatively) academic training and to emphasize dedicated caring and concern. The first of these aspects put these occupations at a disadvantage in relation to knowledge and indeterminacy, and the second tended to vitiate the professional's claim to objectivity. Finally, as these occupations became more important with increased concern in society for health and welfare, the British response in the form of the Welfare State balanced any advantage that might have accrued from their increased social value by placing them within state control, thus circumscribing their freedom of action by the constraints of 'mediation'.

Social closure in nursing and midwifery

These two occupations are key examples in Witz's (1992) analysis of social closure as it applies to professional women, and they provide good illustrations both of the utilty of her conceptualization and of the empirical facts of women's battle against patriarchy. Taking these cases means that attention will be focused on the right-hand column of Witz's diagram (see Figure 5.1 above), for both occupations were engaged in dual closure strategies. Witz exemplifies the inclusionary/exclusionary conflicts in the left-hand side of the diagram by the cases of medicine and radiography; this aspect of closure will be considered below in relation to the legal profession.

Nursing

A recurrent (though not inevitable) feature of the professional project is the internecine strife that occurs in the early stages, as different occupational strands or professional philosophies contend for power. Such divisions can even become embedded in the structure of the profession, as in the case of architecture in Britain, as was shown in Chapter 4: in the case of nursing they were much in evidence in the first stages of the project, became muted as one party gained the upper hand, and show signs of re-emerging in a new form in the 1990s.

The two strands in nursing were, on the one hand, that led by Mrs Bedford-Fenwick, with her vision of occupational professionalism based on expertise, which was opposed on the other hand by a range of interests with a variety of motives and prejudices, and led somewhat surreptitiously by Florence Nightingale. This group was opposed to nurse registration, because they saw nursing as involving caring and as being hospital-based, rather than as a nationally organized, knowledge-based occupation.

The question of nurse registration was first considered by the General Medical Council in 1872, but it did not become an issue until 1887, when the British Nursing Association was formed by a group breaking away from the Hospitals Association which had been founded the previous year. Their objective of statutory registration was the first step in their professional project, and was opposed by the hospitals who foresaw that they would lose control of training if this measure was enacted. Witz (1992: 133) regards this as an exclusionary move, which would also enhance the social status of the occupation by making it attractive to educated women, thus furthering the other side of the professional project, collective social mobility. But this on its own would not give nurses control over their occupation, so it was also necessary to aim for a majority of nurses on the governing council set up by the legislation, and to ensure that there was only one gateway by which members could enter the profession, which would then allow nurses to control admission and training.

But nursing is an example of a 'dual closure' project, and so these exclusionary objectives were linked to complementary aims of usurpation, that challenged the existing power relations in nursing. Their intention was to remove, at least in part, the authority of male doctors over female nurses, and the control that hospitals had over nursing labour, while on the societal level of patriarchy there was the intention to move a female occupation out of the control of men. They aimed to achieve both some authority over the hospitals in which they worked and some autonomy in the tasks that they performed. The details of the events that go to make up this story of this professional project can be found in Dingwall et al. (1988) and its analysis in terms of the concepts of social closure forms part of the central theme of Witz (1992); so it would be otiose to recount them here. What may be usefully added at this point is to recall that the project was only partly successful, and to note some points that may help to explain why.

First of all, among the factors working against the project, there is the presence of patriarchal practices in all their manifold forms. The usurpationary strategy which aimed at curtailing the existing influence of doctors and restricting it in any future structure was to an important degree a matter of gender. Not only did the medical profession resist the efforts of women to join their ranks, it also, together with the state, reacted to the initial efforts of nurses (and other groups) to enter the labour market for more prestigious jobs, and to organize their members in that market, by dragging their feet.

Then there is the point mentioned above, that there was opposition to the registration tactic, which came partly from the more elite section of the medical profession, but probably more importantly from the Poor Law Hospitals and the nursing reformers, who took their lead from Florence Nightingale. It is significant that this important figure in the history of British nursing, having received her initial inspiration from the traumas of the Crimea and Scutari, sought inspiration for her programme of reform by visiting the hospitals of France and Germany and actually taking a six-month course of training in the latter. The reason for going to these countries will be clear from the account given in Chapters 3 and 4, namely, that the development of medicine was much more advanced there, because the state had taken an active interest in the public provision of medical care. It is therefore not surprising that Nightingale's view was that nursing should be tied to the organizations that provided the service, rather than put into the hands of the practitioners: for as Abbott (1988) points out, in modern society knowledge and the control of it, may reside in individuals, in machines, or, as in this instance, in organizations.

In this case the organizations were the Poor Law Hospitals and the reform of the Poor Law in 1919 brought the state more effectively into the picture, and gave the Minister of Health considerable powers, as the British state belatedly (starting with the National Insurance Act of 1911), followed in the path of France and Germany. These hospitals operated on a two-tier system of certificated and untrained nurses, and any one-portal entry, such as that proposed by the registration movement, would have seriously undermined the operation of many hospitals. In addition the voluntary hospitals found the development of nursing as a trained occupation greatly to their advantage – provided that they could retain control of it. It provided hospitals with a cheap source of labour, in the form of probationers, and in the early days the trained nurses gave them a valuable additional income, because their sevices could be rented out to outsiders, people or institutions that could afford to hire them.

But in addition to the opposition of the hospitals on the basis of their economic and organizational interests, the matrons and the more career-minded nursing staff were also opposed, because the ambition of Florence Nightingale to achieve authority for nurses over their own activities was well on the way to being achieved. By 1880 matrons had acquired control over a number of important areas of medical and administrative work, and a nursing chain of command had come into existence. The independence of the occupation was being attained on the basis of the organizations in which they worked, and this in the eyes of many nurses provided a greater likelihood of success than an independent professional body.

It was against this array of opposing forces that the proponents of nurse registration had to fight, in addition to facing the problems that confront many occupations pursuing their professional project of defining themselves, their work, their jurisdiction and their market in a way that will satisfy all interested parties. The activists were mainly those who worked in the voluntary hospitals, but for the reasons just mentioned there was also a sizeable proportion of these nurses who were either apathetic or opposed. While the elite groups in medicine – the Royal Colleges – were opposed on the whole, the British Medical Association was in favour. Medicine and nursing supported these proposed arrangements for different reasons; Mrs Bedford-Fenwick saw the nurses' proposals as modelled on the medical profession, while the BMA regarded the nurses' proposals as based on the principles that they endorsed for their own occupation, and which challenged the elitism of the Royal Colleges. The BMA therefore wished to see a unified, homogenous occupation, with one portal of entry and governed by a state instituted General Council.

The nearly equal balance of forces deployed resulted in this struggle being prolonged from 1887 to 1919. It was eventually concluded by a Nurses Registration Act that was nominally a victory, but a defeat in practice.

The nurses' campaign for registration was a 'dual closure' professional project, being both usurpationary and exclusionary, and within those dimensions, pursued both credentialist and legalistic tactics. These features and their outcomes may be summarized as follows.

1   Exclusionary aims:
    (a) Centralized control over the occupation, established by legislation (heteronomous legalistic means).
    (b) Self-government by means of a majority of nurses on the governing body (heteronomous legalistic means).
    (c) One-portal entry controlled by the governing body (credentialist means).
2   Usurpationary aims:
    (a) Training: challenge to the autonomy of voluntary hospitals on content and standards.
    (b) Employment: undermining of the relationship between hospitals and nursing labour and obtaining some influence over pay and conditions.
    (c) Formalizing the relation between medicine and nursing in a way that would give nursing both recognition and some measure of autonomy.

As in the case of some other professions, such as architecture and dentistry, the formal achievement of statutory registration turned out to be a broken reed. While these other occupations were able to recover from their setbacks by pressing for further legislation, nursing found itself locked into a system which effectively vitiated its apparent success. A General Nursing Council was indeed created but it neither contained a majority of nursing members nor was it given control over those issues listed above that were crucial to the achievement of the professional project, because such decisions had to be ratified by the Minister. So the attainment of 1(a) above actually involved failure on 1(b), while the

Nurses Registration Act specifically allowed for multiple portals of entry to various branches of nursing and allowed for the creation of more.

The usurpationary aims were only achieved in a most limited way, while the power of the state was considerably enhanced. Witz succinctly concludes:

> Credentialist tactics, which pivoted round the one-portal system of entry, were subverted and legalistic tactics of state sponsorship backfired on nurses. At this critical historical juncture, nurses' professional project had failed. (1992: 167)

In the years since that failure the situation has not changed greatly and the way that things have developed has confirmed the importance of the factors that shaped the outcome just described; namely the dominant position of the medical profession and the inaccessibility of the organizational structure of the hospital, increasingly provided by the state. Until the 1960s, nurses were able to build themselves some professional prestige by emphasizing their dedication and, in an era when women's educational attainment fell considerably behind that of men, requiring a level of qualification only possessed by a small minority. It was therefore an occupation which attracted many middle class recruits and those who trained at the more prestigious teaching hospitals achieved a certain cachet. These pretensions were, however, steadily eroded after the Second World War, by the rising level of women's education and the increase in job opportunities that put nursing in the position of being just one opening among many. The National Health Service also tended to depress the standing of nurses by keeping the pay down, while the creation of this new large-scale public employer provided a ready recruiting ground for trade unions into which the nurses tended to get drawn. Industrial action by nurses, or the threat of it, were inevitably greeted with cries of 'unprofessional'. At the same period, more men began to be recruited to nursing, which both diminished the significance of nursing as a female professional project, and played into the hands of the other anti-professional strand in nursing, managerialism.

As noted above, the notion that the provision of hospital organization was more important than nursing professionalism, was part of the Nightingale ethos, and was certainly the emphasis in health provision in Europe. The conception that it was the organization rather than the profession that should be the locus of knowledge was reinforced by the creation of the NHS. The much larger organizational structures that now came into existence at the same time provided career, rather than professional openings, and these career opportunities were increasingly seized by men. However, with the Report of the Briggs Committee 1972 and Project 2000 in the 1990s, it appeared that the professionalist faction in nursing was regaining some ground. Nurse training is now being linked to university education, and there is a wider range of subjects with a more academic and theoretical emphasis. The practical training is also being re-examined, with the intention of ensuring that knowledge of the work is purposefully imparted (involving the notion of each trainee having a 'mentor') rather than relying on the rather more informal methods of the past.

Whether these 'professional' innovations in training will actually enable the occupation to achieve greater autonomy and to succeed in other aspects of the professional project remains to be seen, but it is far from certain that nurses will be in a better position *vis-à-vis* the hospital organization. Not only is the tight management structure still in place, but the Thatcherite emphasis on a market orientation in public service means that the managerial ethos has been strengthened, and professionalism disadvantaged. The salience of cost-based policies means that there is no guarantee that a newly qualified nurse will be offered a nursing grade post, and that she or he may be put on the 'assistant' grade alongside staff who have no qualifications. At the same time, hospital managerialism aims at the routinization and deskilling of nursing tasks, in the search for greater cost-effectiveness. The innovations of Project 2000 may well enhance the educational level of qualified nurses, but it is doubtful if it will do much to alleviate the disadvantages under which nursing labours in its professional project, which were outlined under the headings of mediation, knowledge, indeterminacy and objectivity in the previous section.

Nursing as an occupation has pursued its professional project for over a century, striving to achieve some autonomy and a jurisdiction of its own. Its professional milieu is one which the powerful forces of medicine and the hospitals constantly seek to control, or to change the metaphor, they represent the upper and nether millstones between which nursing has always been ground. If one considers this situation, the constitutional disadvantages just referred to, and the humble and even disreputable base from which the occupation started in the mid-nineteenth century, then the occupation has achievements to be proud of. At the same time, the professional body and its members must work constantly to promote its professional project: like Alice in *Through the Looking Glass*, 'it takes all the running *you* can do to keep in the same place. If you want to get somewhere else, you must run at least twice as fast as that.'

The Red Queen's remark applies to any profession, but in the case of nursing, which was originally made up entirely of women, and in which they are still the large majority, this advice (from one female to another, please note!) is particularly apposite, because patriarchal discourse and practice constitute a pressure which a female profession must constantly resist, if it is not to be pushed into a position of inferiority. This problem has already been discussed above, but in addition to the points made there, it should be noted that Florence Nightingale used the 'feminine' characteristics of the members as part of the drive to make nursing distinctive. In this she was of course successful, and in making nursing into a kind of secularized religious order it was the character and qualities of the members that were emphasized rather than their qualifications. On the other hand, these features made the occupation respectable and middle-class, thereby attracting the right kind of recruit and achieving one part of the professional project. It also received the blessing of the medical profession. Some kind of accommodation with medicine was necessary, but such an acceptance of the patriarchal dominance of medicine contributed in no small measure to what Etzioni (1969) calls 'the caste-like subservience' of nursing to medicine, a simile which nicely catches that pervasiveness of patriarchal practice and discourse that makes it appear 'natural'. So any gains that might be thought to flow from Nightingale's tactic were more than offset by the increase in the size of the task that professionally orientated nursing had to tackle.

Midwifery

There can be no better example of the shift from 'status knowledge' to technical, scientific knowledge than the changes that occurred in midwifery in the course of the transition from agrarian to modern society, nor a clearer instance of the thesis advanced in the opening section of this chapter. The 'mid-' of 'midwife', is the Old English 'with', and so means a woman (and in fact the term 'mid-woman' used also to be current; and it always was a woman until the appearance of man-midwives in the eighteenth century) who was *with* a mother in childbirth. The knowledge possessed by such women was folk knowledge, and like nearly all knowledge in agrarian society, was tied up with the roles and statuses of the practitioners and the institutions in which they participated. There this knowledge remained until the medical men of the Renaissance began to expand their expertise and their jurisdiction into the area of (*inter alia*) the practice of midwifery. After all, with pre-modern rates of infant mortality, midwives must have presided over a sizeable proportion of all deaths, and medical men must have seen an opportunity – and even a duty – to expand their practice in that direction.

Midwifery had probably always been informally stratified in pre-modern society, in that aristocratic births were attended by women of higher status than those of the bourgeoisie, and so on down the scale. But as European societies moved into the modern period, this differentiation became formalized as licensing became widespread, but as it was not universal the births of the poor were handled by the unlicensed. In Britain in the sixteenth and seventeenth centuries, licensing was in the hands of the bishops, who as repositories of probity and learning were seen as the appropriate authorities. The clergy, however, were more interested in the midwife's religious orthodoxy, because with the high rate of infant mortality referred to above, it was often necessary to administer baptism as a matter of urgency: 'In hard labours the head of the infant was sometimes baptised before delivery' (quoted in Carr-Saunders and Wilson, 1933: 122); and it might fall to the midwife to have to perform this rite.

Midwifery was also licensed at this time by the barber-surgeons, but by methods which were much more directed to testing their knowledge and expertise. It was probably this kind of regulation which stimulated midwives in the seventeenth century to make several attempts to obtain a Royal Charter, but the occupation was already under pressure from men-midwives, who with their forceps and other instruments, were already fragmenting and deskilling the profession. Furthermore, by the early eighteenth century the medical profession were beginning to make inroads into the domain of midwifery, starting with royal and aristocratic births and working their way as far down the social scale as was financially worthwhile. Midwifery was thus the victim of the forces outlined at the beginning of this chapter: new knowledge and technology, free from traditional constraints, formed the basis for enterprise in the new market for services, by those who were best able to avail themselves of the opportunities, namely men.

As with all efforts by women to obtain equal rights with men, it is not until the later part of the nineteenth century that the first step towards any formal achievement of this aim was taken. Debates about the state registration of midwives started in the 1860s, but it was not until 1881 that activists founded the Midwives Institute, and it took another twenty-one years of interoccupational conflict before the Midwives Act reached the statute book. In terms of the concept of professional project, this conflict resulted from the clash between the demarcationary strategy of the medical profession on the one hand, and the dual closure strategy of the midwives on the other. As Witz (1992) points out, the complex struggle between these two occupations, together with the intervention of the state, have been chronicled in detail by Jean Donnison (1977), while Witz herself has given a lucid conceptual analysis, so once again it is only appropriate to give an outline here.

It was noted above that doctors did not hold a unanimous view about how they should deal with the nurses' professional project and a similar situation developed in relation to midwifery. The two demarcationary strategies that competed for favour among doctors were (a) that midwifery should be abolished and this entire area should be incorporated into medicine; or (b) that midwives should be registered and their practice severely circumscribed and supervised by medicine. These two views represent the horns of the dilemma that members of an occupation often encounter: should they incorporate an area of practice (or a group of practitioners) even though it (or they) includes a considerable proportion of low status work, thereby risking a reduction in the status of the profession as a whole; or should they rather exclude that area from their jurisdiction, but attempt to deskill and control it? In the event the latter proved to be the outcome in Britain, although in the USA midwifery effectively disappeared and medical obstetrics took over the whole jurisdiction of midwifery. The reason for the divergence of views within the medical profession was, not surprisingly, the variety of practice carried on by its members. On one hand, general practitioners, especially in the provinces, saw qualified, registered midwives as a threat to an important aspect of their practice, and were keen to carry out as much of this work as possible, relying on the assistance of an obstetric nurse working under their direction. On the other hand, doctors in the metropolis and those with aspirations to some sort of specialist status, such as the members of the Obstetrical Society of London, saw their pecuniary interests rather differently and regarded much of the work of midwives as time-consuming and boring. They perceived their interests as best served by a body of well-trained midwives on whom they could rely to deal with 'normal' labour and who could accurately judge when to call in a doctor. The midwives' area of competence and their occupational organization would be defined and controlled by the medical profession.

But the outcome of this debate was not solely the product of the doctors' pursuit of their professional project. On the contrary, midwives had had some sort of occupational identity in earlier centuries and from the 1860s onwards this began to re-emerge and to form into a dual closure professional project, with usurpationary and exclusionary aims, and based on both legalistic and credentialist tactics. This project had clearly to be pursued in the face of the dominance achieved by the medical profession, in consequence of the passing of the Medical Act in 1858. It must be borne in mind that the doctors' position was all the more powerful in that it depended to a significant extent upon their successful manipulation of traditional status criteria, in a society in which modern values were only partly established. Medical knowledge was still quite limited, and did not provide the 'rational' legitimation that it does today. This meant that the conflict took place to an important extent on the basis of tradition and gender, and that legalistic and credentialist arguments were therefore at a disadvantage.

Midwives were no more united in their strategy than the doctors, for – to use the terms of Witz (1992: 117) – both 'revolutionary' and 'accommodative' bases for closure emerged. The former strategy was adopted by the members of the Obstetrical Association of Midwives and the Female Medical Society, and aimed to carve out an area of practice which would be independent of medical men and to establish an organization that would be free from their domination. This dual closure project set the aims of usurpation and exclusion high enough to encroach on the existing jurisdiction of doctors and therefore had the disadvantage that it had no counterpart among the strategies of the latter. The aims of the accommodative faction, on the other hand, associated with the Midwives Institute, ran along lines similar to those envisaged by the Obstetrical Society, which was composed of (male) doctors. This meant that their objectives were, first of all, a distinct area of practice, acknowledgement of which would cost doctors little in financial terms and even less in status, which might even be enhanced because doctors would now have a formal position of control over midwives. Secondly, with the doctors support secured, midwives could hope to campaign successfully for statutory registration, with the guarantees of market control and status that would follow: and thirdly they anticipated that registration would bring in its wake autonomous control over their own affairs via a statutory Midwives Board.

Control of the Board proved to be the most contentious aspect of the Midwives Bill, which went through numerous versions between 1890 and 1902. In the end the midwives' aspirations were dashed, for the Central Midwives Board, when the Act was passed, contained no midwife – merely one doctor who sat as their representative. Midwives had achieved some success – they were after all in existence and recognized by statute – but that success was only attained by conceding some of the most important aspects of the professional project, and accepting a position of subordination to doctors. As noted above the doctors held most of the aces in any contest with an aspirant occupation in the realm of medicine, but as Witz (1992: 126–7) emphasizes in her conclusion, they also held the trump card of the gendered discourse of medical work. The key aspect of this discourse was that 'nursing' was constructed as female and therefore it was always possible for doctors to separate the routine and normal aspects of childbirth and represent them as axiomatically appropriate for women, while anything interventionist or surgical could only be the province of men – and thus of doctors. In this way the female professional project of midwives only succeeded to the extent that medical men would allow it to succeed; that is, to the extent that they felt that it was still under their domination.

A century later, the relation between the two occupations is still much the same, although in practice the subordination of the midwives is all the more pronounced, because the majority of deliveries take place in hospital, where childbirth is thoroughly medicalized and the doctors hold undisputed sway. The gender distinction is still clearly in place, because the subordinate midwives are female and the specialist obstetricians, who are in overall charge, are mostly male.

The position of midwifery is thus of considerable interest for the application of the sociological framework developed in this and earlier chapters, as it represents a balance of power between two professional groups, and illustrates some of the resources that they can bring into play. This example can be even more instructive if a cross-cultural comparison (with North America) is introduced. First of all, there is the success of British midwives in achieving an independent existence sanctioned by the state; there is a Midwives Act, they have their Royal College and so on. In Canada and the USA they have never attained this degree of recognition, although in work on this topic (Rushing, 1993) the reasons for this are not made explicit. However it seems probable that in the USA the populist ethos discussed in Chapter 3 would inhibit the professionalization of the folkways dealing with childbirth. This explanation would have less weight in the case of Canada, but one can envisage that low population density and the vast distances between those centres of population that did exist would not favour the development of an occupational organization that could interact with the state and achieve formal recognition. What did happen in both countries was the development of midwifery teaching in colleges and hospitals, which meant that these skills were kept under the control of the medical profession. The occupation was thus an offshoot of nursing, and its 'services were expressly organized to fill the gaps of medical coverage among rural and urban poor populations in the 1920s and 1930s' (Rushing, 1993: 49). These members of the occupation are termed 'nurse midwives', but there are also 'independent midwives' who have been trained by such methods as self study, formal training in an independent midwifery school and/or apprenticeship to another midwife or (rarely) a physician. Practice by the former is legal in forty-nine states of the Union and by the latter in ten. According to one of Rushing's informants, in Canada independent midwifery is '*alegal*, it's not legal but it's not illegal', and interestingly the situation is the same for nurse midwives – their practice is neither sanctioned nor proscribed.

In these not very promising circumstances, midwives in Canada and the USA seem to have embarked on a professional project. It is difficult to be sure from Rushing's account how vigorously it is actually being pursued, because her main focus is on ideology and she deals with this in terms of currents of opinion as expressed by various writers, public bodies, state agencies and so on; and on the basis of her sample of informants. So while a number of organizations of midwives are mentioned – for example the Midwives Association of British Columbia, Midwives Association of North America or the American College of Nurse Midwives – they do not appear to have been any more active than a number of lay interest groups. But there is no doubt that midwifery finds itself in a web of dilemmas that contains not only the problems that existed for the British profession a century ago, but also the competing ideas of science, natural childbirth and feminism.

The old problem is that the midwives need the sanction of the medical profession – one of the bases of their legitimacy – but they do not want to be dominated by it, nor to act as its low status assistants. Part of the benefit of this connection is that it associates them with medical science, and whatever other resources or skills they may have they cannot dispense with science. On the other hand, it is partly the public response to the perceived inadequacies of medicine that has given midwifery the opportunity to improve its professional position, and it has been able to do this by drawing on two schools of thought, which have a perfectly respectable scientific provenance, but which run counter to the decidedly regimented version of science-based practice which is the norm in hospitals: these are natural childbirth and home birth. This is not say that these practices automatically hand over to midwives a whole area of obstetric work, but they have undoubtedly opened up new opportunities to them which are less attractive to doctors because they are relatively time-consuming.

In addition to the trends which Rushing sees as reflecting the ideology of science, there is the impact of the ideology of feminism. This tends to reinforce the science-based changes just mentioned because they coincide with women's demand to control their reproductive lives, and with the concern of the women's health movement about inappropriate surgery, insensitive medical staff and iatrogenic disease. This coincidence of science and feminism has a certain irony as the two are normally seen as antagonistic, but there seems no doubt that their combination has provided a powerful ideological weapon in the re-emergence of midwifery in North America; powerful enough, Rushing claims, to enable mid-wifery to grow, at a time when it would appear that the market was declining. The plausibility of this account is enhanced by similar develop-ments in Britain, which has seen the emergence of radical midwives groups, criticism of hospitalized births and accommodation to these pressures by the state (Department of Health, 1993; House of Commons, 1992).

Uncaring professions

There is a resounding silence on women in the professions in the standard works on the subject, whether one considers overviews like Carr-Saunders and Wilson (1933) or studies of single occupations like Kaye (1960) on architecture. In the former women are only mentioned in passing or in 'female occupations', such as nursing, while in the latter they do not appear at all. Only in the more recent work, like Witz (1992), is it revealed that women were hammering on the door of, for example, the medical profession: if one wanted to know what happened in the case of architecture, it would probably be necessary to do the research oneself. The history of the ICAEW is slightly more informative, and refers to the wish of the President of the Board of Trade to include the admission of women to the Institute as a provision in the proposed Accountants Registration Bill in 1909; this was Winston Churchill – at that point a Liberal. This proposal came to nothing because the Bill never became law, but the author of the history is typically dismissive of the matter: 'probably the members felt it was not a matter of much importance as it was believed that there were at most six women in practice as professional accountants in England and Wales'.

Solicitors

The Sex Disqualification (Removal) Act 1919 specifically allowed women to become solicitors and in January 1920 the first women were admitted as articled clerks. The number of women employed in professional offices had increased dramatically during the war (from 18,000 to 66,000) and this, combined with pressure from the women's movement and their Liberal male supporters, had given rise to episodes such as the case brought against the Law Society by a Miss Bebb to test the legality of a woman practising as a solicitor in 1913 (which presumably she lost!) and the proposal put to the annual general meeting of the Bar Association in 1917 to admit women, which was defeated by a large majority.

This discrepancy between legislation and the actions of professional bodies exemplifies Witz's (1992: 21) conclusion that in the defence of professional patriarchy, the state proved to be the weak link. From the quotation given in the preceding section, and from similar points made by Witz, one may conclude that an important part of the defence of patriarchy by professionals was their discursive practices. What the accountants and the doctors before them were doing was to define their practice and the characteristics of women in ways that made the two incompatible, in order to justify their exclusionary and other practices. Now these may be appropriately described as 'discursive strategy' (Witz, 1992), but it should also be noted that this is the formal, public aspect of discursive practice and that such practice is also embedded in everyday interaction and it provides the mechanism that men employ and women experience in the maintenance of patriarchy. This is admirably demonstrated in a study by Spencer and Podmore (1986), which explores the ways in which women solicitors are marginalized in their profession by their male colleagues.

The discrimination against women is particularly pronounced in the law, partly because the profession is unusual in that the career structure is extended by the addition of the judiciary at the upper end; only 2 or 3 per cent of judges are women, and there are no women Law Lords. Spencer and Podmore interviewed thirty-two men and seventy-six women lawyers and from these drew out the main themes of the everyday discursive practices of male lawyers, which displayed the definitions of lawyering and of women that female solicitors have to live with. Within these general orientations they identified the following strands.

1 The nature of the legal profession

- 'It's aggressive – and it's male.' Many aspects of legal work were seen as actually requiring aggression to carry them out satisfactorily, and some men referred to the need for physical size and strength.
- 'It's objective, logical, and pragmatic – and it's male.' While these characteristics are less objectively those of men, male lawyers tend to see them as pertaining to both the law and men.
- 'Prejudice is just a fact of life.' Informants were inclined to see clients, other lawyers, judges, magistrates as prejudiced against women lawyers, and believed it was so widespread that it was not possible to do anything about it.
- 'Since prejudice is a fact of life, it is women's problem, not men's.' The ethos of the law is 'masculine' and women must accommodate to that if they wish to succeed; they will just have to work harder and adjust their behaviour.
- 'Women take work away from men and then just leave in order to marry and start a family.' This is a rationalization of prejudice, used to

support the assertion that women in the profession are 'problematic'.

2   Male lawyers' definitions of women

- Women as sexual objects. This theme takes two forms: either women are seen as having an unfair advantage, because their sexual attractiveness will enable them to obtain clients and influence courts' decisions (which carries with it the implication that women who are less sexually attractive will be even further disadvantaged); or they are dismissed as being just a pretty face.
- Women as different kinds of beings. Women are regarded by many lawyers as having far more differences than similarities with men, and that their whole emotional make-up is entirely different from that of men leading them to see things from a different perspective. This is partly that women are seen as being warmer and more 'people-orientated' than men (and this can be seen in the tendency to guide women towards particular kinds of work, and to make them judges in the Family Division); and partly that they are inferior to men and less able to participate in the shared understanding that exists between men.
- Women get emotionally involved. Part of women's difference from men is their more emotional nature, and their tendency to get too 'involved' in a way that impairs their professional judgement.
- Women aren't tough enough – or else they're much too tough. This is a familiar expression of male prejudice, which leads to a 'no win situation' for women, which is really a particular case of the themes that women are different from men, that it is a man's world and that it is up to women to adjust. Women's lack of toughness makes them basically unsuitable, and when they try to adjust they get it wrong.

Spencer and Podmore conclude that the picture is a depressing one, and the best hope of improvement comes from the slow but steady increase in the proportion of lawyers who are women. They were writing when there were plenty of opportunities for the educated labour force and it was thought that there was every prospect of a shortage of graduates due to demographic factors, which led to a favourable situation for women. In the recession of the early 1990s, however, the employment situation for women may well deteriorate, with a corresponding deceleration in the retreat of patriarchy.

Accountants

The one positive piece of information about women that the history of the ICAEW provides is about the effect of the Sex Disqualification (Removal) Act 1919, which must have opened up considerable opportunities to women, but about which studies of the position of women have little or nothing to say (for example,Witz, 1992, or Spencer and Podmore, 1986). This Act provided that no man or woman should be disqualified by sex or marriage from the exercise of any public function, or from being appointed to or holding any civil or judicial office or post or from entering any civil profession or vocation or from admission to any incorporated society. It also made women liable for jury service and opened the Civil Service, Parliament and the universities to them, but not the armed forces or the Church and possibly not the Diplomatic Corps. One woman, Miss Harris Smith, who had been in practice as a public accountant since 1878, was at once admitted to Fellowship of the Institute and occupied the strange position of being the first and only woman Chartered Accountant in the world. In the next year, five women applied for articles of clerkship, and in 1924 the first woman was admitted to membership by examination.

The Society of Incorporated Accountants took a rather more liberal view of women becoming members, and actually revised its Charter to admit them a year before the legislation obliged them to do so. Earlier attempts by some members to admit women had been made in 1889, only four years after the founding of the Society, which had led the Council of the Society to hold a plebiscite: 309 votes were cast, of which only 88 were in favour. None the less, this figure may be thought surprisingly large, in view of the fact that

> a leading member of the Society averred that women could not be 'duly qualified'. He held that 'accountancy was amongst those professions which required for their proper fulfilment those masculine qualities and experience of the world and intellectual capacity and courage which were rarely to be found in members of the weaker sex'. (Garrett, 1961: 7)

Contemporary accountants[3] seem to be rather more open-minded than solicitors were in the early 1980s, when Spencer and Podmore (1986) did their research. They have certainly opened their doors, because in some firms 50 per cent of students are women. Some, but not all; in smaller firms the percentage seems to be as high as this but in the national firms it was nearer a third while in multi-national firms it was thought to be about one in five. This gradient has consequences for the number of women qualifying because the examination success rate is considerably higher for the giant firms than for the smaller ones, partly because the former have the pick of the graduates, and partly because they are able to put more time and money into their training programmes. But as is often the case in examination contests of this kind, women outperform men if they are given a fair start. So in the late 1980s and early 1990s, women from the big firms were taking up to half the examination prizes. Since the recession and the reduction in recruiting by accountants, the proportion of women prize winners has declined, which may be a reflection of the tendency of recruiters to take men with high levels of attainment if they are available, rather than women. Certainly the composition of the membership is only changing slowly, from about one woman in twelve in the early 1980s to about one in ten a decade later.

The career prizes, as opposed to examination prizes, are much harder for women to obtain. In 1987, one multi-national firm had three or four women partners in the UK, out of a total of 222. Although a national firm was said to have 'quite a few', and two out of the four partners in one outer London office were women, there are plenty of smaller firms with no women partners: the women partners referred to had all been appointed in the previous three or four years. In the mid-1980s, women were elected to the Council of the Institute for the first time, and by 1992 there were five women out of a total of seventy-nine Council members.

Nevertheless, there seems to be a rather less prejudiced view of women among accountants, than among the solicitors studied by Spencer and Podmore. The most positive opinion came from a student in the London office of a multi-national firm,[4] who felt that there were actually some advantages in being a woman, but there were actually no women students or managers who felt disadvantaged: indeed some of them felt that their male colleagues regarded them in a positive light. It was interesting that they also refuted the opinion sometimes expressed by male accountants to the effect that it was not they, but their clients who objected to women accountants, by quoting cases of clients who actually preferred women auditors. Women managers felt rather differently about the future, however, because they either could see the prospect of the problems of taking a career break to have children, or had experienced them already. A senior woman manager explained the effort that had to go into keeping up to date with changes in law and practice in the course of, say, a six-year break. Both she and others felt that firms – controlled by men – were unsympathetic and unhelpful, as well as being shortsighted in relation to the waste of talent and experience.

In the USA the door was opened to women much earlier, but for some time there was only a trickle passing through it. The first woman received her CPA certificate in 1899, but by 1909 the total had only risen to ten. By 1924, fifty-four women had become CPAs, but the exclusionary tactics of patriarchal firms kept them out of public practice. An editorial in the *Journal of Accountancy* (December, 1923), while acknowledging the ability of women accountants, asserted that 'women are not wanted on the staff of practising public accountants', because of:

> The need to be ready to serve whenever and wherever called on to do so.
> The requirement to travel with groups of staff members.
> Working at night in places of difficulty and inconvenience.
> Embarrassment caused by working with heterogeneous personnel.
> Objection by some clients to women.

These specious objections have a similar ring to those of British lawyers in the 1980s, but as has so often happened with the exclusion of women from an area of employment, if there is a labour shortage, women suddenly become quite acceptable. Such a change took place during the Second World War, and may be epitomized by the case of Pearl A. Scherer, who started off as a clerk in the Army Corps of Engineers, and who worked her way up to responsibility for the first computer installation on the West Coast. At the end of the war she was posted to the Philippines as Chief Accountant, responsible for the reclamation of all equipment and supplies from the battle zones.

By this time women CPAs had formed their own association (1933), but it was not until the 1960s that anti-discrimination legislation opened up the field to women. It was also at this period that the journal *Woman CPA* was launched, that the first woman became a partner in a major accountancy firm (1962), and that a woman became a partner in one of the Big Eight international firms (1967). In the 1970s and 1980s recruitment was genuinely opened up to women, and although, as in Britain, career advancement lagged behind that of men, by 1985 one in six of CPAs who were partners in public practice were women.

The AICPA was still raising, in 1984, such points as 'There is no question about women's technical ability. But traditional beliefs and attitudes regarding other abilities raise questions. For example, are women at a competitive disadvantage in comparison to men in obtaining new audit clients and maintaining existing ones?': and 'Are males as willing and cooperative when their manager is female?' On the other hand, the questions were being asked by an Institute committee, set up to examine the matter of women's careers in accountancy. In Britain, women are still pressing for such a committee to be established (Ried et al., 1987).

Conclusion

The advent of modern, industrial society opened up the possibility for an occupational group to pursue a professional project and, at the same time, a shift in values was under way that now emphasized achievement as a basis for social status as well as ascription. These changes resulted in a multiplicity of disadvantages for women, leaving them with a closely circumscribed rump of ascription-based status and hardly any access to the achievements on which the new form of status was based. It was not until the middle of the nineteenth century that women were able to mount a challenge to the formidable position that patriarchy had achieved, and there is a pleasing irony in the fact that in the realm of work they were able to open up some chinks in the bastions of patriarchy by employing the very means by which men had achieved their dominance – the professional project and social closure.

The early efforts of nurses, led by Florence Nightingale, used a form of social closure that involved the high risk strategy of using gender as the principal basis for closure, not as one of several as men had done. This was successful, but only up to a point, because while it did facilitate the definition of an occupation that women could call their own, it also put them in a position of disadvantage by reason of the discourse of patriarchy, which axiomatically put them in a position of subordination. Other groups within the occupation took a different line by emphasizing the need for qualifications and registration, the well-established strategies of professional projects, hitherto used by men.

In most other occupations men had also used these credentialist and legalist strategies to achieve occupational exclusivity, and they were thus ready at hand for men to use in resisting the usurpationary efforts of women. These were employed successfully by most occupations until 1919, when the political efforts of the women's movement resulted in the passing of the Sex Discrimination (Removal) Act. Since then the main barrier that women have faced has been patriarchal discourse which has been used to install and legitimate a whole range of barriers; formerly these could actually be used to keep women out of an occupation altogether ('I'm not opposed to admitting women, but the clients . . .'), but nowadays they are more likely to be excluded by these means from the main stream of activities ('Women do much better in the "back room" work where they don't have face the rough and tumble . . .').

As noted at the start of this chapter, such patriarchal practices and discourse have deep roots and are all the more hard to eradicate because they are part of women's as well as men's socialization. However, as Witz (1992: 207–10) observes, female projects have a better chance of success in relation to the state than elsewhere, for the state is (nominally at least) based on legal-rational principles and should therefore be open to institutional change that can erode the multiple inequalities from which women still suffer.

Notes

1 *Roxana, the Fortunate Mistress*, Daniel Defoe, 1724.

2 *Commentaries on the Laws of England*, Sir William Blackstone, 1765. It is interesting that his codification of the law adhered to the form of the new scientific approach, rather than its spirit. The *Encyclopaedia Britannica* (1911) observed 'Blackstone was by no means what would now be called a scientific jurist. He had only the vaguest possible grasp on the elementary conceptions of law. . . . he is always to be found a specious defender of the existing order of things. Bentham accuses him of being the enemy of all reform, and the unscrupulous champion of every form of professional chicanery.' One reason for the acceptance of his view of marriage may be found in the next paragraph.

3 The material that appears in the following paragraphs is drawn from the author's unpublished research on accountants in practice. It is based on forty-one interviews conducted in 1987, with partners, managers and students in three offices of a multi-national firm, one office of a national firm and one of a local firm. It is backed up by a number of interviews carried out between 1979 and 1986 with a number of sole practitioners, and with

the author's erstwhile fellow articled clerks, who now hold senior, or even exalted, positions in the profession.

4 'If anything, it's been a slight advantage ... I'm being sent out to Luxembourg and I think they like ... you know, it's a bit boring having an all male office out there, and it's a slight advantage then.'

6
Knowledge and the professions

An emphasis on knowledge as a 'core generating trait' of professionalism (Halliday, 1987: 29) is to be found in all sociological treatments of the professions and is certainly endorsed by recent writers on the topic such as Larson (1977: 40), Abbott (1988: 9) and others. Sociologists generally take a model of rational, formalized scientific knowledge as their starting point in the study of the epistemological base of the professions, and then elaborate in relation to a number of other features of professions and their social context. This is the path that will be followed in this chapter, but note must also be taken of the chief exception to this mode of analysis, namely Michel Foucault, for whom, according to Turner (1987: 10), 'like all forms of human knowledge, science is simply a collection of metaphors'.

The first consideration will be the nature of the epistemological and cognitive base of professions and how it is characteristically different from knowledge in all earlier forms of society. The focus will shift next to the specific nature of professional knowledge, and then to the relationship between knowledge and professional work and to the concept of *indeterminacy*. Then follows a consideration of the consequences of the nature of different epistemological bases for social and political influence of professions, and after a consideration of the contribution of Foucault to the study of professional knowledge, a summary of the model of professional knowledge as it contributes to the concept of the professional project.

Modern society and knowledge

Professions became possible only when knowledge emerged as a socio-cultural entity in its own right, independent of established social institutions, and when society came to be based on knowledge in a way quite different from earlier periods; and when the market had reached sufficient salience as a feature of society for the private provision of knowledge-based services to become viable. This change has been termed 'the great transformation' by Polyani, (1957) and the European miracle by Jones (1981).

The origins of the professions may be traced to the feature of modern society that Gellner (1988) sees as possibly the most important, namely the development of knowledge as an independent element in society, rather than something bound into a number of other social institutions. Gellner's thesis may be précised as follows:

> *In modern society, the cognitive referent – i.e. our yardstick for assessing the truth or validity of knowledge – is the empirical world of nature: in all earlier forms of society that reference point was one of a number of social institutions.*

This formulation offers an explanation for a variety of puzzling features in pre-modern societies. It can account for the apparent childish modes of thought of some tribal societies, because it demonstrates that their contradictions stem not from a failure to grasp the nature of reality, but because they have two (or more) systems of ideas which they bring to bear on the world according to circumstances. Different circumstances are governed by different social institutions and hence by different modes of thought. As societies became more complex and more technically advanced, thought systems became more elaborate, extensive and unified, but remained as watertight as ever, and within those compartments fact and value are fused, joining together social, moral and cognitive hierarchies. In such societies

> a Nature independent of society cannot be avoided; but there is no need normally to systematize it into a single, socially independent, unified system, and indeed societies do not normally do anything of the kind. When it does happen, it constitutes a historically rare and difficult achievement. It is in no way any kind of baseline of the human condition, a natural birthright of mankind. (Gellner, 1988: 51–2)

In other words, the cognitive system that has been essential to European culture for the past 400 years (and which has since spread to the rest of the world) is practically unique in human history, and it disinguishes the contemporary form of knowledge from that of previous forms of society. Without it modern science would be impossible, because earlier forms of cognition were not unified, nor were they distinct from other social institutions, but were intrinsically bound up with them.

Such a cognitive system would render impossible the establishment of an *independent* group of specialists in a particular branch of empirical knowledge, because all approaches to the empirical world are already foreclosed and tied to the normative and moral structure of the society. Gellner offers a Durkheimian explanation for this integration of knowledge and social structure by arguing that the overriding consideration in a pre-agrarian society (and even in an agrarian society) is the survival of the group, not the manipulation of the natural world and the drive for economic advance that dominate in a modern industrial society, where nature has largely been tamed. So survival in a pre-modern society is achieved by group cohesion; and therefore loyalty to the group, and thus to its norms, is paramount; and into those norms, that which we call 'knowledge' is inextricably bound. In such circumstances, a query about received knowledge, however much it might seem to us a matter of empirical fact, is to a tribal group a challenge to moral orthodoxy and a threat to the all-important social cohesion.

Even in the large scale agrarian-based societies that immediately preceded the modern period there was no independence of knowledge.

The multi-stranded perceptual systems of tribal societies gave way to a unified doctrinal system, but the referential content is small and the power of the clerisy[1] over knowledge is almost total. The ultimate source of the codified theologies and cosmologies is 'surrounded with such awe and reverence that the questioner is, in general, silenced. Political sanctions may silence him if doctrinal ones fail to do so' (1988: 93). Not only is knowledge relatively static in such societies, it is also normal for them to have a low rate of technological innovation.

With the Enlightenment came the change in cognition. Knowledge was no longer locked into compartments of the social, moral world but was the autonomous means by which the world was seen. Furthermore, it was a knowledge that was unified and value-free. 'The world is to be located within knowledge. The criteria of sound knowledge are independent of the structure of the world, and *precede* it' (Gellner, 1988: 119). The way became open for the exponential growth in knowledge that characterizes modern society. But that opening could only be exploited because there arose at the same time that systematic restless striving that Weber saw as the outcome of the Protestant Ethic, and which Durkheim regarded as the cause of anomie. Equally important (or even more important) was its place in the realm of cognition; the corollary to the autonomy and sovereignty of knowledge, that most important theme of the Enlightenment, was **cognitive growth** (Gellner, 1988: 116).

> Modern society is the only society ever to live by, through and for continuous cognitive and economic growth. ... Cognitive growth alone made it truly possible to follow through with the pervasive domination of a society by the market. This constitutes the element of partial truth in the Marxist doctrine that the growth in the 'forces of production' engendered the radical social transformation. (Gellner, 1988: 129,131)

This transformation starts with the Renaissance (early fifteenth century) and continues with the Reformation (early sixteenth century) and the Enlightenment (early seventeenth century) and is largely in place by 1800, although some relics of agrarian society still stood out against it.

Once these changes in the nature of cognition had occurred it became possible for individuals to develop an area of learning and expertise and to become repositories of knowledge in their own right and, in a society like Britain, to form groups of specialists, although as is apparent from Chapter 2, there were few societies, even in the industrialized world, where this could occur. Such groups were then able to take advantage of the other salient characteristic of such a society, the free market, to sell the services they could offer based on their knowledge.

In a society where these changes have occurred, those who are engaged both in the pursuit and in the economic exploitation of knowledge at the same time comply with and embody some of the central values of the society, and it therefore is not surprising that Functionalist sociologists, such as Durkheim, Carr-Saunders and Wilson, and Parsons, place great emphasis on the social value of professions.

It must be emphasized that modern professional organizations bear only a superficial resemblance to the guilds of agrarian society, even though some of them – the Royal College of Physicians is a notable example – have retained (or possibly even invented) all the medieval flummery associated with the guilds and Livery Companies. The difference lies in the social structures of knowledge. In the guild, the members achieved a mastery of their trade, which interestingly enough, was called a 'mystery' in those days, and even today the titles Mister and Master are closely allied: and the masters of the mysteries were effectively beyond challenge in the matter of their guild knowledge. Now, although modern professions attempt to maintain the maximum control over their knowledge, essentially their knowledge is in the public realm, may be challenged or compared or linked up with knowledge that is in the realm of other professions, sciences or specialisms, and indeed universities. This state of affairs is partly the consequence of the modern conception of the unity of science and the applicability of its canons to all forms of knowledge, and partly due to the fact that modern professions are, as has been noted in Chapter 4, licensed by the state, and therefore the autonomy of professional bodies and their monopoly of knowledge and practice is conditional on their keeping their side of the regulative bargain. In this they differ from the guilds of the past, whose autonomy was much more complete and whose guardianship of knowledge was much more exclusive: they were always subject to the arbitrary depredations of the state, but so of course, was everyone else.

The nature of professional knowledge

Professions are knowledge-based occupations and therefore the nature of their knowledge, the socio-cultural evaluation of their knowledge and the occupation's strategies in handling their knowledge base are of central importance. Having indicated what is distinctive about modern knowledge, it will be useful to have a definition of this concept, and for this purpose one may cite that of Murphy (1988).

> The process of formal rationalization has generated a new type of knowledge, namely, the systematic, codified, generalized (which implies abstract) knowledge of the means of control (of nature and of humans). Most importantly, it has resulted in knowledge of how to acquire new knowledge of such means. Science and technology are important elements of this new knowledge, but it cannot be reduced to science and technology. Knowledge of how to calculate market profitability, to organize and plan in bureaucracies, and to develop, apply and predict the abstract codified laws of the legal system have all been developed under the process of formal rationalization. This *formally rational abstract utilitarian knowledge* has resulted in new means of control (over nature and over other groups) and is a form of knowledge which is quantitively and qualitatively different from the previous practical knowledge and the status-cultural knowledge. (Murphy, 1988: 246–7) (emphasis added)

This definition is not only valuable in its own right but it also refers to the unique and revolutionary change that occurred in cognition as part of the 'European miracle', outlined above. The term 'status-cultural knowledge' corresponds to Gellner's view of pre-modern knowledge being compartmentalized and incorporated into social institutions, which means that it inheres in culturally defined statuses, rather than being an independent unified system, theoretically open to all, irrespective of status. It conceives of knowledge as abstract, generalizing and self-expanding; any part of it is available to be applied to any problem or aspect of the world.[2]

Knowledge and credentials

There are a number of related features of the knowledge that provides the basis for professional practice, which need to be identified individually for analytical purposes, but are indissolubly linked in the real world. This amalgam is considered by Turner and Hodge (1970) in their examination of the ways society may make distinctions between occupations, one element of which is 'the degree of substantive theory and technique'. This conceptualization seems to lack a cutting edge, because it does not specify any means of characterizing the kind of knowledge that they are referring to. However this was a matter on which Weber (1978) was quite explicit: the knowledge in question is that which is *certified and credentialled*. Credentials can be very explicitly chacterized – they may be degrees, diplomas, certificates etc. – and these may be obtained from establishments or organizations whose standing is widely known and understood. So the kind of knowledge that can underpin a claim to professionalism in the modern world is that which is credentialled by a relatively high level qualification, typically a degree, or by a relatively high-ranking establishment. If the qualification is one that is granted by the professional body itself, then the entry standards required constitute the basis for judgement. Thus there are everyday, practical means of distinguishing between the knowledge base of doctors, bank officials, printers and plumbers, and there is no great sociological puzzle to be solved, as Turner and Hodge seem to imply, when they state in their conclusion, 'The problem of defining an occupation is a highly contentious matter.'

However, the sociologist can add the observation that, generally speaking, the services provided by holders of high level knowledge do not involve manual work, and where they do, that work is carried out on the body of the client; for example by surgeons, dentists, physiotherapists etc. So if there is thought to be any problem in understanding why society distinguishes between doctors and plumbers, it may easily be solved. More problematic might be thought to be the case of bank officials (Turner and Hodge, 1970: 41), whose knowledge level might be thought to be on a par with lawyers or accountants, and who have to pass exams of the Institute of Bankers if they are to succeed in their careers. Once again, Max Weber's conception is of value, because it is (credentialled) knowledge on its own that he sees as the base on which an occupation can establish social closure and enhance its social status. In other words, members of such groups *carry the means of production for their line of business in their heads*. It follows that in banking, where the means of production is essentially a large sum of money, what is in the heads of the members of the Institute of Bankers does not enable them to embark on a professional project. A somewhat analogous group, computer workers and systems analysts, have in the past appeared to be placed under a similar handicap, but with the dramatic fall in the cost of computing capacity in recent years, the possibility has emerged for this occupation to launch a professional project, although it seems as though there may well be other problems that they would face.

The notion that those whose qualifications are their 'means of production' can embark on a professional project may seem quite acceptable in the case of a solicitor or an accountant; a qualified member of the professional body, who has been granted a practising certificate, can put up a brass plate and wait for the clients to knock at the door. All they need is the working capital to rent an office and buy some office furniture. But the case of medicine is quite different. It is obvious that contemporary medicine is to a large extent carried on in hospitals, using extremely expensive equipment and administering costly regimes of treatment; no one could argue that the means of production is all in the doctors' heads, although important aspects of it are. In this case one must look back to the period when the medical profession was established in its modern form, namely in the mid-nineteenth century in Britain and slightly later in the USA. At this period, medical practice was carried on largely outside the hospital and the doctor was in the same position as the lawyer or accountant today. It is a tribute to the remarkable strength of the dominance that the profession established at that time, that they still have the control they do over the practice of medicine in a context where they manifestly do not own the means of production. This particular instance provides two important points to note in the study of the professions; first, that this general point about the nature of professional knowledge has to be taken in historical context, for the power position achieved by an occupation may enable it to extend its power in other directions – in this case to achieve control over tangible means of production that they do not, in fact, own: and secondly, that changes occurring in the 1990s in the British health care system may significantly shift the power in hospitals away from doctors and in favour of administrators and nurses. The ability of doctors to maintain the powerful position that they achieved in the nineteenth century can be explained in part at least by the nature of their 'knowledge mandate', (Halliday, 1987), a concept to be discussed below.

Work, knowledge, science and abstraction

As noted in the previous section, Turner and Hodge (1970: 26), start their paper with a discussion of what they refer to as 'substantive theory', but by the time they reach the summary of their paper this feature of professional occupations seems to have dropped out of sight entirely. A more systematic analysis of what is involved in this aspect of a profession's resources is to be found in Abbott (1988).

Abbott's point of departure is to challenge the mainstream of socio-logical work on the professions, because it had normally (there were exceptions) taken a theoretical starting point which relied on what he calls 'this synthetic professionalization concept' (1988: 16). This is a theoretical stance of such an all-embracing kind that the result of any study that relies on it is bound, in his view, to be an artefact of the initial theory. His valuable critical analysis of this work has already been discussed (Chapter 1); the emphasis to be picked up here is that in the same way that, in the sociological enterprise, the empirical work must be allowed to shape the theory, rather than being wholly shaped by a theoretical conception of the structure of a profession; so in understanding professions the starting point must be professional **work**. The content of professional work, the control of that work, differentiation in types of work and the notion of **jurisdiction** that the profession attempts to claim for its work are the heart of the matter and the raw material of theory (1988: 19, 31). But in addition, the quality that characterizes professional work (and here we get back to the topic of knowledge) is **abstraction**.

> For abstraction is the quality that sets interprofessional competition apart from competition among occupations in general. Any occupation can obtain licensure (e.g. beauticians) or develop a code of ethics (e.g. real estate). But only a knowledge system governed by abstractions can redefine its problems and tasks, defend them from interlopers, and seize new problems – as medicine has recently seized alcoholism, mental illness, hyperactivity in children, obesity, and numerous other things. Abstraction enables survival in the competitive system of professions. (1988: 9)

In Abbott's definition of his subject matter, the emphasis is on the knowledge system and its degree of abstraction: 'Abstraction enables survival' (1988: 30). The actual tasks of professions are human problems that are amenable to expert service – individual problems like illness or neurosis, social problems like vandalism, group problems like fundraising or auditing. But to turn them into problems that fall with in its jurisdiction, a particular profession must engage in 'cultural work' that will ensure that clients, competitors, the state and the public will acknowledge that the qualities of the problem warrant the granting of that jurisdiction.

> the jurisdictional claims that create these subjective qualities have three parts: claims to classify a problem, to reason about it, and to take action on it: in more formal terms, to diagnose, to infer, and to treat. Theoretically these are the three acts of professional practice.

It will be appreciated from Abbott's style, and especially perhaps from his use of the word 'acts' in the last sentence, that the emphasis in his analysis of knowledge is very much concerned with the active work that professionals have to put in all the time to maintain their claims to a special niche in society; and that knowledge must be seen or, is at least capable of being seen by those who know how and where to look, as having a special character. It must also be noted that in addition to the knowledge in practice, there must also be seen to be an academic version – the formal, abstract knowledge system.

The details of Abbott's analysis cannot be recapitulated here and there is only space to sketch in an outline.

> Diagnosis and treatment are mediating acts: diagnosis takes information into the professional knowledge system and treatment brings instructions back from it. Inference, by contrast, is a purely professional act. It takes the information of diagnosis and indicates a range of treatments and their predicted outcomes. (1988: 40)

Abbott emphasizes that at each stage procedures of classification and abstraction are employed, and appropriate modes of relating the particular case to the formal knowledge system are adopted. This is the 'cultural work' that has to be employed by the practitioner, but at the same time the academic, formal, abstract knowledge system must not only exist but be actively advanced, since it provides both legitimation and the scientific development that is necessary to maintain the professional jurisdiction of practice.

These quotations may give the impression that Abbott is overly concerned with medicine, but in fact any such view is countered by the actual examples that he gives. These certainly include medicine, but there are at every juncture instances from law, psychiatry, architecture, librarianship and other areas including even military strategy, as well as plentiful comparisons with the work of automobile repair and maintenance to show that the necessary 'cultural work' and knowledge base is lacking for that kind of occupation to make a claim to a professional jurisdiction.

One last quotation will serve to sum up Abbott's valuable contribution to the sociological analysis of professional knowledge:

> behind the world of professional work lies a rationalizing, ordering system that justifies it with cultural values, at the same time generating new means for professional work. As custodian of professional knowledge in its most abstract form, this academic centre is uniquely situated to claim new jurisdictions. But the claims are cognitive only. They cannot become recognized jurisdictions without concrete social claims and legitimating responses. Interprofessional competition, that is, takes place before public audiences. (1988: 58)

Knowledge and indeterminacy

Abbott's approach to the question of professional knowledge puts the first emphasis on professional work, but also gives an important place to theoretical knowledge, going so far as to declare that 'abstract knowledge is the foundation of an effective definition of professions' (1988: 102). He goes on to develop the significance of the polarity between abstraction and concreteness, and to review the forces that 'push abstraction in professional knowledge towards an equilibrium between extreme abstraction and extreme concreteness'. At either extreme, the profession tends to lose credibility; too great abstraction appears to be mere formalism, too great concreteness is judged to be no more than a craft. At some nicely chosen spot in the middle, the possessor of knowledge and technique can successfully exercise professional judgement.

The exercise of professional judgement is a point that is also picked up by Larson, who observes that 'the leaders of the professional project will define the areas that are not amenable to standardization; they will define the place of unique individual genius and the criteria of talent "that cannot be taught" ' (1977: 41). At this juncture she turns to the concept developed by Jamous and Peloille (1970: 113) of cognitive *indetermination*, which has certain affinities with Abbott's view of the need for a balance between abstraction and concreteness. In this case the distinction is between 'indetermination' and 'technicality', and Jamous and Peloille put forward the idea that any occupation has a ratio of the two – an I/T ratio – and that those occupations that claim to be professions need to be high on indeterminacy. Once again this concept is set in the context of the professions' need for a body of formal rational knowledge, but they observe that this kind of modern knowledge has a built-in tendency towards codification that renders it more accessible to the (educated) public, thus potentially undermining the professional's privileged position. In the view of Jamous and Peloille, this tendency is counteracted by the emphasis in professional selection and training on 'individual and social potentialities, experience, talent, intuition etc.' (1970: 139) all of which are controlled and evaluated by existing members, largely by reference to qualities that they themselves possess. When it comes to professional practice, the quality of outcomes is regarded by the profession as more dependent on the 'potentialities and talent' of the practitioner than on 'techniques and transmissible rules' (1970: 140). What seems to be implied in this formulation (and this is not wholly clear, because the paper in question appears to have undergone transliteration rather than translation from French), is that a high I/T ratio enables the members of a profession to claim the exercise of professional judgement and thus to put themselves and their actions and their decisions beyond the scrutiny of their clients and the lay public.

There is no doubt that this view of professional knowledge has received a sympathetic reception in many quarters and the paper is often quoted. On the other hand, it is difficult to see how a body of professionals could maintain their knowledge base at a high level of indeterminacy indefinitely, because they would have to acknowledge the primacy of scientific knowledge if they were to maintain their legitimacy in the modern world; and it should be noted that Jamous and Peloille developed their concept in

an historical study of the French hospital system and applied their model
to changes in that system in the 1950s. Perhaps it needs to be recognized
how successfully the public have been hoodwinked in the past; and how much
things have changed since these authors did their research in the 1960s.

On the other hand, there is another line of explanation for the
indeterminacy argument, put forward, amongst others, by Boreham
(1983). Boreham is in full support of the indeterminacy thesis, and draws
on the work of Freidson (1973) and Goldner et al. (1973) as well as that of
Jamous and Peloille (1970). The explanation for him is to be found in
Marxian theory, which, of course, has no truck with the (Weberian) notion
that credentialled knowledge is 'an opportunity for income' (Weber, 1978:
304) and hence a source of power. In this view, professionals exercise
power, obtain rewards and are accorded status because 'global capital'
finds it in its interest to let these things occur. Professionals run the legal
system, regulate economic activity, maintain and supervise the labour
force and perform many other functions that are conducive to the working
of capital. At the same time, professions, as Durkheim, Carr-Saunders,
Parsons and others have noted, are repositories of important social values,
and as such are valuable in maintaining capitalist ideology and hegemony.
In so far as indeterminacy contributes to these things and helps thereby to
obscure the real nature of capitalist relations, then indeterminacy will
flourish as an aspect of professional knowledge:

> Thus, a critical analysis of the professions must be firmly located in theorizing
> the conditions for indetermination, in identifying the pivotal element of the
> professions' support of capitalist regulatory mechanisms both in the labour
> process itself as well as in broader, hegemonic processes of control of social and
> political structures. (Boreham, 1983: 701)

The sociological world has taken a couple of turns since that was written
and the sun has now almost set on the theoretical Marxism that generates
such circularity of argument (if it occurs, then it is because it bolsters
capitalism; if it does not occur, it is because it is of no value to global
capital). But even at that time, work of this kind was coming under fire
from, for example, Sacks (1983). Sacks, writing at the same time as
Boreham, was obviously not able to criticize the paper quoted above, but
he finds very similar faults in Johnson (1977) who argues that professionalism as a form of occupational control 'can only arise . . . where core work
activities fulfil the global function of capital with respect to control and
surveillance, including the specific function of the reproduction of labour
power' (1977: 106). While accepting the truth of some of what Johnson
had to say, Sacks finds him 'rather superficial' and presenting an argument
that 'must contain an element of tautology', and considers it 'surprising
that Johnson's argument is cast in such a dogmatic form' (1983: 15). But
Sacks reserves his big guns for sociologists of the professions generally, not
just the Marxian, for his strongest attack is against the lack of empirical
rigor; and here again the work of Boreham is at fault. One general

statement after another about the relationship between the professions and other features and institutions of the society they inhabit, goes unsupported by any reference to empirical work. One is led to conclude that Marxian theory supplies the warrant for its own assertions, rather than deriving them from empirical data.

It follows that such advocacy of the concept of indeterminacy is self-defeating, and one must conclude that it can only be accepted in a rather weaker form. The notion certainly has plausibility, but its place may well prove to be as a subsidiary hypothesis to Abbott's conception that successful deployment of knowledge requires that a balance be achieved between abstractness and concreteness.

Knowledge mandates and professional influence

The answers to these questions about the nature of the knowledge base give, in part, the basis for assessing how far an occupational group can get with its professional project, other things being equal (which, of course, they never are!). They provide some of the building blocks of a model of professional knowledge which would enable a researcher to hypothesize an explanation of a group's success or failure in creating an organization, establishing a defined area of knowledge over which they can then claim monopolistic rights, limiting admission and other aspects of the professional project; and by extension explaining its relative power *vis-à-vis* its clients, the state, competing occupations and other groups.

But the model is incomplete. From Abbott we may derive one important dimension – theory versus concrete practice – and another from Boreham and others – judgement versus formalized rules. But there is another aspect which Halliday (1983, 1987) sees as having far reaching consequences; this is the balance between **fact** and **value**. Halliday shows how the evaluation of occupational knowledge by reference to cultural values, combined with the organizational form adopted by a profession, has significant consequences for a profession's success in its interactions with the state and for its influence in society. He applies his argument to six occupations – law, medicine, the clergy, engineering, the military and academe.

At first sight it may seem strange that a profession's epistemological base, a topic which hitherto has been dominated by the factual matters of knowledge and practice, should be invaded by its antithesis. But a moment's reflection will bring the realization that if one thing is thought to characterize a profession besides knowledge, it is a code of ethics: professionals are people who act ethically and therefore questions of value are of the essence in professional practice. Furthermore, some professions are very much concerned with 'ought' questions. The clergy are the most obvious example, but lawyers are not far behind, for their work is also concerned with what is 'right'. In societies where the traditions of Roman or positive law obtain, it might be argued that this is still a matter of fact, but in the Anglo-American world, where principles of equity and the common law are applied, the use of value judgement is inherent in the system. But even in medicine, which is regarded as being essentially science-based, moral judgement continually intrudes and may take over. For example, scientific procedure would require the application of one treatment at a time, so that the cause or nature of the complaint can be established, but at the same time ethics demand that the patient should be cured as soon as possible. So in many cases the doctor does not attempt to find out if a patient's symptoms are caused by an allergy or an infection; he prescribes both an antihistamine and an antibiotic; in fact the pharmaceutical industry has probably rendered this course of action all the easier by making a preparation that contains both. The condition disappears, but the doctor does not know what it was. Value has taken precedence over science.

Halliday is interested in professional knowledge, or what he refers to as 'knowledge mandates' (1987: 28), because of the importance he attaches to them as one of a profession's bases for political mobilization: the other three, which are linked to the first to a greater or lesser extent, are the forms of professional authority, the institutional loci of professional activity and lastly the attributes of politial organization. Although most sociologists see science as the prime cognitive foundation of profession-alism,

> Yet the success of contemporary professions cannot be attributed primarily to science *per se* because two of the three longest-standing professions – law and the clergy – are not scientific in any narrow sense of the term ... Law ... has enjoyed virtually the same spectacular success as leading scientific professions on most indicators of professional success ... (1987: 29–30)

When it comes to explaining the differential success of various occupations, that which they have in common – science-based knowledge – only takes one so far. Philosophers have been correct to distinguish fact from value, but the sociological study of professions must take account not only of the point made above that professions have to deal in both, but that 'To put it oversimply, the professions divide into classes depending on whether the cognitive base is primarily of the descriptive or the prescriptive' (1987: 37).

On one side of the divide, according to Halliday, lie the **scientific** professions, such as engineering or medicine, whose methods are epito-mized by the natural and biological sciences; on the other lie the **normative** professions, such as clergy and law, which are primarily concerned with matters of value; with questions of how one should obtain salvation or how individuals or groups ought to behave towards one another. Two other points about this classification are (a) that position in relation to this philosophical divide is by no means the only significant factor of a profession; and (b) that in both categories normative judgements are made, and in both, professions have bodies of codified knowledge that constitute a formal basis for their work.

There are, however, those occupations that straddle the scientific/ normative divide and display what Halliday terms a **syncretic** epistemological foundation: his examples here are the military and academic professions. The role of the military requires a coupling of the best ideas from advancing technology and a doctrine or concept of their tactical or strategic application, while the academic profession remains in an increasingly specialized world, the sole profession that embraces the whole gamut of knowledge and professional skills (1987: 36). But Halliday concludes his initial classification by noting the irony that appears in the relation between the epistemological base of these groups of professions and their capacity for action. For the more scientific the knowledge base of a profession, the greater the likelihood that society will see that as a reason why they should not be granted any great influence in matters of moral judgement; their expertise is in the realm of fact: at the same time those occupations whose empirical base is relatively insecure will probably be attended to on general social issues because of the moral component in their work. It would seem to follow from this that the occupations with the greatest share of public influence will be those who have a foot in both camps, and who can call on the authority of science, while at the same time having a breadth of normativeness. In fact, the academy and the military do not have as much effect on public affairs as the model might lead one to assume, while it is also the case that the members of each group differ among themselves in this respect. The epistemological dimension must therefore be taken in interaction with the other dimensions.

The first of these dimensions is that which has at one pole **technical** and at the other **moral authority**. Technical authority stems from scientific knowledge and expertise in its application and can be exercised in those spheres to which the expertise applies or those closely adjacent to it. Moral authority is exercised when professionals pronounce or intervene in areas outside the immediate purview of their professional work; when doctors attempt to influence the nature of the health care system or when lawyers pronounce on constitutional reform, or when physicists enter the debate about the use of nuclear energy as part of a fuel policy. If a scientific profession can add a moral tone to its pronouncements and public actions it can gain considerable influence, but this in turn is dependent on the actual epistemological base, from which it starts. If the expertise relates fairly directly to the issues over which there are moral concerns (such as health or the environment) then the chances for effective action are increased. Likewise, the profession with a normative base can enhance its influence if it can clothe the moral issues it promotes in the cloak of technical complexity.

The form of authority is linked to the next dimension, that of primary or secondary institutional context; that is, a profession has a context in which it chiefly operates – medicine in the hospital, the law in the courts, for example – while there are other contexts in which members of a profession may work, but which is not the main locus of professional activity. Halliday suggests that there is a range of legitimacy of professional influence, which ranges from the complete legitimacy that obtains when expert authority is exercised in the context of a primary institutional sphere, to the marginal legitimacy that can be exercised when moral authority and secondary institution coincide.

The final factor affecting professional influence is professional organization, and here there are three important aspects.

1   The degree of national professional integration: this is the question of whether the recruitment boundary and the level of recruitment have resulted in the profession constituting merely a small elite of practitioners or whether it includes every conceivable eligible. There are all sorts of variants to be found; nearly every British lawyer is a member of a law organization – the Law Society, an Inn of Court etc., but they are many such organizations, while in the USA there is one American Bar Association – but only about half the nation's lawyers belong to it. British engineers are divided amongst numerous Institutes in their 'Balkanized' profession, while the military is the most highly organized association in the state, but it is not distinct from the organization that employs it: and so on.

2   Professional mobilization is the next factor. If the epistemological base of the occupation is narrow then mobilization is easier to achieve, because there is more likely to be a common area of interest; but it also restricts the range of issues about which they can speak legitimately. On the other hand, a normative profession may have so many topics that can be seen as its legitimate interests that the capacity for influence is dissipated; and the same would apply to a syncretic profession, such as academics.

3   Finally there is the capacity for making alliances, which will depend on a number of factors, such as the profession's contacts with other influential groups, the degree of consensus within a profession, the number of members who work outside public practice, but in adjacent fields, and so on.

It can be seen from this model that the variations in professional influence derive from a number of factors, which vary according to circumstances. To take just the most obvious example of the exercise of influence by a profession – the medical profession in anglophone countries – the features which lead to success are often, though not inevitably, present: a scientific base, which none the less is brought to bear on an area of life that is shot through with moral and normative issues; a professional inclusiveness/exclusiveness that results in a relatively homogenous group with a high degree of agreement about important issues and priorities; and one that is well placed to make alliances with other influential groups.

Halliday's thesis that the key to this constellation of factors is the epistemological base of the profession is more than plausible.

While this was the end point of Halliday's original paper on this topic (1985), in *Beyond Monopoly* (1987), he applies it specifically to the American legal profession, with the aim of showing that it too is favourably placed in the matrix of factors from which influence is derived. But he takes his analysis one stage further in this case, for his objective is to show that the legal profession is not only distinctive in terms of this model, but in addition it differs from other professions in that (a) it is constitutive of the state, at least in part; in the Anglo-American context, only the military profession is fully constituent of the state: and (b) in spite of having a highly advantageous position in the model of professional influence, outlined above, it shows a considerable degree of altruism in the exercise of its advantages, which leads Halliday to 'propose a theory of professions beyond monopoly and beyond ideology' (1987: 54). The consideration of the evidence in relation to the American, and more especially the Chicago Bar occupies the rest of his book and leads to the confirmation of his thesis.

Location of knowledge

At a number of points in *The System of the Professions*, Abbott (1988) refers to the socially constructed locations of knowledge, and how it may reside in people, in organizations or in commodities. Ever since there has been specialized knowledge, there has been a tendency for those who possessed it to organize into exclusive groups, or as in the case of ancient empires, for them to work under the control of the temple or the state. Specialist religious and other arcane knowledge, and military expertise, were located in elite controlled organizations. With the development of modern knowledge and the market for services in it, the possibility for the members of an occupation to pursue a professional project arose, but at the same time industrial and commercial entrepreneurs appeared on the scene, who might find the opportunity to provide the same services as the professional in organizational form, or develop the technology to offer it in commodity form. It was also open to the state to set up organizations to provide knowledge-based services for its citizens. So while knowledge has for millennia been located in people and in organizations, it is only in the modern period that it has been incorporated into commodities, and only in recent decades with the development of information technology that commodification has posed a serious threat to professions.

Generally speaking, innovations in technology and organization have benefited professions by providing them with fresh opportuities for work, rather than by usurping their existing functions. However, there have been many ways in which such advances have affected professions. One of the first inroads created by commodification was the development of printed legal forms, for such things as wills, conveyancing landed property, contracts and other legal procedures. Lawyers objected that these documents were too rigid and merely encouraged later litigation, but law stationers flourished from the sales of these forms to accountants and other agents, who made inroads into lawyers' jurisdiction as a result. This occurred both in Britain and the USA, while in France there arose a special type of lawyer, *le notaire*, who specialized in legal forms. Doctors, by their insistence on avoiding any taint of 'trade', opened the way for apothecaries to encroach on their territory by incorporating their knowledge in pills, and later for the marketing of patent medicines. But after the the inclusion of apothecaries in the profession (by the Medical Act of 1858), and later by the statutory definition of types of medication that could only be obtained on a doctor's prescription, this commodification of medical knowledge was limited.

The enormous expansion of knowledge that arose from the invention of printing raised the possibility of the commodification of knowledge of all kinds, but the professionals are practictioners, and so as long as they could retain control of practical training in the use of their knowledge, then they could withstand this kind of threat. Textbooks on anatomy or auditing only provide the starting point, and while untrained charletans are unmasked from time to time, they are really relatively rare. None the less, the rate of expansion of knowledge is so great that the practitioners of any knowledge base need to be updated, and this means that there is a continuous stream of publications with information on innovations and their applications which increases the likelihood, not of pirating by quacks, but of marginal expansion by practitioners of adjacent bodies of knowledge.

This possibility is all the greater since the advent of computers and their capacity for interactive systems, expert systems and artificial intelligence. Some of the most successful of these applications have been in medicine, where expert systems have been developed that will mimic diagnosis and interpret the results of high technology investigations. It is, however, an open question how far individual patients would actually trust a computer, and eventually their own non-medical judgement, because judgement will often enter into diagnosis, sooner or later. Developments such as computer aided design (CAD) are more likely to impinge on the practice of professionals, such as engineers and architects. The most general outcome of this way of embodying knowledge in artefacts is likely to be a more pronounced version of the effect of books and technical up-dates; that is, it will be those activities at the margin of a jurisdiction, where one occupational group depends on another, that the service provider will be supplanted by an expert system. Many professionals have realized that computers open up new opportunities for them, and that provided they are aware of the potentialities for innovations in practice, they can benefit from computers (for example, by computerizing routine activities) rather than suffer a reduction in jurisdiction.

Organizations have long been a way of embodying religious and military knowledge, but in the modern period both state and commercial organizations emerged as possible locations of professional knowledge. Some of the earliest examples come from Germany and France, where both university education and medical services – especially hospitals – were sponsored by the state, which regarded such things necessary to the pursuit of its political and military objectives, rather than from any direct benign concern for its citizens. However, it was not until the latter part of the nineteenth century that threats to professional monopolies from organizations actually materialized in Britain and the USA.

In these societies, in the late nineteenth and early twentieth centuries, the jurisdictions of law and accountancy came under threat. The administration of trusts was the most important of a number of areas of work that commercial organizations realized could be run by a staff who were not fully trained lawyers, provided the clients regarded them as honest and dependable. Some organizations were set up specifically for the purpose, while certain other organizations such as banks created departments or subsidiary companies to do this work. In Britain, in addition to these developments, the state also took a hand and created the **Public Trustee**, in the face of vociferous opposition from both lawyers and accountants to what they termed 'officialism'. Accountants in Britain also suffered inroads into their practice from other public officials, namely the **Official Receiver** and the **Public Auditor**. Competition from commercial organizations, on the other hand, was aimed much more at the practical adjuncts of legal work (rather than activities based on legal knowledge), such as debt collection, and aspects of land transfer. This vulnerability was one reason for lawyers' opposition to the Land Registry – they believed it would make practice simple enough for it to be carried out by non-lawyers. Today, these particular forms of completion seem less serious – in the case of the state organizations, because they failed to provide a cheaper service, which was part of their *raison d'être*. But they illustrate the possibility of this kind of competition, which can arise whenever an entrepreneur sees an area of professional work that can be detached from the main jurisdiction.

The other circumstances in which an organization can successfully encroach on a professional market is when technological advance provides new means of doing a professional task, which requires a large capital investment that would normally be outside the financial range of a professional firm. Thus in the 1970s accountancy firms, especially the smaller ones that provided accountancy services as well as auditing the accounts of small organizations, found that the banks, with their large computing facilities, were trying to take over this activity. This encouraged the move to larger accountancy practices that could afford the hardware, but the threat did not last long, because the rapid advances in computer technology soon rendered the large main-frame machines unnecessary for this work, enabling accountancy firms of all sizes to handle it.

Abbott concludes by framing his main question as 'how do societies structure expertise?' The answer, for modern Western societies, is that professions are probably the most important feature, which leads on to the further question, 'Why professionalism?' (1988: 323–5). His answer to this is that modern Western market society 'favours employment based on personally held resources, whether of knowledge or wealth', to which he adds the observation that 'competing forms of institutionalization have not yet overwhelmed it'. True enough, but from the action perspective this sounds rather like *Hamlet* without the Prince of Denmark. Abbott's version of systems theory seems only to say professionalism survives because other institutions are not strong enough to diminish it, whereas action theory shows that it is the conscious pursuit of the professional project that holds its competitors at bay, advances into new fields as they emerge, and remains the chief repository of knowledge and expertise for the provision of expert services to deal with human problems.

Foucault on power and knowledge

Foucault is seen by some contemporary sociologists as having important insights about the nature of knowledge and its relation to certain occupations, especially medicine. They regard his conceptualizations as having generated new perspectives on professions, their knowledge and practice and their power, and so it would be appropriate to consider briefly some of this work. The examples to be considered are Nettleton (1992) on dentistry, Arney (1982) on obstetrics, Armstrong (1983) on medicine and Johnson (1994) on accountancy. The issues raised by these studies will be reviewed collectively at the end of this section.

1 *Power, Pain and Dentistry* (Nettleton, 1992) takes up one of Foucault's themes, namely, the need to see the history of a profession as part of the way in which knowledge was reconstituted in the modern period. Nettleton therefore moves away from the themes to be found in earlier work on dentistry, which has only been examined in terms of individual or collective power struggles. Earlier writers have seen the growth of a discipline, such as dentistry, as involving the development of technology, correct knowledge and the acquisition of power, although dentists themselves emphasized their altruism in improving the general level of health. These approaches ignore the mouth and the teeth, and such everyday practices as tooth-brushing. Nettleton's work is therefore concerned with dental techniques that explore and work upon the mouth, and with how a discourse was developed that brought about the constitution of the mouth as an object, which is structured by dental practices. This stage was reached by about 1900, when dentistry began to move on to other concerns such as dental prophylaxis and the control of pain. In the case of pain the profession saw its work as 'the attempt to reduce pain and fear of dentistry [which] has been seen as part of a move

towards a more caring and less violent practice, reflecting a more humanitarian society' (1992: 65–6). But in the theoretical framework of this analysis it is seen as follows:

> it was through the very processes involved in the elimination of painful dentistry, that its key attributes (pain and fear) have become objectified, and a prolific discourse produced about them. Furthermore, this discourse, like that which focused on dental health education, contributed to the production of the subjective patient. The object of dentistry was thus relocated from the mouth with teeth, which had been discovered in the mid-nineteenth century, to a mind that was linked to the oral cavity, and finally to a social space which surrounded and transcended the mouth and the patient. (1992: 65)

The study of dentistry enables Nettleton to draw out six main themes.

1 The disembodied dental 'gaze' that has reconstituted the object of its attention.
2 'Spacialization', that is, the location of the object of the gaze (the mouth) in its social context.
3 'The individual' that has been shaped within the dental discourse.
4 The 'disciplinary power' that dentistry exemplifies.
5 The notions of 'exile enclosure' and 'the plague' with which dentistry is congruent.
6 'Surveillance', the fundamental dimension of disciplinary power.

Nettleton then goes on show how these themes can be found in her study. The sociological aspect of these concepts is clear to see, but as the exposition continues, it leads in the direction of the philosophical topics of epistemology, including the notion of the interrelatedness of knowledge and power, and of ontology, especially how the individual, or in the case of dentistry one part of a person, becomes an object and an object of knowledge. So this study is to be seen as an example of Foucault's conception of the nature of modern society. It is a society in which knowledge has come to be applied to human beings in a manner hitherto unknown. The application of scientific method to the human sciences turns human beings into objects; and while this is for their own good – or at least for society's good – they are thereby subjected to discipline, and collaborate in their own subjection. They also come under surveillance, which Foucault sees as being modelled on the panopticon design for a prison produced in the early nineteenth century by the Utilitarian philosopher Jeremy Bentham.[3] An important aspect of this is *le regard medical*, which is translated as 'the gaze', and this for Foucault is the 'programme' of the panopticon applied to psychiatry, medicine and, as Nettleton shows, dentistry. This would also be an example of the way knowledge is intertwined with power, and is dependent on surveillance. Thus in Nettleton's example, dentistry constructs a discourse which constitutes part of the human body as an object, locates that object in a social space that dentistry defines and by the exercise of 'the gaze', disciplines and controls this aspect of human existence. This is all the easier to achieve because objects of that control collude with the controllers.

Nettleton concludes that dentistry practice in its early days continued the process that Foucault believes started at the end of the eighteenth century, whereby the patient and the patient's body were constituted as objects of knowledge. Dentistry's contribution was to bring the mouth with teeth into existence, by means of the 'medical gaze'. This in turn was part of the 'surveillance' that characterizes modern society, which is itself one feature of the 'discipline' that is imposed by this means and by means of the 'examination' and by 'normalizing judgements' (the ability to assess and rectify those who deviate from the norms). More recently, from the 1930s onwards, the conception of the mouth has been extended to include its context in the individual patient and the patient's home and social context. This apparently humanitarian concern in fact extends the area of surveillance and causes 'discipline' to 'rely increasingly on the patient, the prisoner or the student to assess themselves – to monitor their own progress or their own lifestyles' (Nettleton, 1992: 149).

2   This development of the modern *episteme* was not, so far as I am aware, considered by Foucault, who confined himself to 'the two great discontinuities in the *episteme* of Western culture: the first inaugurates the Classical age (roughly half-way through the seventeenth century) and the second, at the beginning of the nineteenth century, marks the beginning of the modern age' (Foucault, 1973: xxii). None the less, it seems entirely consistent with Foucault's line of thought, and it forms the theme of Armstrong's (1983) treatment of his *Political Anatomy of the Body*. This work covers a wider range of subject matter than Nettleton's – children's health, psychiatry, general practice and geriatrics – but within these it focuses on a particular development of 'the gaze'. It is concerned with the way, after the First World War, a 'medicine of the social' was developed, and how it relied on one particular technique of knowledge acquisition, the survey. While there are particular aspects to all four areas of the study, the common theme is the emergence of epidemiology, and in consequence, 'the community gaze'. While Armstrong does not invoke Foucault to anything like the extent to be found in Nettleton, he none the less arrives at similar conclusions; that medical knowledge is also knowledge about individuals and is concerned with a discourse whereby the patient is constituted as an object of medical enquiry and knowledge. It is therefore tied up with surveillance and discipline.

> In the twentieth century the human body has been subjected to a more complex, yet perhaps more efficient, machinery of power which, from the moment of birth (or, more correctly, from the time of registration at an ante-natal clinic) to death, has constructed a web of investigation, observation and recording around individual bodies, their relationships and their subjectivity, in the name of health. (Armstrong, 1983: 112)

3   Both Nettleton and Armstrong follow the model that is set by Arney (1982) in *Power and the Profession of Obstetrics*, in which he elaborates

Foucault's idea about the development of modern knowledge by the introduction of a stage in the first third of the twentieth century where individuality of the obstetric patient (or other object of 'the gaze') and her social context is taken into account: but once again this is seen as producing greater discipline, rather than humanizing the person's condition.

Arney shows that in the case of obstetrics, as we have seen with other branches of medicine, the nineteenth century witnessed a rapid improvement in the technology of childbirth, which combined with the constitution of the pregnant woman as an object of the 'medical gaze' resulted in greater control of this aspect of women's lives. This is a particularly interesting case, because as we have seen in Chapter 5, midwives in North America suffered much more than their British and European counterparts, in that they were not merely reduced to a position subordinate to medicine, they were practically driven out of existence altogether. Once again, from the 1920s onwards, the pregnant woman was redefined, to make her a whole person, with a home and a social background. But this meant that she was even more subjected to surveillance, because there was all the more to be controlled. Arney then looks at the alternatives provided by the natural childbirth movement and finds that they are just as rule controlled and, at least in some cases, require a surrender of personality, not merely of body.

Like the other authors discussed above, Arney draws on the notion of the panopticon, which implies continuous supervision (of a prisoner in the original plan drawn up by Jeremy Bentham in about 1790), in such a way that the subject knows he or she is under observation; a condition, which according to Arney, leads the inmates to cooperate in their own discipline. (More of the panopticon below.) He quotes Foucault on the subjection that is imposed by the panopticon. 'He who is subjected to a field of visibility and knows it, assumes responsibility for the constraints of power; he makes them play spontaneously upon himself ...' (How can you *make* something happen spontaneously?) Arney comments:

> Who is in control? Certainly not the prisoner; but not the guards either. To speak of an agent of control in the panopticon is absurd since the machine is in control. ... Rather *the situation is controlled* by the fictitious relationships created through history, in our case through the deployment of monitoring with its reformation of the doctor-patient relationship. (Arney, 1982: 231, emphasis in the original)

But this critique is not aimed at conventional medicine alone, for it is actually developed in a passage that deals with the natural childbirth movement, started by Dr Grantly Dick-Read in the 1930s, and achieving popularity some twenty years later. Arney argues that while natural childbirth appears at first glance to put the mother in charge of her own body enabling it to function naturally, it actually involves a personal commitment to the doctrine and a surrender to those who monitor pregnancy and parturition. What seems to be a move away from the impersonal rationalism of science in fact subjects the individual to emotional constraints in a system of rules which is no less intrusive than those of conventional obstetrics.

A rather different example of the use of Foucault's ideas in the study of the professions can be found in Johnson (1994), who examines the notion of 'governmentality'. This term refers to a mode of state action, which, like 'surveillance', emerged with modern society. Foucault rejects any idea that the state is a purposeful actor – no 'executive committee of the bourgeoisie' for him – but rather:

> the state is viewed as an ensemble of institutions, procedures, tactics, calcula-
> tions, knowledge and technologies, which together comprise the particular
> direction that the state has taken; the residue or outcome of governing. One
> strand in the plethora of such outcomes has been the institution of expertise in
> the form of professions. (Johnson, 1994: 140. A page later Johnson repeats this
> list, with the addition of 'analyses' and 'reflections'.)

As in Armstrong's (1983) study of epidemiology, this is 'the gaze' applied not to individuals but to populations, and Johnson's objective is to show how the 'deregulation' of professional activities (in medicine, law, account-ancy, welfare and education) that the Thatcher administration undertook in Britain, in the 1980s, was in fact not a reduction in state control of knowledge-based activities, but merely a redeployment, which increased state control without reducing the part played by professions.

> From a Foucauldian perspective, both state and professions are, in part, the
> emergent effects of an interplay between changing government policies and
> occupational strategies. This is a view that undermines the dominant conception
> of the state–profession relationship in sociology, wedded, as it is, to a notion of
> the state ... whose interventions are inimicable to the development of
> autonomous professionalism. (Johnson, 1994: 145–6)

Curiously enough this is exactly the same as the position adopted in Johnson (1982), with substitution of Foucault for Marx. The 'dominant conception' that he attacks was given only one reference (Jessop, 1977) in the earlier work and it is given none in this: this is not surprising as, to the best of my knowledge, there are none. The object of this critique was and is a straw man.[4]

As with other Foucauldian concepts, governmentality has an attractive ring to it. But a closer examination reveals that it is as much a rhetorical device as an analytical concept. In many respects it is no more than the application of modern techniques to government, as the 'gaze' was their application to medicine and other areas of life, while at the same time it seems that it may well be a sort of pun, because it is also referred to as 'a certain *mentality*' (Foucault, 1979: 20).

The empirical studies reviewed above make a significant contribution to the sociology of professions, by examining the changes in the character of their knowledge base and in the nature of their relation to their clients or patients. In particular the notion of 'discourse' is valuable in enabling us to understand one basis of professional power: those who can develop and monopolize the language and concepts to be used in an area of social life do indeed have power rooted in knowledge. This aspect of social relations is often underemphasized, although it can be seen from Witz's (1992) study of nurses and midwives (discussed in Chapter 5) how important it can be. In following this course, the authors discussed above are adducing evidence which confirms Foucault's conception of the development of knowledge, but they go further than this and show how modern professional knowledge has taken another turn since the 1930s. It has moved in a more 'social' and even humanitarian direction, but at the same time, it is argued, has achieved even greater compliance by clients in their own surveillance and powerlessness.

At this point, problems begin to emerge, because the empirical discovery of changes in the nature of knowledge that do not appear in the theory raises doubts of one kind, while the notion of an increasing level of compliance in groups in the population who are said to be under surveillance is at odds with the daily reports of the amount of trouble being caused to (for instance) doctors and prison officers by those in their charge. This warrants a look at the ideas of Foucault, from which these studies take their origin, because it is from there that these problems arise.

In taking Foucault as a starting point for sociological work, there is the assumption that he himself was a sociologist and social historian. In fact he was neither. He was a philosopher, who used aspects of historical and sociological knowledge to pursue his interests in epistemology and ontology.[5] In addition he could write brilliantly and by all accounts was an enthralling performer in the lecture hall and the interview; but to many, it was his talents as a *performer* (on the page or in the flesh), rather than the coherence of his ideas that captured minds (Baudrillard, 1977; Jay, 1993; Kellner, 1989). One cannot fail to be impressed by his use of dramatic, insightful and incisive accounts with which he opens the reader's eyes to the significance of Velazquez's painting of 'Las Meninas' (*The Order of Things*, 1973), the execution of Damiens (*Discipline and Punish*, 1977b), or the confession of *I, Pierre Riviere, having slaughtered my mother . . .* (1978). With the audience captivated, Foucault can (quite legitimately) go on to expound the relevance of these examples to trends in modern society, which support his view of topics in the nature of knowledge and existence. And as a philosopher he is under no compulsion to remind his audience that what he says is 'for the sake of argument'.

Unfortunately, this does not provide an adequate base from which to mount a sociological study, first of all because it does not open up the possibility of falsification, nor is it concerned with 'why' questions. Its objective is to convince, and those who *are* convinced devote their efforts to showing that his account is reinforced by the cases they have studied. When, as happens in the three examples above taken from medicine, a new facet emerges, it is fitted into the Foucauldian *gestalt*, with little attempt to explain it. This deficiency is not to be wondered at, because it reflects the tenor of the original. That original may be contrasted with the approach to be found in Gellner (1988), whose account of the development of human cognition is not only firmly based in historical and sociological material, but makes its methodology explicit ('the method of deduction'), thus making it clear how one would set about reordering data and arguing otherwise. Furthermore, it engages the question of *why* cognition should change, which leads to a plethora of interrelated causal influences on the emergence of modern cognition, which is seen as being interconnected with changes in the economic and political order and religion – to mention some of the most salient. This view does not attach particular significance to Foucault's change from 'Classical' to 'Modern' knowledge, nor would the developments of the mid-twentieth century be unexpected, because in Gellner's account modern cognition, like other aspects of modern culture, embodies the principle of constant striving for advance. An increment in knowledge is not only an end in itself, it is also a stepping stone to further progress.

The comparison of a sociological account with Foucault's philosophical mode also exposes the unidimensionality of the latter as well as the opacity of his central concept of power/knowledge. It is evident enough what this might mean in a loose, general way – if one has knowledge of some technique, then one may have a certain market power; if one has knowledge about an individual, then one may have some power over him or her. But in sociological terminology both power and knowledge have a number of meanings and applications, and while this gives rise to certain problems, they seem as nothing as compared with the difficulties that even Foucault specialists seem to have with 'power-knowledge'. For example, it appears from Smart that Foucault has an entirely new insight into power and claims that 'It does not represent a reformulation of the idea that knowledge is relative to its socio-historical context', but that:

> Knowledge is inextricably entwined in relations of power and advances of knowledge are associated with advances and developments in the exercise of power. . . . knowledge and power are mutually and inextricably interdependent. A site where power is exercised is also a place where knowledge is produced. . . . knowledge and power are inextricably and necessarily linked. (1985: 64)

This passage explains nothing. In its entirety it is only one hundred words long, but what is effectively the same statement is repeated four times and the word 'inextricably' is used three times. In one respect Smart is not to blame, because it is not clear – at least to the reader of English translations – what Foucault's point is.[6]

Foucault's view of power, as was noted above, is connected with surveillance, and he and his followers take the panopticon as the model, or the 'programme' for the exercise of this kind of power. In *Power/ Knowledge* (1980) he comments on the frequency with which late-eighteenth-century reformers refer to the panopticon (well before Bentham started his attempt to get the idea accepted by the British government in fact) and expands on its potential and its importance as a 'programme'. But in fact the idea met with considerable opposition in Britain, partly because of Bentham's political views, which did not endear him to the Prince Regent and other powerful figures. According to the *Encyclopaedia Britannica*, only one example of his prison was built (Millbank) and as time went on it was the other aspect of his plan – solitary confinement – that was widely adopted.[7] It does not seem to have been applied to schools or army camps, as Foucault claims; it may of course have been more widely used in France, and indeed Haussmann's rebuilding of Paris after 1871 certainly employs that layout.

The idea of the panopticon as a programme, and even more the claim by Foucault (1977b: 71) that 'Panoptism was a technological invention in the order of power, comparable with the steam-engine in the order of production', seems weakened by its lack of practical application. On the other hand, many writers see it as a valuable metaphor of the way control systems have developed in modern societies; and certainly the notion of the reinforcement of control by the compliance of the subjects is intelligible enough. On the other hand, this idea is well known from Durkheim.[8] The difference is that Durkheim was strongly of the opinion that social control of this sort was on the decline, giving rise to what he saw as the bane of modern societies, the problem of anomie. As for the implication of the loss of freedom, this would appear to be as nothing compared to the degree of constraint that existed in classical society, according to another French authority, Fustel de Coulanges. 'The citizen was subordinate in everything, and without any reserve, to the city; he belonged to it body and soul' ([1864] 1955: 219).

Arney (1982: 230) takes up the notion of the panopticon, which like Foucault he extends from prison to other institutional settings, which are actually quite different. So Arney applies the notion of surveillance to obstetrics, but as he argues that surveillance must be seen as a relationship, the professionals themselves are bound into the rule system as well as the patient. This he expresses in the abstract terms typical of Foucault: 'Natural childbirth controls'. This gives a view of what goes on which is much the same as, say, a tribal society, where everyone is bound by the rules and everyone's actions are visible to everyone else. What *is* different is the quality of the knowledge available and the benefits that it bestows – as may be seen from the infant mortality rate where modern obstetrics are not available.

Nineteenth-century philosophers were much more concerned with freedom than they were with the panopticon, and one conclusion was that, to some extent, people have to be forced to be free; and that in particular their freedom of choice over what they are allowed to do to their children has to be restricted in order to allow the latter the full range of opportunities that society offers. One of those opportunities is for a level of health that is far and beyond what any previous society could have dreamed of. Most people willingly trade in 'the freedom to be invisible' (Arney, 1982: 241) in return for greatly increased chances of staying alive and healthy, and thus able to exercise the multiplicity of freedoms available to them.

Childbirth is a good case to examine because it is such an important personal life experience, and modern sensibility demands that the mother should be able to gain the most possible from this experience. But at the same time it is a universal human tendency to turn individual life events into public social rituals in order to put a cultural seal of approval on them: because after all these are the very means by which society continues to exist and by reason of which individuals change and adjust their social roles.

So what Arney and Foucault are *really* talking about is the modern way in which age-old social practices are carried out. Modernity involves a level of knowledge and expertise that was undreamed of in the past, and a division of labour that puts control into the hands of specialists. But that does not justify the near-paranoia of Foucault's account, because it is hard to believe that the oppression of specialists, even if linked to the state apparatus, is greater than the tyranny of community that all pre-modern societies experienced.

Arney's conclusion, loaded with Gouldner's (1955) 'metaphysical pathos', prompts him to comment briefly on the future; and he starts by stating that 'As a social analyst, I have outlined the situation as I see it.' Unfortunately, this vision is seriously affected by the theoretical stance adopted, that of Foucault; and, as noted above, the latter is not really a sociologist, but a philosopher. In view of this, it is not surprising that Arney's concluding paragraphs are taken up with a discussion of the philosophical topic of freedom, for which one could certainly construct objective measures, but which is also inescapably a subjective experience. 'Free' is something we feel.

Arney (1982: 14) discusses the idea that knowledge or the possession of truth may be used to oppress, and argues that the remedy is to expose the ways in which this oppression occurs, so that at least the folk know about it. But there is the implication that knowledge/truth should be in the hands of the folk, but this is either impossible – because they are not intelligent enough to handle it – or it is a return to Jacksonianism and the freedom of quackery (see the discussion of law in the USA in Chapter 3).

It may be concluded that, while Foucault's conception of power/ knowledge has led to some interesting studies, such work is handicapped rather than helped by the use of this starting point, because power/ knowledge has been developed as a philosophical tool rather than a sociological one. After all, according to Turner (1987: 12), 'for Foucault, sociology is merely a branch of social medicine'. There are indeed those, such as Baudrillard (1977: 11–12), who even regard the philosophical content of his work as having little value.

In short, Foucault's discourse is a mirror of the powers it describes. That is its strength and its seduction, not at all the 'index of truth', that is its *leit-motiv*: the procedures of truth have no importance, for his discourse is no more true than anyone else's – no, it is in the magic of an analysis that unwinds the subtle meandering of his topic, which describes it with a tangible, tactical exactitude, in which seduction feeds the analytical power and the language itself brings forth the operation of new powers. This is also the operation of myth, with all the efficacy of the symbol described by Levi-Strauss, and it is not a discourse of truth but a discourse of myth, in the strong sense of the term, and, I secretly believe, without illusion about the appearance of truth that it produces. That, moreover, is what is lacking in those who, following in Foucault's footsteps, leave on one side this mythic construction and return with the truth, nothing but the truth.[9]

And Baudrillard's title? *Oublier Foucault.*

Conclusion

The significance of the change in cognition that is crucial to the emergence of modern society renders more intelligible the importance attached to the professions by functionalist sociologists; because as the bearers, exponents and developers of knowledge, professionals had the potential to ally themselves with possibly the key element in modernity and thus with the central values of modern society. But modernity took centuries to develop into its maturity, especially, perhaps, in Britain, for Britain did not experience the leap into modernity and the discarding of tradition that accompanied the American and French revolutions. This British characteristic illuminates another aspect of the professional project, which may be seen from a further consideration of Larson's (1977) diagram, reproduced in Chapter 1. The traditional means of furthering the professional project are particularly important for British and pre-revolutionary French professions as they have to make headway against the traditional inertia, hostile to modern knowledge. Especially notable was the achievement of physicians in achieving and maintaining a high status at a time when their knowledge was meagre at best, and in some respects downright wrong.[10]

As the modern conception of knowledge gained acceptability (towards the end of the eighteenth century), medicine in France and Prussia benefited, because the state came to see the value of applying this knowledge to the population in general in order to ensure a supply of healthy young men for military service. In France, and even more so in America, this trend was counteracted by the democratic spirit of the times, which promoted the populist notion that specialists are unnecessary; a notion reinforced by the revolt against the traditionalism of the *ancien régime* in France and against all things British in the new United States of America. In these circumstances, it was necessary to re-establish professional standing, not on the grounds of tradition and gentlemanliness, but on the basis of education in scientifically, or at least systematically and rationally based knowledge; and so the 'modern means' in the second and third rows of Larson's matrix come into prominence. It is thus only after the lapse of several decades that, in the USA, the appropriate law and medical schools (accompanied by genuine advances in medical knowledge) establish sufficient reputation for professions to claim the cognitive distinctiveness requisite for the founding of professional associations and the pursuit of the professional project. As we saw in Chapter 3, the same is broadly true of France, although there the fledgling professional associations were hamstrung by the state control of education and the high prestige of the civil service.

Exclusivity is essential to the professional project and one aspect of this is cognitive exclusivity. But in the same way that monopoly in the market is antithetical to modern economic thinking, so cognitive exclusivity flies in the face of the spirit of science. So the professional project involves the need to demonstrate that the knowledge in question would be dangerous in the hands of the untrained and the unqualified; while this may be demonstrated where risk to life, limb or property exists, if the state considers that the ordinary citizen, or the state itself, could provide the service in question, then the profession has an uphill task, as in the case of accountancy. Exclusivity is not solely that of the knowledge base itself: it is also the need to prevent other occupations – especially other established professions – from poaching parts of the market that they believe can be supplied with services based on their knowledge, and it is also required to prevent the entry of ineligibles to membership. These ends are achieved in part by means of a discourse that defines the profession and its activities, but discourse is also a concept, as we have seen from the work of Foucault, that can be applied to the activities of defining, collating and applying the knowledge base itself. Foucault sees it chiefly in relation to the exercise of power over patients, but many of the aspects of professional knowledge reviewed in this chapter can be seen as part of this activity. In a sense it starts with the work of certifying and credentialling the members in terms of the knowledge they have acquired, ensuring that it is difficult to obtain – intellectually, financially or socially according to circumstances. (For instance, when medical knowledge was relatively slender, a prodigious number of hours of the curriculum were devoted to learning the minutiae of anatomy.) The features of abstraction and of diagnosis, inference and treatment that Abbott (1988) discusses, as well as the balance between indeterminacy and technicity that Jamous and Peloille (1970) focus on, are all part of 'the cultural work' (Abbott, 1988: 30) that must be carried on in relation to knowledge.

This last point – association of technique with knowledge – is one of the potential weak points in the professional armour, for if the technique can be separated from knowledge then the door is open for other occupations to encroach. Examples of this are the way dentistry in Britain was invaded by the manufacturers of false teeth in the 1920s, until the Dentists' Act was amended to give the profession the protection it required: a contrary case was the failure of doctors to achieve full control of the application of X-ray technology, which they dealt with by hiving off the operation of the machinery to a paramedical group.

Threats of this kind to the professional project are linked to the feature discussed above in the section on knowledge and credentials, namely that the means of production of a profession's knowledge-based service is contained in their heads: this point is linked to Abbott's discussion of the location of knowledge, which shows that it may reside in people, organizations or commodities. In the earliest specialized occupations of religion and the military, knowledge was located in organizations, and for modern professions this possibility is always a threat. Once again it is linked to technique and technology. If advanced technology requiring high capital investment becomes necessary for professional activities, then the possibility for capitalist or state organizations to encroach on professional jurisdictions arises. This has notably occurred in the case of medicine, but to a large extent the strength of professional bodies has been such that the doctors have managed to retain control of hospitals and other organizations. At the same time, events such as these demonstrate the value of Halliday's work on the relation between the nature of a profession's knowledge and its influence *vis-à-vis* the state and other actors in the professional arena, and hence its ability to pursue the professional project successfully.

Finally, it must be noted that the phrase from Halliday (1987) with which this chapter was introduced – that knowledge is 'a core generating trait' of professionalism – needs to be put in context. On the one hand this should not be taken to imply that once blessed with knowledge an occupational group is thereby assured of a opportunity for income for evermore. It cannot even be sure of reward in the short term unless it is constituted as the province of the profession by means of discourse, exclusion and a whole battery of other devices, perhaps including legislation. It must be made into an essential part of the professional project if the occupation is to be able to claim it for its own. Once this is achieved, the knowledge base may become the central resource of the profession, and will remain so as long as the profession can maintain its exclusive rights to it. But the exercise of the power thus acquired, whether in defence of its rights in its knowledge and the market that it claims for the provision of services based on that knowledge, or for pursuing its interests and exerting influence in society at large, will in turn be constrained by the nature of the knowledge base, as demonstrated by Halliday (1985), and by the characteristics of the professional organization. The contingent nature of a profession and its power may be illustrated graphically by comparing the position of the legal profession in the USA with its moral and market independence, while at the same time effectively constituting an arm of the state, with the legal profession in Germany (especially prior to 1948), which was not an arm but merely an instrument of the state and whose potential power and status descended instead on the civil service and the university professorate. Professional knowledge is only what the occupational group can annexe and hold on to. The advantages they derive from it are only those that their professional project can achieve in a particular historical context.

Notes

1 The **clerisy** (Gellner, 1988) are specialists in literacy who, in the earliest civilizations, started off as what Gellner calls 'accountants', but once writing developed from a system of record-keeping to a *script*, then religion and law were committed to written form and the clerisy achieved a much greater significance and extended their expertise to mathematics and astronomy.

2 The principle that the search for knowledge may reasonably and legitimately be pursued in any context by any means is a commonplace in contemporary society, but earlier in the modern period it was one of Swift's targets for satire in *Gulliver's Travels*; as for example in the philosophers who were attempting to extract sunbeams from cucumbers.

3 'A proposed form of prison of circular shape having cells built round a central well, whence the warders in a central tower could at all times see all the prisoners.' The Oxford English Dictionary ascribes the origin of the word to the Utilitarian philosopher Jeremy Bentham in 1791, but Foucault says that the idea was in use in France before that date. Bentham himself got the idea, in about 1786, from his brother Samuel, who used it to supervise the shipwrights under his command as a engineer colonel in the Russian Navy. It is interesting that for Bentham solitary confinement was as important as supervision, that his plan sprang from a desire to remove the horrors of transportation as a punishment, and that the British government saw the key elements in its new prison at Millbank as seclusion, employment and religious instruction. It is not clear from the *Encyclopaedia Britannica* that the building was in fact in the form of a panopticon.

4 Jessop certainly refers to other authors, but these, and Poulantzas (1973), who is quoted later, are writing about the concerns of political scientists, which apart from Johnson, have not attracted the attention of sociologists of the professions, nor stimulated 'the way sociologists have conventionally conceptualized the relationship between the state and the professions'.

5 This may be gauged from the references to be found in the 'Afterword' by Gordon to *Power/Knowledge* (Foucault, 1980), where there are twice as many references to philosophers as to anyone who could remotely be described as a social scientist.

6 Turner (1987) writes in similar terms: 'power produces knowledge ... power and knowledge directly imply one another ... there is no power relation without the correlative constitution of a field of knowledge'. And so on. The last part of this statement seems to me to be simply untrue. As Goldthorpe (1974: 132) says in another context, the power exercised by the dropping of napalm bombs requires no social relation between the two parties, and certainly no correlative field of knowledge.

7 It should be noted that Bentham's motives in proposing the panopticon scheme stemmed from a moral and humanitarian opposition to transportation as a punishment. After working on the plan for the best part of twenty-five years, the British government paid Bentham £23,000 to go away. In spite of the statement in the *Britannica*, another panopticon was built – Pentonville Prison. It is also noteworthy that Bentham was made a French citizen in 1792.

8 In the apt phrase of my friend Christopher Jenks (Goldsmiths College, London), 'Foucault has nothing to add to Durkheim, except suspicion' (personal communication).

9 Author's translation.

10 The appalling treatment of George III for the rare condition porphyria, as portrayed in Alan Bennett's play *The Madness of George III*, is a case in point.

7

A professional project –
the case of accountancy

> Robinson Crusoe, having rescued a watch, ledger, and pen and ink from
> the wreck, begins, like a true-born Briton, to keep a set of books.
>
> (Karl Marx, *Capital*, Vol. 1)

This concluding chapter aims to bring together the themes that have been
discussed in earlier chapters by means of an empirical example of the
professional project. This will be the case of English accountancy, with
some comparative material from Scotland and the USA. It might be more
conventional to conclude a discussion of topics that arise out of a concept,
such as the professional project, by presenting a theoretical and relatively
abstract synthesis. On the other hand, this is already to be found, in large
measure, in Chapter 1, and it is hoped that an empirical case study will
bring the theoretical strands together in a more enlightening way than a
recapitulation along the lines of an 'ideal type'.

So, after a brief conceptual outline, there follows the story of English
accountancy; how an occupational group was formed and how it launched
its professional project, how it established its respectability and its
expertise, marked out its knowledge base and its jurisdiction and obtained
state recognition. From its national base it then succeeded in establishing
itself in the Empire (as it then was) and in the USA; although American
accountants are now in the majority in the international firms, these are
for the most part Anglo-American in origin. The story has no end, for the
occupation – individuals, firms and professional body – have to continue
their efforts to maintain their present position and to seize and even create
opportunities for professional work, if the professional project is not to
fail.

The concept of a professional project

1 **The starting point**. The concept of a professional project draws
together a number of ideas from various sources. First, there is Max
Weber's general conception of society as an arena in which classes, status
groups and other social entities, such as political parties, compete for
economic, social and political rewards. One category of competitor is
the **occupational group**, and, in contrast to Marx, he draws attention to the

holders of educational qualifications, which provide an opportunity for income (1978: 302–5).

2 **The overall objective**. So the occupational group is seen not just as a fact of social life, but as an entity whose members have to work at bringing it into existence, and who then have to keep up a continual effort to maintain and if possible enhance the position of the group. In other words, the group has to pursue a **project**. (This may be seen as cognate to the notion of career – deriving from the Symbolic Interactionist tradition – and extended in the work of Hughes (1958), Freidson (1970b) and Larson (1977) to professions.) The elite of the group articulate its objectives and set in train the work needed to achieve them, and although the individual members may pursue their own personal ends and may not be fully conscious of the group goals, they are normally sufficiently in tune with the group objectives for these to be pursued. There is also the meaning that 'project' is given in Existentialist philosophy, by Sartre for example, which is not specifically mentioned in the authors just referred to, but probably implicit; that it is pursuit of a project that gives existential meaning and moral value in the philosophical case to the individual, and in this instance to the group.

In practical terms, the occupational quest is for a **monopoly in the market** for services based on their expertise, and for **status in the social order**, as Weber terms it. These two objectives are linked in two interesting ways. First, as Larson observes, an action on the part of the would-be profession often serves both purposes and has both economic and status advantages: 'the two dimensions are inseparable' (1977: xvii). For example, if any occupation manages to set a university degree as an entry requirement, then this will be good for business in that it provides a warrant of the abilities of the practitioners, but a degree also carries with it a certain social cachet, which will raise the standing of the occupation as a whole in the eyes of the community. Secondly, social standing and economic success have a unique connection for knowledge-based occupations, because of the problem of the intangibility of what they have to sell. These occupations are offering services which not only cannot be seen in advance in the shop-window, as it were, but which also require the customers to trust the practitioner with their lives, their health, their money, their property and even their immortal souls. As there are no goods for inspection, the customer has to trust the practitioner himself (and in the formative period it was 'him')[2] and trust is bestowed on those who appear to be respectable. The professional group has therefore to try to get into a benign spiral of interaction between these two aspects: if they seem respectable, they can attract business; if they are economically successful they can afford more of the outward signs of respectability. These dual objectives can, at the same time, be seen as manifestations of the underlying strategy of **social closure**, whereby 'ineligibles' are excluded from the group and thus denied access to its knowledge, its market and its status.

3 **Sub-goals**. Then there are a number of other objectives that the aspirant profession must strive for and, once established, must maintain. In the first place, it has to carve out for itself a **jurisdiction** (Abbott, 1988: 33). This requires economic activities in the establishment, and retaining of a market in their services, and this in turn involves competition and accommodation with rivals; but it also necessitates 'cultural work' to establish the legitimacy of their practice. At the same time, it must set about **producing the producers** (Larson, 1977: 71), that is, ensuring that all future entrants have passed through an appropriate system of selection, training and socialization, and turned out in a standardized professional mould. This will involve the attempt, at least, to control the educational input and is closely connected to the development, definition and **monopolization of professional knowledge**.

The attainment of these three goals will play a part in the achievement of a fourth, namely **respectability**. The kind of work, the sort of person and the quality of the knowledge of the aspirant occupation will all have consequences for the way it is perceived by the rest of the world, the relative importance of these factors being conditioned by the values of the society at the time. But in addition, there will be other activities, which may be undertaken in ways that will be of significance for the evaluation of the occupation by others, or for the morale and self-image of the members. Whether their offices are located in Milton Keynes or in the City of London, the granting of a coat of arms or the eating of lavish dinners are examples of things that may have consequences for the profession's perceived respectability.

4 **Other actors**. Then there are other actors in the field where the group pursues its professional project. Relations with them may have both market and status consequences and none is more fateful than those with **the state**, with whom a regulative bargain (Cooper et al., 1988: 8) must be struck. This is because in a modern Western culture monopoly is normally unacceptable, and so the exceptional nature of the professional activity has to be recognized and regulated. A professional monopoly is dependent upon state recognition (Cooper et al., 1988: 1), but at the same time such acknowledgement confers status and even moral authority.

The occupation must also have dealings, sometimes cooperative, sometimes competitive, with **other occupations** in and around their potential jurisdiction and with **educational institutions**. Both may have important influence on the course of the professional project. Finally, the occupation needs to present itself to the **public** in the way most likely to maximize its business returns and its social standing; the most significant section of the public is clearly its potential **clientele**.

5 **Context – social, political, cultural**. The other social actors just described are really only the most active elements in a social context composed of factors which range from social values to legislation and from the history, tradition and power position of other social actors to the latest technological innovations to impinge on professional work.

The occupational group

> Particular groups of people attempt to negotiate the boundaries of an area in the social division of labour and establish their control over it. (Larson, 1977: xii)

The particular group of people in this case are 'public' accountants, those who in Britain are termed Chartered Accountants and Certified Public Accountants (CPA) in the USA and who are in public practice, that is, they are selling their services to the public. The precursors of these practitioners can be seen emerging as an identifiable profession about 200 years ago, but in order to appreciate the way accountancy started and developed as an occupation, it will be helpful to start by outlining the activities that contemporary accountancy includes.

1   The basic skill of bookkeeping. Most enterprises employ clerks, most of them unqualified, to do this task, but in order to do any of the work of accountancy the practitioner must have this skill. At the same time, the preparation of the accounts of a large group of companies is a matter of considerable complexity, requiring wide and detailed knowledge of financial practice and of the legal requirements, often of more than one country. This leads to one of the curiosities of accountancy, as compared with other professions, that the clientele, as represented by the finance directors of large corporations, is as well-qualified and experienced as the public practitioner.
2   The substance of that first point (knowledge of accounting practice and the relevant legal provisions) is that it enables the accountant to carry out what is the bread and butter of most practices, namely auditing.
3   Again it is these areas of knowledge that enable the accountant to provide services in the fields of taxation, insolvency and bankruptcy, trusts and probate as well as the manifold tasks that come under the heading of management consultancy.

The knowledge and skills on which accountancy services are based are very much a concomitant of modern industry and business, and do not therefore have their antecedents in the agro-literate society, from which modern society developed, as in the cases of law and medicine. Accountancy had played an important part in the administration of ancient empires and the earliest surviving records from both the Middle East and Europe are accounts of tribute, distributions and possessions. Medieval Europe took some time to catch up on the standards of antiquity, but by the end of the fifteenth century there is evidence that, in Northern Italy at least, systematic bookkeeping, including double-entry, had been developed.

Accounting skills at this date were part of literacy and numeracy, and some evidence of this can be found in Chaucer's descriptions of the Canterbury pilgrims, the majority of whom appear to have been literate. Chaucer's characters were mostly 'middle class' (in so far as this term can be applied to the fourteenth century), and several of them are described as having commercial qualities, which the author clearly sees in a favourable light. So the merchant, the maunciple (financial and administrative officer of an Inn of Court), the frankeleyn (estate manager who had been both a 'shirreve' – i.e. county clerk – and a 'countour' – i.e. an auditor) and so on, were men of business and it was people who were described as 'men of business' who appear in the early modern period as prototypes of accountants. Such figures were also factors or agents and therefore played a more active role in their clients' affairs than a modern accountant; as a specific occupation they seem to have been more prominent in Scotland than in England, and quite a few can be found in the city directories of Glasgow and Edinburgh by the latter part of the eighteenth century. However, it is England that claims the first practising firm of accountants. It was founded in 1780 by Josiah Wade, in Bristol, and built up a practice auditing the books of merchants in the city.

Auditing, now the mainstay of accountancy practice, was not in fact nearly so important for the early accountants (or accomptants, as they were termed in those days), for this activity was often carried out by a person whom the interested parties – that is to say the shareholders – saw as appropriate, and this was often one of their own number. It was rather the application of accounting skills to bankruptcy that provided the opening for professional practice, and perhaps the first official mention of the accountant comes in the Bankruptcy Act of 1831, where accountants are listed, along with merchants and bankers, as suitable people to draw up the bankrupt's statement of affairs, which was required to sort things out. One of the founders of the English profession, looking back to 1864 when he started work, wrote:

> We may disregard the then current jibes, that if an accountant were required he would be found at the bar of the nearest tavern to the Bankruptcy Court in Basinghall Street, and that an accountant was a man who had failed in everything else ... but an accountant was regarded as associated with and dependent upon insolvency, and I well remember that to be seen talking to or having your office visited by an accountant was to be avoided, especially in the stressful times of 1866. (Ernest Cooper, quoted in Margerison, 1980: 9)

Those stressful times saw some dramatic financial crashes, and work for accountants became plentiful. Demand for accountancy services was further augmented by the passing of the Companies Act of 1867 and it was at this juncture, in 1870, that English accountants formed professional organizations on a local basis, first in Liverpool and later that year in London. But these were not the first such bodies to be established in Britain, for these had been founded in the early 1850s in Scotland, and Royal Charters were granted to the local bodies in Edinburgh (1853) and Glasgow (1855). In this case too, the Bankruptcy laws (which were different from, and more stringent than, those in England) were an important stimulus to the activity of accountants.

So by the middle of the nineteenth century as a result of the growth in economic activity, and the concomitant regulation through legislation, a number of skills and an area of knowledge had emerged, in which its practitioners saw the possibility of monopoly. But these attributes were ones that any intelligent, enterprising 'man of business' could acquire, and that indeed was what most mid-nineteenth-century accountants were. Some were in fact merchants whose businesses had failed (Brown, 1905), and if, for example, that failure was a matter of bad luck, who better to guide a fellow-unfortunate through the tangled paths of insolvency? Others were auctioneers or dealers, stock brokers or lawyers who found in accountancy an additional outlet for their talents.

Launching the project: respectability and expertise

At this point the people who were practising accountancy could not be regarded as a 'particular group', nor was accountancy a defined area in the social division of labour. The manner in which these things came about can be more fully described in the case of Scotland, because the data are more readily available; it is also more appropriate because that was where the occupational identity first emerged.

From the accounts given by Brown (1905) and Stewart (1977), it appears that in 1850 accountants in Edinburgh started to hold meetings with a view to forming an association of practitioners in the city, and in spite of some debate and disagreement, by January 1853 they had settled their differences and formed the Edinburgh Society of Accountants. It may seem surprising from our point in time that anyone should have doubts about the value of forming a professional body, but when the field is wide open, those who perceive themselves as being established in a strong position in it may feel reluctant to surrender their advantage. Even those who do not feel impregnable and who wish to circumscribe the membership, in order to protect what they hold, may disagree about where the boundary line should be set. For this is the inevitable dilemma facing an occupation; if too many are included as eligible, it may downgrade the whole membership, while if the line is drawn too narrowly, those left out may be of sufficient ability to form a rival body (which is exactly what happened in England, thirty years later).

So the initial move in crystallizing the membership is similar to the creation of an exclusive club: the founding coterie then select those whom they believe have the necessary qualities and qualifications to match up to themselves. It is possible to show fairly clearly the sort of people who went to make up this first professional body of accountants (Macdonald, 1984); the initiators are men who are connected with the landed gentry and many of them are lawyers. Most of those who were then regarded as eligible were upper middle class in Edinburgh, although fewer fell into this category in Glasgow which formed a similar society the following year.

Aberdeen, which followed suit about twelve years later actually included a peer among their number. The impression one forms of the relation between the founding clique and the whole membership is that the solid respectability of the former was used to provide a warrant for the equally able but less well-connected members. The quality of the future members was assured by the need to pass exams, but in case it might be thought that the door was now open to any man of ability (no women at this stage!), the mechanism of 'serving articles', that is, training by means of an indentured apprenticeship, ensured that entry was only possible to someone deemed acceptable by an existing member, and one whom that member was prepared to have in their office for five years. As articles usually provided no wage for the clerk, he had to come from a family of sufficient means to support an adult for five years.

The other means of delimiting the membership and making it 'professional' was to insist that a member practise accountancy and nothing else. New members, especially in Glasgow, tended to have other occupations, such as auctioneer or merchant, and while these occupations were by no means disreputable, it was felt that pluralism of this kind detracted from the aura of professionalism. Some years later, in the 1880s, English accountants were complaining in the columns of their professional journal of the same problem (*The Accountant*, 27 October 1902: 1369), but in that instance the second string to an accountant's bow was the trade of rent-collector or fishmonger!

But the desire to rid themselves of pluralism and the taint of trade was only one aspect of what seemed the major thrust of the Scottish accountants' campaign for professional status, and that was the quest for respectability. This is exemplified with great clarity by a content analysis of the petitions presented by the Accountants Societies of Edinburgh, Glasgow and Aberdeen. Table 7.1 shows that the two chief points of emphasis were their connections with the law and the courts and their respectability. The former received such prominence because it was connected with an undoubted area of technical expertise and knowledge, but it is also a very prestigious aspect of work, and in view of the emphasis on respectability itself – apparently twice as important as accountancy skills – it is reasonable to infer that the legal connection was also to do with respectability.

The drive for achieving and maintaining a high status for the profession was also much in evidence in the English branch of the profession, although in this case the medium was not so much the petition to the Privy Council as conspicuous consumption, in the form of their headquarters building (Macdonald, 1989). There seems little doubt from contemporary comment that they succeeded in their objective, which made such an impression that the second ranking body of English accountants found it necessary to emulate them, by buying a building in a positively flamboyant style, at a price they could barely afford. The Scots chose not to follow this path in search of high social status, and elected, typically one might

Table 7.1   *Factors mentioned in the petitions for charters to the Privy Council by Scottish Societies of Accountants in 1853, 1854 and 1867*

	Number of times mentioned
Connections with law and the courts	32
Respectability, professional standing	13
Accounting skill	7
Importance of work content	7
Importance of liberal education	3
Incorporation would achieve:	
Unity	3
Qualifications	2
Public benefit	2

Source: Macdonald, 1984

suppose, the more sober tactic of using the printed word. The reason that it is possible to document the respectability of the origins of the founders of the Scottish profession is that certain of their members took care to publish this information. The USA is different again. In this case accountants relied almost entirely on modern sources of prestige, namely educational qualifications and state licensure; a course of action in keeping with their history and culture.

The course followed by accountants in launching their professional project was quite typical, but to consider briefly the ways in which some other professions came into being may illustrate the variation to be found at this stage in professional formation. As noted in Chapter 3, the medical profession has its origins back in the Middle Ages,[3] but by the end of the eighteenth century, was divided into physicians, surgeons and apothecaries, who collaborated in their practice, but could not agree organizationally until the middle of the nineteenth century. When unity was finally achieved, their resulting professional position was greatly enhanced by all the work that had gone into improving their status in earlier decades. British doctors therefore had a head start in pursuing the professional project in the modern period.

Architects provide yet another variation on the theme. The founding, in 1791, of the first association in Britain was initiated by four architects of undeniable distinction, who then invited another eleven to join them in The Architects' Club. The club was only open to Fellows or Associates of the Royal Academy or its Gold Medallists in architecture, or members of the Academies of Rome, Parma, Bologna, Florence or Paris. But the variety of interests within the occupation resulted in a number of other bodies being founded, and even the founding in 1834 of the Institute of British Architects (Royal Charter in 1837) could not achieve complete amalgamation, and there is another body, the Architectural Association, that flourishes to this day. The problem of achieving unity is a reflection of the diversity of traditions that fed into the occupation at the start and which have never entirely disappeared. It was only with the spread in

Britain in the mid-seventeenth century of Palladio's ideas, that the design of buildings began to be taken out of the hands of master masons, a movement in which Inigo Jones was the key figure. Notions of style in buildings became current among the upper classes and some young men, travelling abroad on the continent, became interested in architecture to the point that it became part of the educational equipment of a gentleman. Designing his house thus became a gentlemanly thing to do. Some were good at it, others were not; the latter could have their plans 'ghosted' by an architect. In this way the occupation of architect came into being, but it was also something that gentlemen undertook, often as rather more than a mere pastime, while there were still many buildings that were designed by master masons.

The first step in the pursuit of the professional project is therefore the creation of a **formal occupational group**. The occupational field is inchoate and more than one group is often formed in the early stages, or may have survived from the pre-modern period. This is true not only of the cases reviewed above but also of the American accountancy profession, which also displays another feature, one that occurs less often in Britain, namely the presence of an academic group, with a concern for professional education and who may play a large part in professional formation. Internecine strife may ensue, which has often taken a long time to settle, or may result in the uneasy symbiosis that can be seen in British architecture. Establishing credentials, displaying collective and individual respectability and obtaining legal recognition are soon under way.

Qualifications: producing the producers

Accountants seem to have hit on effective means of establishing their claims to professional status, if one may judge by the speed with which they obtained official recognition. Scottish accountants, first in Edinburgh (1853) and then in Glasow (1854), obtained Royal Charters within a year of the founding of their societies, while in 1880 English accountants first unified their several societies into a single professional association, and then succeeded in obtaining a Royal Charter. It is hard to explain why seventeen years should pass between the founding of the Edinburgh Society and the first English one in Liverpool in 1870: the ten year gap between that date and the formation of a national association is not so surprising as it took the Scots the best part of a century to achieve national unity, and local and other divisions are frequent in professional bodies, especially in the early years.

The Charters granted to both the Scottish and the English Accountants included provision for the establishment of a system of training and qualification. Training took the form of a five-year period of 'articles', during which the would-be accountant received training on the job from his 'principal' (a Fellow of the Institute in public practice). The articled clerk took intermediate and final exams and if he passed, would be admitted to the Institute as an Associate; in due course he could apply for a practising certificate and set up on his own in practice, or be made a partner in an existing firm. Education to provide the range of knowledge to pass the exams was obtained by private study, which soon came to be organized by correspondence colleges and by the Institute and its local societies. In today's conditions where graduate entry to accountancy is the norm, as it is to most other knowledge-based occupations, this must seem a rather unimpressive method of training, but in the context of a century ago, it must be realized that this training system had the great advantage for an infant profession of being highly visible to the audience who mattered most, that is the business community who purchased the profession's services. So in their early years the accountancy profession put a lot of effort into '**the production of producers**' (Larson, 1977: 31–9). It thereby legitimated its claim to a monopolistic position, by demonstrating the standard of training, and at the same time drew on a 'modern' source of prestige. This was enhanced by the entry educational qualification, which was regarded as high in those days, and by the requirement of the payment of a premium, of a considerable sum for the larger, better-known firms, which together with the absence of a salary for the articled clerk, ensured that he came from a relatively well-to-do family. Accountants thus drew on both **traditional and modern sources of prestige** (Larson, 1977: 68), in pursuing their professional project.

In following the apprenticeship model, accountants were taking a typically British course, and one which was also adopted by architects. This may seem a mode of training more usually found among trades and crafts, but it remained the norm in law until quite recently; only a minority of solicitors aged over fifty have degrees, while entry to the English bar until the mid-twentieth century only required secondary education to age 16 – in addition that is to showing that he is 'a gentleman of respectability' (Carr-Saunders and Wilson, 1933: 7). This discriminatory terminology was apparently still in use, in spite of the Sexual Discrimination Act of 1919. At that date a Bar student was still only 'recommended' to become a pupil of a barrister: so although many pupils had law degrees, there were plenty who had degrees in other subjects and others who had none, and all were expected to learn their profession by means of tutelage to a practising member.

Accountancy (and other professions) in America relied much more on the 'modern' source of prestige to be obtained from college education and a directly relevant degree. The more pragmatic and anti-traditional attitudes to be found in America, even in colonial times, allowed the emergence of the new specialism of accountant to emerge at a much earlier date, *and* offered positive encouragement to women. This is not to say there was anything like equality, but by 1910 ten women had become CPAs (Ried et al., 1987). But equally striking is the way that formal accountancy education actually preceded the formation of the first accountancy body. The first accounting course was offered at the University of Pennsylvania (Wharton School of Finance and Economics) in 1883, the first organization – the American Association of Public Accountants – was established in 1887,[4] and the first official registration and examination law was passed in New York State in 1896. American educators and practitioners rejected the British apprenticeship form of training and were convinced that college or university affiliation was critical to the long-run viability of the profession. At the same time they believed that it was necessary for the practitioners to define the university's role in accounting education, and in these early years they persuaded New York and North-Western Universities to provide courses, which reflected the requirements of the CPA exam (Langenderfer, 1987).

While the history of American accountancy confirms that the formation of a professional organization is an essential element in the professional project, it also shows that the American culture produced much more active and innovative educational establishments. Higher education thus played a part in the establishment and legitimation of the profession in America. In the 1920s the American Association of Instructors in Accounting came into being and in 1926 started its own journal, *Accounting Review*. This group (now called the American Accounting Association) has become an important element in the American profession which has no real counterpart in Britain.[5]

The professional project, in the formative stage, contains the same elements in Britain and the USA, but their relative salience and mode of deployment displays distinctive differences that may be attributed to cultural variation. The **production of producers** and their **certification and legitimation** are features which the occupation strives to establish and control, by one means or another.

Building respectability

The tactics described in the previous section were designed to enhance and display the valuable characteristics of both individual members and the profession collectively. But some actions are purely to improve the standing of the collectivity, and this was very marked in the case of the English accountancy profession, which chose to draw on the traditional resource of conspicuous consumption in the gentlemanly practice of patronage of architecture. *Building Respectability* (Macdonald, 1989) is a punning way of referring to the decision by the ICAEW, soon after obtaining their Royal Charter, to acquire a prestigious site in the City of London, and to hold a competition, with the most eminent of assessors, to design a building for it. The outcome was a building that was regarded both as an architectural landmark and as the embodiment of the prestige that was so essential to the advancement of the accountants' project.

Any doubt about the motives of the budding profession may be dispelled by the words of their own professional journal, and by those of outsiders.

> It is our pious hope [wrote the Editor of *The Accountant*] that as the new building rises, so will the reputation of the profession gradually ascend in public estimation, and that both may be established on equally solid foundations ... It is the actual and visible embodiment of the astonishing growth of a profession, young but already of commanding power, and capable of almost unlimited extension. May men say with Shakespeare 'There is nothing ill can dwell in such a temple'. (*The Accountant*, 12 July 1890, p. 353)

And from an outsider:

> The Institute has obtained those outward and visible signs of respectability that are of so much importance in England, although they are too often neglected ... They have gained the means to impress everybody who gazes on the building that the business of Chartered Accountants has been underrated. Instead of the commonplace affair ... [that] might be supposed from its practitioners, it is now shown to be a great power of which the relations are worldwide. (*The Architect and Contract Reporter*, reported in *The Accountant*, 2 September 1893, p. 753)

One thrust of the professional project, *collective social mobility*, was clearly well under way.

The building continues to have importance for Chartered Accountants, as may be seen from the number of pages devoted to it in the annual List of Members. It likewise continues to attract considerable favourable attention from works on architecture such as Pevsner (1973) and Service (1977). The former includes the 1960s extensions to the building in his encomium of praise, which illustrates the fact that English accountants have continued to use this method of claiming public attention. In doing so they are following the practice of other English (and, to some extent, Scottish professions) of buying a prime building site in a location appropriate to their activities, erecting an imposing building designed by a leading architect and equipping it in a way that is more appropriate to a Pall Mall club than to an office (Macdonald, 1989).

Once again the contrast may be drawn with American professions. The Institute of CPA's offices are situated in a handsome office block in mid-Manhattan, but it is an office and not their own purpose-built accommodation. Its rooms and corridors are not decorated with valuable paintings and *objets d'art*, but with framed posters. The headquarters of the American Bar Association is an unobtrusive part of the University of Chicago campus, while the American Medical Association operates from a building in a part of Chicago that makes the visitor glad that the metro station is just across the street. Conspicuous consumption, at least of this kind, is not part of the professional project in America.

Professional unity, jurisdiction and state licensure

Generally speaking, professional unity is necessary if a professional body is to be sufficiently impressive to obtain state recognition, but in the case of British accountancy it was in fact only local or regional. By 1887 there were five bodies of Chartered Accountants – in Edinburgh, Glasgow, Aberdeen, England and Wales, and Ireland. Furthermore, the English profession in particular seemed to have misjudged the crucial question of where to draw the line in admitting or excluding members, when the Institute was founded. Only five years after the granting of the Charter, there were enough 'ineligibles' of sufficient standing as accountants to form a rival body, the Incorporated Society of Accountants and Auditors. This group never seriously threatened the standing of the Institute, but on the other hand they were not merely a body of technicians, carrying out a lower level of work. They were engaged in doing the same kind of work but on the whole for the smaller business. They continued to shadow the progress of the Chartered Accountants and they eventually succeeded in achieving amalgamation with them on terms of practical equality in 1957. In the early days however, they and one or two other smaller associations of accountants, together with the Scots (and to a lesser degree, the Irish), played an important part in curtailing the advance of the English Institute.

The objective at this period was to achieve a monopoly in the market for services based on accountancy knowledge. The sure way to do this was to persuade the legislature to pass a statute that would define its **jurisdiction** and those who would be allowed to do it. But the legislators had to be convinced that both these things could in fact be clearly defined, and such definitions are actually quite problematic. They also had to be sure that there was good reason for overriding the inherent antipathy of liberal democracy to the idea of monopoly, which as Lord Salisbury said in debate on the Accountants Registration Bill in 1909, would only be overcome 'if there is great good to be performed or great evil to be remedied'.

By 1905, Chartered Accountants were auditing about 95 per cent of all public companies, but even this high proportion still left the possibility for this work to be carried out by others. In addition, other aspects of accountancy work, that they would liked to have monopolized, were capable of being performed by solicitors, banks and of course those accountants who were not Chartered: and again, some activities were actually also undertaken by state agencies – liquidations by the Official Receiver, and trust accounts by the Public Trustee – and in spite of determined opposition, the Institute was unable to stop this intrusion of 'statism' into their claimed jurisdiction.

The English Institute fought a long battle to obtain state registration of accountants, by introducing legislation into Parliament, but they found themselves constantly at daggers drawn with the other accountancy bodies – Chartered and otherwise – who always found the draft bills too inimical to themselves, and who therefore opposed them and sometimes introduced bills of their own. This struggle continued, with the English Chartered Accountants leading the way, but continuing to fail to take into account their colleagues and competitors, especially those north of the border. As recounted in Chapter 4, the outcome was the failure of accountants to achieve what Parkin (1979: 57) seems to regard as the *sine qua non* of professionalism: 'the professions . . . generally seek to establish a *legal monopoly* over the provision of services through licensure by the state'. But accountants are nothing if not careful people, and in this case they were relying on both belt and braces; when the belt of statutory registration let them down, their monopolistic trousers were sustained by the device of ensuring, through their advocates in Parliament, that wherever legislation called for a professional auditor, as in the case of a newly created local authority or public utility for example, that duty was required by the Act to be carried out by a member of the Institute. By the 1930s, Chartered Accountants had come to the conclusion that this strategy of building their monopoly piecemeal was in practice achieving their aim, and the risky business of getting legislation through Parliament could be dropped.

So after something over a century, British accountancy reached a position where **the organized profession held a monopoly of provision of services**. The 'organized' profession was in fact divided up regionally, but no longer horizontally because in 1957 the major anomaly of the existence of the Incorporated Accountants was removed by merger with the Chartered: and the monopoly was not sustained by a statutory register as in the case of doctors or solicitors, but by the Companies Act and via the schedules of many other Acts dealing with particular corporations, which specified that the duties of a statutory audit should be carried out by a Chartered Accountant.

Once again the USA took a different course. Instead of legislating about company accounts and leaving it to the company to decide who was competent to do audit work, it was the accountants who were the subject of legislation, thereby leaving the company little option but to use a CPA if they wished their accounts to carry conviction. The crucial point came in 1903, 'when the shareholders of the newly formed US Steel Corporation, then the nation's largest corporation, decided in their first annual meeting that a full disclosure of the firm's financial facts, properly attested to, would enhance its public acceptance' (Davidson and Anderson, 1987: 113). The practice of employing CPAs to carry out audits was thus a matter of good company practice, rather than statutory requirement, but legislation was not far behind and regulatory bodies were created within the next five years or so, who greatly extended the work that auditors were required to do.

Professional knowledge

If accountancy was to establish its credentials as a knowledge-based occupation, it was necessary to assemble, define and isolate a particular cognitive domain to which it could restrict access. This was quite problematic, and as mentioned above the difficulty in defining the occupation, its jurisdiction and its knowledge base was one of the stumbling blocks that halted the progress of the registration legislation that British accountants drafted so often, around the turn of the nineteenth/twentieth centuries.

In fact their 'esoteric' knowledge was less than esoteric on the face of it, because there was scarcely an aspect that they did not share with some other occupation. Bookkeeping, company law, insolvency, taxation, trust accounts – lawyers, company secretaries and a host of bookkeepers and clerks with modest qualifications could be found to deal with each of these. So the Chartered Accountants' case had to rest on the claim that they were the only group who could do them all. The general public probably thought (as the quotation on p. 198 shows), that accountancy 'was a commonplace affair', but this impression was steadily rendered less tenable by the growth in the size and complexity of business organizations, and by the corresponding expansion of the legislation to regulate them. By the outbreak of the First World War, those with any knowledge of the requirements of a large company audit can have had no doubt that there was only one kind of person to carry out this task. The war itself generated enormous demands from government for the monitoring of supply contracts and rationing and so on; demands that accountants were called on to fulfil as the chief repository of business knowledge.

> From the first it was apparent that by reason of their training and qualifications accountants could make a significant contribution to the war effort in a variety of ways, and as time went on and months lengthened into years, their services were in demand as never before. (ICAEW, 1966: 59)

Seven leading Chartered Accountants were knighted for war work of this kind.

As the economic world which gave rise to accountancy became increasingly complex and the legislation required to regulate it followed suit, professional practice came to entail an **esoteric collection of areas of knowledge**, rather than a basis in esoteric knowledge. In recent years attempts have been made to establish *theories* or conceptual frameworks for financial accounting, but it is clear from the review of such efforts in Roslender (1992: 116–26) that they have been less than wholly successful. He quotes a definition from the US Financial Accounting Standards Board of a conceptual framework as being:

> a constitution, a coherent system of interrelated objectives and fundamentals that can lead to consistent standards and that prescribe the nature, function and limits of financial accounting and financial statements.

This does not really seem to meet the same criteria as a theory in the sciences – natural or social – and perhaps one must conclude that the underpinning of accountancy knowledge is not so much theory, as practice raised to the level of a theory; or that its essence is scientific method, rather than a science *per se*.

Accountants can thus be said to have an esoteric collection of knowledge, even though they share most specific components of that knowledge with one of a number of other occupations: and that this cognitive base is applied by methods that are capable of statement in abstract terms, rather than the content of their practice. Another aspect of the knowledge base is the standards to which it is examined. Accountancy exams are notoriously difficult to pass – the pass rate rarely reaches 50 per cent. It is well known that recruitment to the profession is very competitive, and if a highly selective entry finds it hard to achieve a pass, then this makes it appear that it is difficult to acquire the professional knowledge. To some extent this is an artefact of the need to memorize a great deal of material, but it is also true that the ability to apply both principles and practical techniques to a wide range of inherently complex problems requires considerable intellectual capacity.

A worldwide profession

> a great power of which the relations are worldwide.

This phrase, reported in *The Accountant* of 1893 and quoted above on p. 198, sounds like a bit of journalistic hyperbole; but whether the writer knew it or not, this statement was about to come true in a fashion that makes accountancy unique among professions, for accountancy was the first profession to operate cross-nationally.

The 1890s was the period when Britain clearly lost its world economic lead, notwithstanding its Imperial political power, and was overtaken by Germany and the USA. As appeared in Chapter 3, American culture until the end of the nineteenth century was less than favourable to the professions, with the result that while the economy was industrializing with great rapidity, there was very little in the way of accounting expertise to provide the regulatory mechanisms that had become necessary – especially in view of the spate of enormous frauds and defalcations that occurred in this period. State certification of accountants was provided for by legislation in individual states, but these newly professional people found themselves decidedly short of experience and organization of a standard to cope with the already very large American industrial corporations. In this predicament they turned to their British counterparts, and a number of accountants from the leading British firms crossed the Atlantic, originally as advisers and consultants, but in due course as partners.[6] These links appeared so beneficial to both sides that a number of Anglo-American firms were set up, with such success that they soon became much larger than the purely British or American firms, and eventually developed into the eight giant multi-national firms of accountants that in the last third of the twentieth century have dominated not merely the accountancy scene in Britain and the USA, but, as that journalist wrote so prophetically a century ago, worldwide (Montagna, 1975: 477).

Although this situation makes accountancy rather different from other professions, it follows from the logic of the professional project and the drive for monopoly in the provision of services. At the same time this does nothing to lessen the other aspect of the project, for the need for a cultural guarantee of probity is greater than ever when the clients are multi-national corporations. In this respect too accountancy is an egregious profession, because in no other is such a large proportion of the clientele made up of giant corporations, who require a service provided worldwide. It is the pursuit of the professional project in this context that has led to the emergence of the huge accountancy firms, who in turn have disproportionately great interest in the direction that the professional project takes. At the other end of the scale, sole practitioners in accountancy are content if their professional body maintains the status quo, provides them with the services they need and does not ask for too large a subscription. The big firms, by contrast, are keen to see a pro-active professional association, one that is sufficiently ahead of the game to forestall any increase in state involvement in setting the accountancy agenda, and to ensure that accountancy improves its position in the competition for 'jurisdiction'. This leads to the interest that the large firms show in having their partners actively involved in their professional association: in consequence, the big firms have a disproportionate say in its affairs, although this is partly due to their much greater ability to spare the personnel to perform these duties. It is not much of an exaggeration to say that in Britain the big firms – the worldwide firms – *are* the Institute, both Scottish and English, and the same is true of other Western industrial societies.

The wide reach of British accountancy can also be seen in the sizeable proportion of members (in the region of 7 per cent) residing in the Empire or Commonwealth. This is seen by Johnson (1982) as the imperial British state exercising its hegemony over the colonial and dominion territories, and indeed the colonial administration does seem to have taken a quite different attitude to the state registration of accountants from the home Parliament. Statutes were passed for the dominions and colonies which required that very registration to which the government was so indifferent at home. The British accountancy bodies also took a different stance, because they saw such Acts as preventing their members from practising in these countries: ironically, once passed, they used them as an argument to support their own case for registration. The view advanced by Johnson is that the extension of British accountancy to the Empire, and the statutory registration of accountants there, demonstrates the fact that 'modern professions are a product of state formation' (1982: 208), and indeed this fits with data that he adduces about other professions. On the other hand there is no doubt that the British accountancy bodies were at best ambivalent about it: furthermore, some of the overseas members must have been the local members of home firms (or at least their representatives), and thus part of their quest for monopoly: others will have been overseas residents seeking to enhance their own careers. 'Imperial bodies with imperial interests' (1982: 198) is a stronger verdict than the evidence will stand.

The continuing project

Accountants have undoubtedly succeeded in achieving, to a very large extent, the objectives of their project: they have a monopoly in the most important of accountancy services, auditing, and in Britain (less so in the United States) they have a firm grip on a number of other services – taxation and management consultancy, insolvency, company flotations, mergers and share issues, for example. The counterpart of this, the quest for enhanced social status, has likewise been attained. What does the profession do next?

In the same way that the rewards of the professional project are attained by steady, constant effort on the part of members and their organization, they are only retained by comparable exertion. The condition of professional monopoly, like that of liberty, is eternal vigilance.

All the points which go to underpin the jurisdiction of the profession must be maintained and even improved. For example, since the 1960s, entry to the English profession has been almost entirely confined to graduates, and while this has been made possible by the increase in the size of the university population, accountancy firms, especially the large ones, have been able to offer such handsome starting salaries that the recruits are of the highest ability. At the same time the increase in the volume and complexity of the legislation that governs the accountants' jurisdiction has increased and the exams required to test this knowledge have become correspondingly difficult. Firms put more time, money and effort into the training of their student members, and they are anxious to get value for the money they are investing in their young staff and therefore do all they can to ensure their examination success. It therefore becomes known that the quality of the practitioners is probably going up and their range of knowledge even more extensive.

At the collective level, the English and Scottish Institutes attempt to maximize cooperation, because while the memberships refuse to amalgamate (in particular the Scottish CAs voted against such a proposal, probably because they feared the loss of their valued distinctive identity, and loss of autonomy if merged with the English Institute), it is clear that many Members of Parliament regard accountants as over-privileged, and would prefer to see both more state intervention and more competition of accountancy services as well as regarding the regionalization of a national profession as a time-wasting anachronism. In these circumstances, a united front is essential. Externally, its aim is to keep ahead of the state in standards of financial regulation, in a world of increasingly diverse economic and professional activity. Internally, one of its objectives is also stimulated by diversity, because accountants work in a variety of specialisms and contexts, and the ICAEW has struggled for years with the problem of structuring itself and its activities in a way that will best serve the manifold interests of the membership. It also sees a need to ensure that its members are primarily involved in the Institute and that they are not seduced into such specialist organizations as those concerned with taxation or insolvency.

These points can be illustrated by considering some of the remarks of the President of the ICAEW in his annual statement to the AGM in 1990. First, there were declarations of overall purpose that reflect the need for steady effort mentioned above.

> I would summarise the work of your Council in a single corporate objective – to enhance the value of membership, the description 'chartered accountant', to each member and to do that in the public interest ... we are always vigilant of the public interest in the name of the membership generally.

This is interesting in that it emphasized the pursuit of the professional project, and at the same time asserted that this was altruistic.

> The major changes in Company Law, affecting the audit practices of our members, seem to me an opportunity ... These changes, must in the long run, benefit our members as they expand into Europe and compete on level terms with professions in that great market place.

Here the President was uttering an implied exhortation to the members, but the intention seems very similar to that in the previous extract.

Secondly, there were statements of specific objectives;

> the two great strategic initiatives of merging with the Chartered Institute of Public Finance and extending the training of our students into industry.

There were a number of factors prompting these initiatives, and it would be difficult to assign causal weights to them. The proposed merger with CIPFA was both an attempt to extend the jurisdiction and a response to a possible threat from a competitor. At the same time it would have served the purpose of deflecting government and Civil Service criticism that the ICAEW does not speak for all accountants – especially those involved in government and the Civil Service!

The other objective also sprang from a mixture of motives. This innovation was intended to extend involvement in training to the considerable proportion of the membership who work in industry and commerce (rather than in public practice), thus expanding the base of this important professional function. At the same time it would silence criticism that there was a serious deficiency in the practical training of

Chartered Accountants if almost the whole of their time was spent working on audit teams, without learning the accountancy work of the organizations whose records they audit. It would thus strengthen the ties between 'non-practising' members and the professional body and forestall any possible tendency on the part of accountants in industry to form their own professional organization.

The statement of these objectives concluded with a further endorsement of the professional project. 'Surely, these two major initiatives must fulfil the corporate objective of enhancing the value of "chartered accountant" to us all.'

Finally, the President outlined the changes in the Institute's internal organization that have been put in hand 'so that we can respond to members' needs effectively and comprehensively'. Once again, the first target seems to have been the members in industry, and the language (for a Chartered Accountant) becomes positively florid. 'It was thrilling to see in January the launch of the Board for Chartered Accountants in Business . . .'. 'The formation of the Board's Senate, a grouping of senior members, whose wisdom and experience we can tap, is imaginative and far-reaching. In parallel to this we will shortly launch a Board for General Practitioners.' He then went on to outline a proposal for 'Faculties' – specialist groups within the Institute – that would provide the organization and activities that specialists might otherwise seek outside the Institute, thus reducing its value and cohesion. The first of these, the Tax Faculty, came into existence in 1991 and others soon followed.

Although this is only a brief analysis, the stance of the ICAEW is clear; and it is equally clear from a perusal of other annual reports that this one is a typical example. They are all concerned to maintain their members' commitment to the profession and to make it clear that the Council is working hard at expanding and improving the infrastructure and organization that it provides, and ensuring that membership is a valuable asset for individuals and firms. In terms of the conceptual model of professional project, it can be seen from the President's report that work is going into protecting and extending the market or jurisdiction and ensuring that the status of Chartered Accountant will in no way diminish, but will probably improve. The need to consider the boundaries of membership seems to be constantly under review, and the failure of the ICAEW's two attempted mergers – with CIPFA and the Scottish CAs – does not mean that the professional body has lost its way: on the contrary, it can be taken to mean that the elite of the profession have a clearer view of the collective interest than the individual members, for whom their professional socialization and qualification is so important that they are not prepared to dilute it by admitting outsiders.[7]

Pursuit of these goals and sub-goals brings the profession into relations with other actors in the professional arena, and especially in the case of the state, that relationship leads to the formulation of goals. As can be seen from the above account, the expectations of the state about the representativeness of the professional body and it capacity to provide the regulatory and other services required of it, is a constant stimulus to reform and improvement. In short, the aspirations, initiatives and exhortations of the ICAEW President all have their place within the framework of the professional project.

The Institute and its members still work likewise at 'respectability'. Their handsome and prestigious building has been improved and extended over the years and it features in various ways in their publications and their activities. They continue to patronize the arts, to hold dinners and to conduct conferences in distinguished locations: by these means they display the qualities of a cultured, learned, responsible body. At the level of the firm and the individual, accountants ensure that they can be seen to be people of substance and seriousness. They send out newsletters to their clients with information about the latest Budget changes and accounting practice and so on; their offices are soberly furnished with paintings, or more often reproductions, on the wall that are guaranteed to offend no one. Accountants adhere to a strict code in personal appearance: men wear grey or blue suits and beards are extremely rare; women do not wear trousers.[8]

The minutiae of personal conduct and appearance might seem unimportant but in fact they are as crucial as the firm's procedures and proformas that guide an auditor through the daily work, or the process for the selection and training of staff. Great care is taken to get the right work performed, in the right way, by the right people, wearing the right clothes. Of such stuff is the garment of professionalism made: and such is the display of knowledge and trustworthiness that justifies monopoly.

Notes

1   Bottomore and Rubel (1963: 117).

2   Until 1920 there were no women members of the chief bodies of accountants, so they will be referred to as 'he' when dealing with the profession's early years.

3   Chaucer's portrait of the Doctour of Phisyck is interesting, because although he is well-read in the classical authorities on medicine, and therefore presumably a university man, Chaucer is heavily ironic about his profitable association with his apothecaries, and indeed about the whole basis of his practice. (I put it in modern English:)

In all this world there was no one like him
To speak of physic and of surgery;
For he was grounded in astronomy.

4   Both the centenary and the half-centenary of the AICPA was acknowledged by a letter from the President of the United States – Roosevelt in 1937 and Reagan in 1987. Roosevelt's letter contained ten sentences with a mean length of 36 words; Reagan's eleven sentences contained an average of 18 words each.

5   British accountancy now has close links with universities, and the Scottish Institute for a long time led the way in making it a graduate profession; but this does not detract from the striking difference between Britain and the USA for half a century and more after the founding of their professional bodies.

6   Carey (1969) in his history of American accounting cites an example of an audit certificate from the 1880s covering the accounts of St Louis Breweries, signed in London by the British firm Price, Waterhouse and Co.

7   In fact, it was the rank and file Scots CAs who rejected the latter merger. There are similar examples to be found in the history of other groups, such as the relative reluctance of the laity of the Church of England, as compared with the Bishops, to amalgamate with the Methodists in 1972 (Hastings, 1986: 610).

8   Brown suits are anathema. While engaged in researching a large accountancy firm, I was accustomed, after a couple of visits, to go straight into the lift and make my way to a desk that had been allocated to me on the fourth floor. I normally wore a grey suit, until one warm day I put on my lightweight suit – which was brown. As I came into the entrance lobby, a commissionaire bore down on me with all the subtlety of the Bismarck intercepting a convoy, and the phrase 'Can I help you, *Sir*?', in that tone which really means 'I don't think you ought to be in here'.

Beards are not much better. An informant (a partner in a multi-national practice and since then elected to the Council of the ICAEW) told me that in another firm where he had worked at one time, the senior partner had, one year at the firm's Christmas party, presented all the bearded men in the firm with electric razors. Those who appeared clean-shaven at the office function the following Easter, received an expensive bottle of after-shave. My informant was the bearded exception that proved the rule!

Bibliography

Abbott, A. (1988) *The System of the Professions*. London: University of Chicago Press.

Abbott, P. and Wallace, C. (1990) *The Sociology of the Caring Professions*. London: The Falmer Press.

Abel, R. (1979) 'The rise of professionalism', *British Journal of Law and Society*, 6: 82.

Abel-Smith, B. and Stevens, R. (1967) *A History of the Nursing Profession*. Cambridge: Harvard University Press.

Abercrombie, N. and Urry, J. (1983) *Capital, Labour and the Middle Classes*. London: George Allen & Unwin.

Abercrombie, N., Hill, S. and Turner, B.S. (1988) *The Penguin Dictionary of Sociology*, (2nd edn). Harmondsworth: Penguin.

Acker, J. (1989) 'The problem with patriarchy', *Sociology*, 23(2): 235–40.

Adams, D. (1979) *The Hitch-Hiker's Guide to the Galaxy*. London: Pan.

Armstrong, D. (1983) *Political Anatomy of the Body*. Cambridge: Cambridge University Press.

Armstrong, D. (1987) 'Bodies of knowledge: Foucault and the problem of human anatomy', in G. Scambler (ed.), *Sociological Theory and Medical Sociology*. London: Tavistock.

Arney, W.R. (1982) *Power and the Profession of Obstetrics*. London: University of Chicago Press.

Arnstein, W.L. (1973) 'The survival of the Victorian aristocracy', in F.C. Jaher (ed.), *The Rich, the Well-Born and the Powerful*. Chicago: University of Illinois Press.

Atkinson, P. and Delamont, S. (1990) 'Professions and powerlessness: female marginality in the learned occupations', *Sociological Review*, 38(1): 90–100.

Badie, B. and Birnbaum, P. (1983) *The Sociology of the State*. London: University of Chicago Press.

Baudrillard, J. (1977) *Oublier Foucault*. Paris: Editions Galilee.

Becker, H.S. (1970) *Sociological Work*. Chicago: Aldine.

Becker, H.S., Greer, B., Hughes, E.C. and Strauss, A.L. (1961) *Boys in White*. Chicago: University of Chicago Press.

Berlant J.L. (1975) *Professions and Monopoly: a Study of Medicine in the United States and Great Britain*. Berkeley, CA: University of California Press.

Beshers, J. (1962) *Urban Social Structure*. New York: The Free Press.

Birnbaum, P. (1988) *States and Collective Action*. Cambridge: Cambridge University Press.

Blau, P. (1955) *The Dynamics of Bureaucracy*. Chicago: University of Chicago Press.

Bledstein, B.J. (1976) *The Culture of Professionalism*. New York: Norton.

Boreham, P. (1983) 'Indetermination: professional knowledge, organization and control', *Sociological Review*, 31(4): 693–718.

Bottomore, T.B. and Rubel, M. (1963) *Karl Marx: Selected Writings*. 2nd edn. Harmondsworth: Penguin.

Bourdieu, P. (1973) 'Cultural reproduction and social reproduction', in R. Brown, (ed.), *Knowledge, Education and Cultural Change*. London: Tavistock, pp. 71–112.

Bourdieu, P. (1984) *Distinction*. London: Routledge & Kegan Paul.

Bourdieu, P. and Passeron, J.C. (1977) *Reproduction in Education, Society and Culture*. London: Sage.

Braverman, H. (1974) *Labour and Monopoly Capital: the Degradation of Work in the Twentieth Century*. New York: The Monthly Review Press.

Bridenhaugh, C. and Bridenhaugh, J. (1962) *Rebels and Gentlemen: Philadelphia in the Age of Franklin*. New York: Oxford University Press.

Briggs Committee (1972) *Report of the Committee on Nursing*. London: HMSO.

Brown, R. (1905) *A History of Accounting and Accountants*. Edinburgh: T.C. & E.C. Jack.

Burrage, M. (1988), 'Revolution and the collective action of the French, American and English legal professions', *Law and Social Enquiry: the Journal of the American Bar Foundation*, 13(2): 225–77.

Burrage, M. (1990), 'Beyond a sub-set: the professional aspirations of manual workers in France, the United States and Britain', in M. Burrage and R. Torstendahl (eds), *Professions in Theory and History*. London: Sage

Burrage, M. and Torstendahl, R. (eds) (1990) *Professions in Theory and History*. London: Sage.

Burrage, M., Jarauch, K. and Siegrist, H. (1990) 'An actor-based framework for the study of the professions', in M. Burrage and R. Torstendahl (eds), *Professions in Theory and History*. London: Sage.

Caplow, T. (1954) *Sociology of Work*. Minneapolis: University of Minnesota Press.

Carchedi, G. (1975) 'On the economic identification of the new middle class', *Economy and Society*, 4: 1–86.

Carchedi, G. (1977) *On the Economic Identification of Social Classes*. London: Routledge & Kegan Paul.

Carey, J.L. (1969) *The Rise of the Accounting Profession*, 2 vols. New York: AICPA.

Carr-Saunders, A.M. and Wilson, P.A. (1933) *The Professions*. Oxford: The Clarendon Press.

Carter, B. (1985) *Capitalism, Class Conflict and the New Middle Class*. London: Routledge & Kegan Paul.

Clark, G. (1964) *A History of the Royal College of Physicians of London*, 2 vols. Oxford: The Clarendon Press.

Clarke, A. (1919) *The Working Life of Women in the Seventeenth Century*. Leicester.

Cocks, G. and Jarauch, K.H. (eds) (1990) *German Professions 1800–1950*. Oxford: Oxford University Press.

Collins, R. (1975) *Conflict Sociology: Towards an Explanatory Science*. New York: Academic Press.

Collins, R. (1979) *The Credential Society: an Historical Sociology of Education and Stratification*. New York: Academic Press.

Collins, R. (1981) *Sociology Since Midcentury: Essays in Theory Cumulation*. New York: Academic Press.

Collins, R. (ed.) (1985) *Three Sociological Traditions*. Oxford: Oxford University Press.

Collins, R. (1986) *Weberian Sociological Theory*. Cambridge: Cambridge University Press.

Collins, R. (1990) 'Changing conceptions in the sociology of the professions', in R. Torstendahl and M. Burrage (eds), *The Formation of Professions: Knowledge, State and Strategy*. London: Sage.

Cooper, D., Lowe, A., Puxty, A., Robson, K. and Willmott, H. (1988)'Regulating the U.K. accountancy profession: episodes in the relation between the profession and the state'. Paper presented at Economic and Social Research Council Conference on Corporatism at the Policy Studies Institute, London, Jan. 1988.

Corrigan, P. and Sayer, D. (1985, 1991) *The Great Arch*. Oxford: Basil Blackwell.

Coulanges, Fustel de ([1864] 1955) *The Ancient City*. New York: Doubleday Anchor Books.

Crompton, R. (1987) 'Gender, status and professionalism', *Sociology*, 21: 413–28.

Crompton, R. and Jones, G. (1984) *A White Collar Proletariat?* London: Macmillan.

Crompton, R. and Sanderson, K. (1989) *Gendered Jobs and Social Change*. London: Unwin Hyman.

Dahrendorf, R. (1959) *Class and Class Conflict in Industrial Society.* London: Routledge & Kegan Paul.

Dangerfield, G. ([1935] 1961) *The Strange Death of Liberal England 1910–1914.* New York: Capricorn Books.

Daniels, A.K. (1973) 'Professionalism in a formal setting', in J.B. McKinlay, *Processing People.* London: Holt, Rinehart and Winston.

Davidson, S. and Anderson, G.A. (1987), 'The development of accounting and auditing standards', *Journal of Accountancy, Centennial Issue,* May, 163(5): 110–27.

Davis, K. (1959) 'ASA Presidential Address', *ASR,* 24: 757–73.

Department of Health (1993) *Changing Childbirth: Report of the Expert Maternity Group.* London: HMSO.

Derber, C. (ed.) (1982) *Professionals as Workers: Mental Labour in Advanced Capitalism.* Boston, MA: G.K. Hall.

DiMaggio, P. (1989) 'Review of Abbott (1988)', *American Journal of Sociology,* 95(2): 534–5.

Dingwall, R. (1979) *The Social Organization of Health Visiting.* Beckenham: Croom Helm.

Dingwall, R. and Lewis, P. (eds) (1983) *The Sociology of the Professions.* London: Macmillan.

Dingwall, R., Rafferty, A.M. and Webster, C. (1988) *An Introduction to the Social History of Nursing.* London: Routledge.

Donnison, J. (1977) *Midwives and Medical Men.* London: Heinemann.

Durkheim, E. (1957) *Professional Ethics and Civic Morals.* New York: The Free Press.

Durkheim, E. (1958) *Rules of the Sociological Method.* New York: The Free Press.

Earle, P. (1989) *The Making of the English Middle Class.* London: Methuen.

Elster, J. (1989) *Nuts and Bolts for the Social Sciences.* Cambridge: Cambridge University Press.

Etzioni, A. (1969) *The Semi-Professions and their Organization: Teachers, Nurses and Social Workers.* New York: Free Press.

Fielding, A. and Portwood, D. (1980) 'Professions and the state – towards a typology of bureaucratic professions', *Sociological Review,* 28(1): 23–54.

Foster, J. (1974) *Class Struggle and the Industrial Revolution.* London: Weidenfeld & Nicolson.

Foucault, M. (1973) *The Order of Things.* New York: Vintage Books.

Foucault, M. (1977a) *The Archaeology of Knowledge.* London: Tavistock.

Foucault, M. (1977b) *Discipline and Punish: the Birth of the Prison.* London: Allen Lane, The Penguin Press.

Foucault, M. (1978) *I, Pierre Riviere, having slaughtered my mother, my sister and my brother . . .* (trans. Frank Jellinek). London: Peregrine.

Foucault, M. (1979) 'On Governmentality', *Ideology and Consciousness* 6: 5–22.

Foucault, M. (1980) *Power/Knowledge.* Brighton: The Harvester Press.

Fox, A. (1974) *Beyond Contract: Work, Power and Trust Relations.* London: Allen & Unwin.

Friedson, E. (1970a) *Medical Dominance.* Chicago: Aldine-Atherton.

Friedson, E. (1970b) *The Profession of Medicine.* New York: Dodd, Mead & Co. ('Afterword' added 1988.)

Freidson, E. (1973) *Professions and their Prospects.* New York: Sage.

Freidson, E. (1983) 'The theory of the professions: the state of the art', in R. Dingwall and P. Lewis (eds), *The Sociology of the Professions.* London: Macmillan.

Friedson, E. (1986) *Professional Powers: a Study of the Institutionalization of Formal Knowledge.* Chicago: University of Chicago Press.

Gane, M. and Johnson, T. (eds) (1993) *Foucault's New Domains.* London: Routledge.

Garrett, A.A. (1961) *History of the Society of Incorporated Accountants.* Oxford: Oxford University Press.

Geison, G.W. (ed.) (1984) *French Professions and the State, 1700–1900*. Philadelphia: Pennsylvania University Press.

Gellner, E. (1988) *Plough, Sword and Book*. London: Collins Harvill.

Giddens, A. (1973) *The Class Structure of the Advanced Societies*. London: Hutchinson.

Giddens, A. (1984) *The Constitution of Society*. Cambridge: Polity Press.

Glaser, B. and Strauss, A. (1965) *The Awareness of Dying*. London: Weidenfeld & Nicolson.

Goldner, F.H., Ference, T.P. and Ritti, R.R. (1973) 'Priest and laity: a profession in transition', in P. Halmos (ed.), *Professionalization and Social Change*. Sociological Review Monograph No. 20. University of Keele.

Goldstein, J. (1984) 'Foucault among the sociologists: the "disciplines" and the history of the professions', *History and Theory*, pp. 170–92.

Goldthorpe, J.H., Lockwood, D., Bechhofer, F. and Platt, J. (1969) *The Affluent Worker in the Class Structure*, Cambridge: Cambridge University Press.

Goldthorpe, J.H. (1974) 'A rejoinder to Benson', *Sociology*, 8(1): 131–3.

Goldthorpe, J.H. (with Llewellyn, C. and Payne, C.) (1980) *Social Mobility and the Class Structure of Modern Britain*. Oxford: Clarendon.

Goldthorpe, J.H. (1982) 'On the service class, its formation and future', in A. Giddens and G. Mackenzie (eds), *Social Class and the Division of Labour*. Cambridge: Cambridge University Press, pp. 162–89.

Goldthorpe, J.H. (1985) *Order and Conflict in Contemporary Capitalism*. Oxford: Oxford University Press.

Goode, W.J. (1957) 'Community within a community: the professions', *American Sociological Review*, 22: 194–200.

Gouldner, A. (1955) 'Metaphysical pathos and the theory of bureaucracy', *American Political Science Review*, 49: 496–507.

Gouldner, A. (1970) *The Coming Crisis in Western Sociology*. London: Heinemann.

Gramsci, A. (1971) *Prison Notebooks* (ed. Q. Hoare and P. Nowell Smith). London: Lawrence & Wishart.

Hall, J.A. (1985) *Powers and Liberties*. Harmondsworth: Penguin.

Hall, R.H. (1968) 'Professionalization and bureaucratization', *American Sociological Review*, 33(1): 92–104.

Hall, R.H. (1975) *Occupations and the Social Structure*, 2nd. edn. Englewood Cliffs, NJ: Prentice-Hall.

Hall, R.H. (1983) 'Theoretical trends in the sociology of occupations', *Sociological Quarterly*, 24: 5–23.

Hall, R.H. (1988) 'Comment on the sociology of the professions', *Work and Occupations*, 15(3): 273–5.

Halliday, T.C. (1983) 'Professions, class and capitalism', *Archives Européens de Sociologie*, 24: 321–46.

Halliday, T.C. (1985) 'Knowledge mandates: collective influence by scientific, normative and syncretic professions', *British Journal of Sociology*, 36: 421–47.

Halliday, T.C. (1987) *Beyond Monopoly*. London: University of Chicago.

Halmos, P. (1970) *The Personal Service Society*. London: Constable.

Halmos, P. (ed.) (1973) *Professionalization and Social Change*. Sociological Review Monograph No. 20. University of Keele.

Halpern, S.A. (1988) *American Pediatrics: the Social Dynamics of Medicine*. London: University of California Press.

Haskell, T.L. (1984) *The Authority of Experts*. Bloomington, IN: University of Indiana Press.

Hastings, A. (1986) *A History of English Christianity, 1920–1985*. London: Collins.

Haug, M.R. (1973) 'Deprofessionalization: an alternative hypothesis for the future', in P. Halmos (ed.) *Professionalization and Social Change*. Sociological Review Monograph No. 20. University of Keele.

Haug, M.R. (1988) 'A reexamination of the hypothesis of physician deprofessionalization', *Millbank Quarterly*, 66 (Suppl. 2).

Heraud, B. (1973) 'Professionalism, radicalism and social change', in P. Halmos (ed.), *Professionalization and Social Change*. Sociological Review Monograph No. 20. University of Keele.

Hickson, D.J. and Thomas, M.W. (1969) 'Professionalization in Britain: a preliminary measure', *Sociology*, 3: 37–53.

Hofstadter, R. (1962) *Anti-Intellectualism in American Life*. New York: Vintage.

Hopwood, A.G. (1987) 'The archaeology of accounting systems', *Accounting, Organizations and Society*, 12(3): 207–34.

House of Commons (1992) *The Health Committee Second Report: Maternity Services*, vol. 1 (Chairman, N. Winterton). London: HMSO.

House of Lords (1909) *House of Lord Debates*, volume 2.

Hoy, D.C. (1986) *Foucault: a Critical Reader*. Oxford: Basil Blackwell.

Huerkamp, C. (1990) 'The unfree professions: German lawyers, teachers and engineers between democracy and National Socialism, 1900–1950', in G. Cocks and K.H. Jarauch (eds), *German Professions 1800–1950*. Oxford: Oxford University Press.

Hughes, E.C. (1958) *Men and Their Work*. New York: The Free Press.

Hughes, E.C. (1963) 'Professions', *Daedalus*, 92: 655–68.

Hughes, E.C. (1971) *The Sociological Eye*. New York: Aldine.

ICAEW (Institute of Chartered Accountants in England and Wales) (1966) *History of the Institute of Chartered Accountants in England and Wales 1880–1965*. London: Heinemann.

Jackson, J.A. (ed.) (1970) *Professions and Professionalization*. Cambridge: Cambridge University Press.

Jamous, H. and Peloille, B. (1970) 'Changes in the French university hospital system', in J.A. Jackson (ed.), *Professions and Professionalization*. Cambridge: Cambridge University Press, pp. 111–52.

Jaques, E. (1976) *A General Theory of Bureaucracy*. London: Heinemann.

Jarauch, K. (1990) *The Unfree Professions: German Lawyers, Teachers and Engineers between Democracy and National Socialism*. New York: Oxford University Press.

Jay, M. (1993) *Downcast Eyes*. London: University of California Press.

Jessop, B. (1977) 'Remarks on some recent theories of the capitalist state', *Cambridge Journal of Economics*, 1 (4).

Johnson, T. (1972) *Professions and Power*. London: Macmillan.

Johnson, T.J. (1977) 'Professions in the class structure', in R. Scase (ed.), *Class, Cleavage and Control*. London: Allen & Unwin.

Johnson, T.J. (1980) 'Work and power', in G. Esland and G. Salaman (eds), *The Politics of Work and Occupations*. Milton Keynes: Open University Press.

Johnson, T.J. (1982) ' 'The state and the professions: peculiarities of the British', in A. Giddens and G. Mackenzie (eds), *Social Class and the Division of Labour*. Cambridge: Cambridge University Press.

Johnson, T. (1989) 'Review of Abbott (1988)', *Work, Employment and Society*, 3 (3): 413.

Johnson, T. (1994) 'Expertise and the state', in M. Gane and T. Johnson (eds), *Foucault's New Domains*. London: Routledge.

Johnson, T. and Caygill, M. (1978), 'The development of accountancy links in the Commonweath', in R.H. Parker (ed.), *Readings in Accountancy and Business Research, 1970–77*. London: ICAEW.

Jones, E.L. (1981) *The European Miracle*. Cambridge: Cambridge University Press.

Joppke, C. (1992) 'Explaining cross-national variations of two anti-nuclear movements: a political process perspective', *Sociology*, 26(2): 311–32.

Kaye, B. (1960) *The Development of the Architectural Profession in Britain*. London: Allen & Unwin.

Kellner, D. (1989) *Jean Baudrillard*. Cambridge: Polity Press.

Kimball, B.A. (1992) *The True Professional Ideal in America*. Oxford: Basil Blackwell.

Kocka, J. (1990) ' "Bergertum" and professions in the nineteenth century: two alternative approaches', in M. Burrage and R. Torstendahl (eds), *Professions in Theory and History*. London: Sage.

Kronus, C.L. (1976) 'The evolution of occupational power', *Sociology of Work and Occupations*, 3: 3–37.

Langenderfer, H.Q. (1987) 'Accounting education's history: a 100-year search for identity', *Journal of Accountancy, Centennial Issue*, May, 163(5): 302–31.

Larkin, G. (1983) *Occupational Monopoly and Modern Medicine*. London: Tavistock.

Larson, M.S. (1977) *The Rise of Professionalism: A Sociological Analysis*. London: University of California Press.

Larson, M.S. (1980) 'Proletarianization and educated labour', *Theory and Society*, 9: 131–75.

Larson, M.S. (1984) 'The production of expertise and the constitution of expert power', in T.L. Haskell (ed.), *The Authority of Experts*. Bloomington, IN: University of Indiana Press.

Larson, M.S. (1990), 'On the matter of experts and professionals, or how it is impossible to leave nothing unsaid' in R. Torstendahl and M. Burrage (eds), *The Formation of Professions: Knowledge, State and Strategy*. London: Sage.

Lewis, R. and Maude, A. (1952) *Professional People*. London: Phoenix House.

Lipset, S.M. (1964) *The First New Nation*. New York: Free Press.

Littler, C.R. (1982) *The Development of the Labour Process in Capitalist Society*. London: Heinemann.

Lockwood, D. ([1958] 1992) *The Blackcoated Worker*. London: Allen & Unwin.

Loft, A. (1986) 'Towards a critical understanding of accounting: the case of cost accounting in the U.K. 1914–1925', *Accounting, Organizations and Society*, 11 (2): 137–60.

Lynd, R.S. and Lynd, H.M. (1929) *Middletown*. New York: Harcourt Brace.

Lynn, K. (1963) 'Introduction to the professions', *Daedalus*, Fall.

Macdonald, K.M. (1984) 'Professional formation: the case of Scottish accountants', *British Journal of Sociology*, 35 (2): 174–89.

Macdonald, K.M. (1985a) 'Social closure and occupational registration', *Sociology*, 19 (4): 541–56.

Macdonald, K.M. (1985b) 'Professional formation: a reply to Briston and Kedslie', *British Journal of Sociology*, 38 (1): 106–11.

Macdonald, K.M. (1989) 'Building respectability', *Sociology*, 23 (1): 55–80.

Macdonald, K.M. and Ritzer, G. (1988) 'The sociology of the professions: dead or alive?', *Work and Occupations*, 15 (3): 251–72.

Mackay, L. (1990) 'Nursing: just another job?', in P. Abbott and C. Wallace (eds), *The Sociology of the Caring Professions*. London: The Falmer Press.

Mann, M. (1973) *Consciousness and Action Among the Western Working Class*. London: Macmillan.

Mann, M. (1986) *The Sources of Social Power*, vol. I. Cambridge: Cambridge University Press.

Mann M. (1993) *The Sources of Social Power*, vol. II. Cambridge: Cambridge University Press.

Mannheim, K. (1936) *Ideology and Utopia*. London: Routledge & Kegan Paul.

Marcuse, H. (1964) *One Dimensional Man*. London: Routledge.

Margerison, T. (1980) *The Making of a Profession*. London: ICAEW.

Marshall, G., Newby, H., Rose, D. and Vogler, C. (1988) *Social Class in Modern Britain*. London: Unwin Hyman.

Marshall, T.H. (1963) 'The recent history of professionalism in relation to social structure and social policy', first published in 1939 and reprinted in *Sociology at the Crossroads*. London: Heinemann.

Marx, K. (1958) 'Manifesto of the Communist Party', in K. Marx and F. Engels, *Selected Works*, vol. I. Moscow: Foreign Languages Publishing House.

Marx, K. (1976) *Capital*. Harmondsworth: Penguin.

McKinlay, J.B. (1973a) 'On the professional regulation of change', in P. Halmos (ed.), *Professionalization and Social Change*. Sociological Review Monograph No. 20. University of Keele, pp. 61–84.

McKinlay, J.B. (1973b) 'Clients and organizations', in *Processing People*. London: Holt, Rinehart and Winston, pp. 61–84.

McKinlay, J.B. and Arches, J. (1985) 'Towards the proletarianization of physicians', *International Journal of Health Services*, 15: 161–95.

McLellan, D. (1977) *Karl Marx: Selected Writings*. Oxford: Oxford University Press.

McLellan, D. (1980) *The Thought of Karl Marx*, 2nd edn. London: Macmillan.

Merton, R.K. (1947) 'The machine, the worker and the engineer', *Science*, 105: 79–81.

Merton, R.K. (1957) *Social Theory and Social Structure*. Glencoe, IL: The Free Press.

Millerson, G. (1964) *The Qualifying Professions*. London: Routledge & Kegan Paul.

Mills, C.W. (1956) *White Collar*. New York: Oxford University Press.

Montagna, P. (1975) 'The public accounting profession: organization, ideology and social power', *American Behavioral Scientist*, 14: 445–91.

Murphy, R. (1984) 'The structure of closure: a critique and development of the theories of Weber, Collins and Parkin', *British Journal of Sociology*, 35 (3): 547–67.

Murphy, R. (1988) *Social Closure*. Oxford: The Clarendon Press.

Murphy, R. (1990) 'Proletarianization or bureaucratization: the fall of the professional?', in R. Torstendahl and M. Burrage (eds), *The Formation of the Professions: Knowledge, State and Strategy*. London: Sage.

Neale, R.S. (1972) *Class and Ideology in the Nineteenth Century*. London: Routledge & Kegan Paul.

Nettleton, S. (1992) *Power, Pain and Dentistry*. Buckingham: Open University Press.

Oppenheimer, M. (1973) 'The proletarianization of the professional', in P. Halmos (ed.), *Professionalization and Social Change*. Sociological Review Monograph No. 20. University of Keele.

Parkin, F. (1971) *Class Inequality and Political Order*. London: Macgibbon and Kee.

Parkin, F. (1979) *Marxism and Class Theory: a Bourgeois Critique*. London: Tavistock Publications.

Parry, N.C.A. and Parry, J. (1976) *The Rise of the Medical Profession: a Study of Collective Social Mobility*. London: Croom Helm.

Parsons, T. (1954) 'Professions and social structure', in *Essays in Sociological Theory*. Glencoe, IL: The Free Press.

Penn, R. (1985) *Skilled Workers in the Class Structure*. Cambridge: Cambridge University Press.

Perkin, H. (1972) *The Origins of Modern English Society, 1780–1880*. London: Routledge & Kegan Paul.

Pevsner, N. (1973) *Penguin Buildings of England: London* (vol. 1). Harmondsworth: Penguin.

Poggi, G. (1978) *The Development of the Modern State*. London: Hutchinson.

Polyani, K. (1957) *The Great Transformation*. Boston, MA: Beacon Press.

Portwood, D. and Fielding, A. (1981) 'Privilege and the professions', *Sociological Review*, 29: 749–73.

Poulantzas, N. (1973) *Political Power and Social Classes*. London: New Left Books.

Poulantzas, N. (1975) *Classes in Modern Capitalism*. London: New Left Books.

Pound, R. (1977) *The Lawyer from Antiquity to Modern Times with Particular Reference to the Development of Bar Associations in the United States*. St Paul, Minn: West.

Pye, L. (1968) 'Political culture', *International Encyclopedia of the Social Sciences*, vol. 12. New York: Macmillan.

Ramsey, M. (1988) *Professional and Popular Medicine in France 1770–1830: The Social World of Medical Practice*. Philadelphia: University of Pennsylvania Press.

Reskin, B.F. (1978) 'Sex differentiation and the social organization of science', in J. Gaston (ed.), *The Sociology of Science*. San Francisco: Jossey-Bass.

Ried, G., Acken, B.T. and Jancura, E.G. (1987) 'An historical perspective on women in accounting', *Journal of Accountancy, Centennial Issue*, May 163 (5): 338–55.

Roberts, K., Cook, F.G., Clark, S.C. and Semeonoff, E. (1977) *The Fragmented Class Structure*. London: Heinemann.

Robson, K., Willmott, H., Cooper, D. and Puxty, T. (1994) 'The ideology of professional regulation and the market for accounting labour: three episodes in the recent history of the UK accountancy profession', *Accounting, Organizations and Society*, 19 (6): 527–53.

Rose, D. and McAllister, I. (1986) *Voters Begin to Choose*. London: Sage.

Roslender, R. (1992) *Sociological Perspectives on Modern Accountancy*. London: Routledge.

Roszak, T. (1969) *The Making of a Counter Culture*. New York: Doubleday Anchor Books.

Rubenstein, W.D. (1977) 'The Victorian middle classes: wealth, occupation and geography', *Economic History Review*, 30: 602–23.

Rueschemeyer, D. (1987) 'Comparing legal professions cross-nationally: from a professions-centered to a state-centered approach', *Law and Social Enquiry: the Journal of the American Bar Foundation*, 3: 415–46.

Rushing, B. (1993) 'Ideology in the reemergence of North American midwifery', *Work and Occupations*, 20 (1): 46–67.

Russell, B. (1946) *The History of Western Philosophy*. London, Allen & Unwin.

Sacks, M. (1983) 'Removing the blinkers: a critique of recent contributions to the sociology of the professions', *Sociological Review*, 31: 1–21.

Salaman, G. (1981) *Class and the Corporation*. London: Fontana.

Sartre, J-P. (1957) *Being and Nothingness*. London: Methuen.

Savage, M., Barlow, J., Dickens, P. and Fielding, T. (1992) *Property, Bureaucracy and Culture: Middle-class Formation in Contemporary Britain*. London: Routledge.

Seebohm Committee (1968) *Report of the Committee on Local Authority and Allied Personal Social Services*. Cmnd. 3703. London: HMSO.

Service, A. (1977) *Edwardian Architecture*. London: Thames & Hudson.

Sheppard, M. (1990) 'Social work and community psychiatric nursing', in P. Abbott and C. Wallace (eds), *The Sociology of the Caring Professions*. London: The Falmer Press.

Shyrock, R.H.(1947) *The Development of Modern Medicine*. New York: Knopf.

Siegrist, H. (1990) 'Public office or free profession; German attorneys in the nineteenth and early twentieth centuries', in G. Cocks and K.H. Jarauch (eds), *German Professions 1800–1950*. Oxford: Oxford University Press.

Smart, B. (1985) *Michel Foucault*. Chichester: Ellis-Horwood.

Smigel, E.O. (1954) 'Trends in occupational psychology: a survey of post-war research', *American Sociological Review*, 19: 398–404.

Smigel, E.O., Wood, R.B. and Nye, B.R. (1963) 'Occupational sociology: a reexamination', *Sociology and Social Research*, 47: 472–7.

Spencer, A. and Podmore, D. (1986) *In a Man's World*. London: Tavistock.

Stacey, N.A.H. (1954) *English Accountancy: a Study in Social and Economic History 1800–1954*. London: Gee.

Stewart, J.C. (1977) *Pioneers of a Profession: Chartered Accountants to 1897*. Edinburgh: ICAS.

Stinchcombe, A.L. (1965) 'Social structure and organizations', in J.C. March, *Handbook of Organizations*. Chicago: Rand McNally, pp. 142–93.

Tawney, R.H. ([1921] 1982) *The Acquisitive Society*. Brighton: Harvester Press.

Thompson, E.P. (1963) *The Making of the English Working Class*. Harmondsworth: Penguin.

Thompson, E.P. (1978) *The Poverty of Theory*. London: Merlin.

Tilly, C. (1990) *Coercion, Capital and European States*. Oxford: Basil Blackwell.

Torstendahl, R. (1990) 'Essential properties, strategic aims and historical development: three approaches to theories of professionalism', in M. Burrage and R. Torstendahl (eds), *Professions in Theory and History*. London: Sage.

Torstendahl, R. and Burrage, M. (1990) *The Formation of Professions: Knowledge, State and Strategy*. London: Sage.

Turner, B.S. (1987) *Medical Power and Social Knowledge*. London: Sage.

Turner, B.S. (1989) 'Review of Abbott (1988)', *Sociology*, 23 (3): 473.

Turner, B.S. (1992) *Regulating Bodies*. London: Routledge.

Turner, C. and Hodge, M.N. (1970) 'Occupations and professions', in J.A. Jackson (ed.), *Professions and Professionalization*. Cambridge: Cambridge University Press.

Turner, R.S. (1980) '*Das Bildungsbergertum* and the learned professions in Prussia, 1770–1830: the origins of a class', *Histoire Sociale–Social History*, 13 (25): 105–35.

Veblen, T. (1970) *The Theory of the Leisure Class*. London: Unwin.

Waddington, I. (1984) *The Medical Profession in the Industrial Revolution*. London: Humanities Press.

Walby, S. (1989) 'Theorizing patriarchy', *Sociology*, 23 (2): 213–44.

Walby, S. (1990) *Theorizing Patriarchy*. Oxford: Basil Blackwell.

Warner, W.L. and Lunt, P.S. (1941) *The Social Life of a Modern Community*. New Haven, CT: Yale University Press.

Waters, M. (1989) 'The concept of patriarchy', *Sociology*, 23 (2): 193–212.

Weber, M. (1949) *The Methodology of the Social Sciences* (ed. E Shils and H. Finch). Glencoe, IL: The Free Press.

Weber, M. (1976) *The Protestant Ethic and the Spirit of Capitalism*. London: George Allen & Unwin.

Weber, M. (1978) *Economy and Society*. London: University of California Press.

Wilensky, H. L. (1964) 'The professionalization of everyone?', *American Journal of Sociology*, 70: 137–58.

Winkler, J. (1977) 'The corporate economy: theory and administration', in R. Scase (ed.), *Class, Cleavage and Control*. London: Allen & Unwin.

Witz, A. (1992) *Professions and Patriarchy*. London: Routledge.

Wood, S. (ed.) (1982) *The Degradation of Work?* London: Hutchinson.

Wood, S. (ed.) (1989) *The Transformation of Work?* London: Unwin Hyman.

Wright, E.O. (1979) *Class, Crisis and the State*. London: Verso.

Wright, E.O. (1985) *Classes*. London: Verso.

Wright, E.O. (1989) 'Rethinking, once again, the concept of class structure', in E.O. Wright et al., *The Debate on Classes*. London: Verso.

Author index

Subject index